ALLEN J. FRANK

GULAG MIRACLES: SUFIS AND STALINIST REPRESSION IN KAZAKHSTAN

ÖSTERREICHISCHE AKADEMIE DER WISSENSCHAFTEN
PHILOSOPHISCH-HISTORISCHE KLASSE
SITZUNGSBERICHTE, 895. BAND

VERÖFFENTLICHUNGEN ZUR IRANISTIK
HERAUSGEGEBEN VON BERT. G. FRAGNER UND FLORIAN SCHWARZ

NR. 84

STUDIES AND TEXTS ON CENTRAL ASIA
HERAUSGEGEBEN VON FLORIAN SCHWARZ

BAND 2

ALLEN J. FRANK

GULAG MIRACLES: SUFIS AND STALINIST REPRESSION IN KAZAKHSTAN

AUSTRIAN
ACADEMY
OF SCIENCES
PRESS

Diese Publikation wurde einem anonymen, internationalen Begutachtungsverfahren unterzogen.
This publication was subject to international and anonymous peer review.

Peer review is an essential part of the Austrian Academy of Sciences Press evaluation process. Before any book can be accepted for publication, it is assessed by international specialists and ultimately must be approved by the Austrian Academy of Sciences Publication Committee.

Die verwendete Papiersorte in dieser Publikation ist DIN EN ISO 9706 zertifiziert und erfüllt die Voraussetzung für eine dauerhafte Archivierung von schriftlichem Kulturgut.

The paper used in this publication is DIN EN ISO 9706 certified and meets the requirements for permanent archiving of written cultural property.

Cover Design: Bettina Hofleitner
Coverphoto: © Allen J. Frank. Gravestone of Mäshhür Zhüsip Köpeyulï, near Bayanaul, Kazakhstan.

Wien/Vienna 2019
ISBN 978-3-7001-8334-1
Druck/Printed: Prime Rate, Budapest
https://epub.oeaw.ac.at/8334-1
https://verlag.oeaw.ac.at
Made in Europe

CONTENTS

ACKNOWLEDGEMENTS

This book originated in the city of Baltimore, from a series of discussions with Jeff Eden about Central Asian history. Jeff was present at every stage of the project, from its inception through to its submission and publication, and he deserves special thanks for his encouragement and for his kind attention and time.

Several other colleagues significantly encouraged and assisted the preparation of this monograph. Ulan Bigozhin and Ashirbek Muminov supplied many important and otherwise unobtainable sources for the project. Devin DeWeese provided helpful suggestions to the manuscript, and his contributions to the history of Central Asian Sufism and Soviet Islam have strongly informed this work, well beyond his reviewer's comments. Paolo Sartori, Florian Schwarz, and Bettina Hofleitner likewise provided kind assistance and encouragement in seeing the work through to publication. Finally, the author wishes to thank the National Library of Kazakhstan for making many crucial publications available.

INTRODUCTION

The crimes of 20th century Nazi and Stalinist totalitarianism enveloped a vast portion of the globe, inflicting mass arrests, enslavement, genocide, ethnic cleansing, and generalized terror and social disruption on diverse populations, communities, and cultures. Among Western historians in particular, the experience of Muslims with totalitarianism, especially during the Second World War, is most commonly addressed with respect to colonized populations. The interactions between Nazi Germany and the Islamic world are often depicted as continuing the Imperial German policy of encouraging Muslims under French and British colonial rule to rebel against their overlords, or otherwise assist in the German war effort.[1] Similarly, we have studies of how the British and French governments, both perpetrators of atrocities in their own Muslim colonies during the Second World War, managed their Muslim subjects, as well as the propaganda threats emanating from Nazi Germany.[2] If we take into account the relatively limited, and – in contrast to the 21st century experience – benign, wartime interactions of the United States with the Islamic world during the Second World War, it is not surprising that from the vast literature on the social impacts of Nazi and Stalinist crimes, one is left with the impression that Muslims escaped relatively unscathed, if only thanks to geography.[3] Muslims, however, made up a significant proportion of the Soviet Union's citizenry, and like every other ethnic or religious community in that country, suffered severely under Stalinist rule. These include Muslim communities in the Crimea, the

---

[1] Nazi-Muslim relations are the topic of the following recent monographs: David Motadel, *Islam and Nazi Germany's War*, (Belknap Press: Cambridge Massachusetts, 2014); Stephan Ihrig, *Atatürk in the Nazi Imagination*, (Belknap Press: Cambridge Massachusetts, 2014); Francis Nicosia, *Nazi Germany and the Arab World*, (Cambridge: Cambridge University Press, 2014); Marko Attila Hoare: *The Bosnian Muslims in the Second World War: a History*, (Oxford: Oxford University Press, 2014.

[2] See, Madhusree Mukerjee, *Churchill's Secret War: the British Empire and the Ravaging of India during World War II* (New York: Basic Books, 2010); Annie Rey-Goldzeighuer, *Aux origins de la guerre d'Algerie: de Mers-el-Kebir aux massacres Nord-Constantinois*, (Paris: La Decouverte, 2002).

[3] For some discussions of religious policy towards Muslim communities under Japanese occupation, see Harry J. Benda, *The Crescent and Rising Sun: Indonesian Islam under Japanese Occupation, 1942–1945*, (The Hague and Bantung: Van Hoeve, 1958); Abu Talib Ahmad, "Japanese Policy towards Islam in Malaya during the Occupation: A Reassessment, *Journal of Southeast Asian Studies* 33/1 (2002), 107–122.

Caucasus, the Volga-Ural region, Siberia, and above all, Central Asia, the region on which this study is focused. In the broad and often quite excellent historical literature devoted to the Gulag, and its impact on Soviet society, the Muslim perspective, and especially the Muslim religious perspective, is largely or entirely absent. One of the goals of this work are to consider this religious facet of Soviet Muslim society, as well as to take into account the experience of totalitarianism for Muslims outside of the Middle East, and the French, British, and Dutch colonies.

To the degree that studies of Stalinist atrocities against Muslim populations in the Soviet Union have been the topic of scholarly study, historians have generally examined them through a secular lens. Scholarly approaches that are sensitive to the religious interpretations of totalitarian crimes are far more evident in studies of Christianity, and especially Judaism.[4] Religious interpretations of the Holocaust as it was experienced by Jewish religious communities, particularly the Hasidim, are relevant to this study, because of some similarities in conceptions and manifestations of religious authority between Hasidism and Sufism, and also due to similarities in the narrative traditions of both communities. Publications of Hasidic tales, a vital compositional genre that serves some of the same didactic and biographical functions in Hasidism as the Sufi hagiographies discussed in this study – and that also share some of the latter genre's demotic qualities – have permitted a broader public to gain insights into religious interpretations of the Holocaust beyond more abstract theology and moral philosophy.[5] In studies of Soviet Muslim communities, the privileging of an ethno-national over a religious conceptual representation is, ironically, at least partially conditioned by Soviet ideology. A secular orientation is no less evident in examinations of earlier

---

[4] For an introduction to the Jewish theological responses to the Holocaust, see: Steven T. Katz et al. eds. *Wrestling with God: Jewish Theological Responses during and after the Holocaust*, (New York: Oxford University press, 2007). Beyond the vast number of works devoted to specifically Christian theological, philosophical, and political responses to the crimes of Stalinism and Nazism, there is also some scholarship on popular religious responses. For example, for the development, among Russian Orthodox communities, of shrines and pilgrimage on the sites of former Gulag prison camps in Siberia, see Galina Liubimova, "Sibirskaia traditsiia pochitaniia sviatykh mest v kontekste narodnoi istoricheskoi pamiati," *Studia Mythologica Slavica* XVI (2013), 27–45; Jeanmarie Rouhier-Willoughby, "The Gulag Reclaimed as Sacred Space: Negotiation of Memory at the Holy Spring of Iskitim," *Laboratorium* 1 (2015), 51–70.

[5] Yaffa Eliach, *Hasidic Tales of the Holocaust*, (New York: Vintage Books, 1988); for an introduction to Hasidic tales as a compositional genre, see Martin Buber, *Tales of the Hasidim: the Early Masters*, (New York: Schocken Books, 1947).

episodes of massive state violence directed against nomads. Such an approach, originating in Cold War Sovietology, continues to generate an ever-growing literature devoted to the deportation of various Muslim nationalities of the Crimea and the North Caucasus.[6] There is an even wider literature, primarily in Russian and Turkic languages, on the persecution of the national – and basically secular – elite: nationalist figures, intellectuals, scholars, the bourgeoisie, etc. These are important studies, that emphasize the personal tragedies of individuals, and sometimes evaluate Stalinist repression more broadly, as it affected Muslim *nations*, either through mass deportations of entire ethnic groups, or the metaphoric decapitation of the nation by the elimination of its supposed national elite.[7] The imposition of secularism on the populations of the former Russian Empire, including its Muslim subjects, was a declared goal of both Soviet cultural policy, and of local elites in varying degrees. In this, the Soviets were largely successful, in part thanks to social disruption brought about through the massive application of state violence. Tellingly, during the Cold War, anti-communist critics discussed Muslim communities and Islam almost entirely within a framework of Soviet definitions, and this framework has by no means lost its appeal, if not its fashionableness.[8] However, as with all cultural policies in the Soviet era, even

---

6 Aleksandr Nekrich, *The Punished Peoples*, (New York: Norton, 1981); Robert Conquest, *The Soviet Deportation of Nationalities*, (New York: MacMillan, 1960); Robert Conquest, *The Nation Killers*, (London: MacMillan, 1970); Alan Fisher, *The Crimean Tatars*, (Palo Alto: the Hoover Institution, 1978); G. Uehling, *Beyond Memory: the Crimean Tatars' Deportation and Return*, (New York: Palgrave, 2004).

7 A few examples of the vast literature devoted in large measure to the secular elite in Turkic communities include, Rafael Khakimov, *Repressiyalängän tatar ädipläre,*" (Kazan: Tatar kitap näshriyäte, 2009); Bolatbek Näsenov, *Khalïq zhaularï: keng dalanïng küyreuĭ* (Almaty-Novosibirsk: n.p., 2006); Bolat Zhünïsbekov ed. *Alash-Alzhir* II (Almaty: Sarïarqa, 2011); Makhmud Dudov et al. *Pravozashchitniki repressirovannykh narodov*, (Moscow: n.p., 1996); Svetlana Alieva, *Tak eto bylo: national'nye repressii v SSSR 1917–1952* I-III, (Moscow: Insan, 1993); A. T. Orymbaev, *Deportatsiia chechenskogo i ingushskogo narodov v Kazakhstan v gody Velikoi Otechestvennoi voiny i ikh polozhenie v poslevoennye gody*, (Astana: Parasat älemĭ, 2006); Zukhra Borlakova, *Deportatsiia i repatriatsiia karachaiskogo naroda*, (Moscow: Reglant, 2005);

8 The influential studies of Alexandre Bennigsen and his circle illustrate this tendency very clearly. The most relevant of these works for our study is Alexandre Bennigsen and S. Enders Wimbush, *Mystics and Commissars: Sufism in the Soviet Union*, (London: C. Hurst, 1985); Devin DeWeese had characterized this approach as "Sovietological Islamology." For an informed critique, see, Devin DeWeese, "Islam and the Legacy of Sovietology: a Review Essay on Yaacov Roi'i's *Islam in the Soviet Union*," *Journal of Islamic Studies* 13/3 (2002), 298–330.

secularization was in some important ways negotiated, and achieved on the ground with a degree of compromise, despite the Soviet state's ability and willingness to unleash violence to achieve its goals. Absent from these studies of the Muslim experience of Stalinism is the religious dimension, and religious responses of the Muslim community.[9] The religious, Islamic, aspects of the topic are relevant to the study of Stalin-era crimes against Soviet citizens because the repression of Islamic institutions and religious figures was a very public aspect of Soviet cultural policy. The destruction of "religion" or "religious institutions" was also explicitly conjoined with the suppression of older, religiously conceived, relationships, forms of identity and cultural practices.[10] In addition to banning Islamic education, and closing down mosques, the Soviet authorities targeted religious leaders of the Muslim community, including the *ʿulamāʾ*, but also expressly Sufi *ishans*. Not only were religious leaders targeted, but their families were, too, threatening the survival of the lineages themselves. Given the existence of strong religious bonds between *ishan* lineages with non-holy descent groups (evident among the Kazakhs in particular, but also among the Turkmens and Uzbeks), violent repression directed against these *ishan* lineages affected rural Kazakh society in profound ways, even beyond the immediate catastrophes of mass famine and collectivization.

---

9 Stalinist violence against Soviet Muslims has been the subject of a substantial literature in Russian and in various Turkic languages of the former Soviet Union, as well as several monographs in Western languages; see, Niccolò Pianciola, *Stalinismo di frontiera: Collonizzazione agricola, sterminio dei nomadi e costruzione statale in Asia central (1905–1936)* (Vicenza: Viella, 2009), Mukhamet Shayakhmetov, *The Silent Steppe: the Memoir of a Kazakh Nomad under Stalin*, (New York: The Rookery Press, 2006); Isabelle Ohayon, *La sédentarisation des Kazakhs dans l'URSS de Staline*, (Paris: Maisonneuve et Larose, (2006); Robert Kindler, *Stalins Nomaden: Herrschaft un Hunger in Kasachstan* (Hamburg: Hamburger Edition, 2014), Valeriy Mikhailov, *The Great Disaster: Genocide of the Kazakhs* (London: Stacey, 2014); Shoshana Keller, *To Moscow, not Mecca: the Soviet Campaign against Islam in Central Asia, 1917–1941,* (Westport, Connecticut: Praeger, 2001). Keller's emphasis is on the "Soviet Campaign," rather than "Islam."

10 There are, nevertheless, some works devoted to the repression of the *ʿulamāʾ*, and sacred lineages; see, Nodirbek Abdulakhatov et. al., *Farghona azizlari taqdiri*, (Tashkent: Abu Matbuot-Kansalt, 2012); *Musul'manskoe dukhovenstvo i vlast' v Tatarstane (1920–1930-e gg.* (Kazan: Akademiia Nauk Respubliki Tatarstan, 2006); M. K. Koigeldiev, *Stalinizm i repressii v Kazakhstane 1920–1940-kh godov,* (Almaty: Zerde, 2009), 194–311.

SOVIET ISLAM

The purpose of this work is two-fold. On the one hand, I seek to explore the experiences and responses of Muslim religious communities under totalitarian oppression, in this case looking at Kazakh holy lineages during the Stalin era. On the other, I hope to challenge, or at least qualify, some of the commonly-encountered ideas that dominate much of the discussion of Islam in the Soviet Union, namely, that the Soviet era severed the link between the Muslim community and Islamic knowledge, that Islamic knowledge was relegated to the "family" sphere, and that, effectively, because of Soviet policies, Islamic knowledge could no longer be transmitted in the communal sphere.[11] This line of thinking, most prominently argued by Adeeb Khalid, holds that Central Asians' understanding of Islam became less a universal body of ethics, relationships, and rituals, than an "ethno-national" conception incubated within the family environment.[12] The Kazakh environment, with its kinship-based social structures, provides good ground to challenge these hypotheses.

While this book focuses in particular on the interpretation by Muslim religious communities of their own experience of Stalinism, including the Gulag experiences of their leaders and ancestors, it is also looks at the collective survival of several Muslim religious communities in Kazakhstan, as narrated in their own treatises. The study highlights 1) the continuity of conceptions and practices rooted in medieval Sufism, 2) the role of these Sufi ideas in maintaining the cohesion of these communities against the challenges of state-imposed secularism and Stalinist repression, and 3) the ways in which Stalinism, and the Soviet system more generally, influenced these selfsame Sufi practices and conceptions. All of these questions are relevant to understanding how these Sufi communities dealt with Stalinist repression, how they adapted to it, and how they survived it.

This study is based primarily on Kazakh-language sacred literature produced by and for Muslim holy lineages. These include hagiographies embedded within genealogical treatises, and shrine catalogs published in independent Kazakhstan. The sources are Kazakh variations of a well-established Islamic compositional genre firmly linked to Sufism, and dating from the 11th century CE. These sources require us to qualify much that has

---

11 This argument is inspired particularly by Paolo Sartori's article, "Of Saints, Shrines, and Tractors: Untangling the Meaning of Islam in Soviet Central Asia," *Journal of Islamic Studies* (2019), 1–40.

12 Adeeb Khalid, *Islam after Communism: Religion and Politics in Central Asia* (Berkeley and Los Angeles, University of California Press, 2007), 82, 104.

been written about Soviet and Post-Soviet Islam, where the apparent success of a type of secularization is thought to distinguish the former Soviet Union from the supposedly insufficiently secularized parts of the Islamic world that remained outside of the Soviet Union. But these sources equally demonstrate that, in keeping with the holy lineages' role in their societies as "Islamizers" and bearers of Islamic norms of behavior and morality, elements of Soviet secularism could become objects of Islamization, even during the Soviet era. In any case, it is evident that older conceptions and expressions of sacred communal affiliations derived from Sufism, from Islamic ideas more broadly, and from Inner Asian social structures, survived the Soviet era, reemerged after 1991, and, remain relevant. On the one hand, these hagiographies and the stories they contain are documents of independent Kazakhstan, and of modern Kazakh society. On the other, as collective documents of Kazakh historical tradition that memorialize older religious sensibilities and historical judgments, they are also *public* documents of descent groups and religious communities, and as such, represent collective understanding and memory. Being historical works, they are informed by the documentary methodology of Kazakh oral tradition, derived in part, from hadith methodologies, with its documented chains of transmission (*isnad*). Such elements are strongly evident in Kazakh Islamic historiography composed before and during the Soviet era, and remains evident particularly in genealogical publications in independent Kazakhstan. To dismiss these accounts as "merely" post-Soviet writings that have no authority for the period they describe would be a failure to appreciate the role and evolution of these narratives in their communities, their historiographical context, and their collective, public nature.

The book is divided into five chapters. Chapter 1 addresses the use of hagiographies as a source for the social history of Central Asia and the Volga-Ural region. To provide an example of fully fledged hagiographical tradition, and the application of hagiographies to social history. The chapter then looks at the inclusion of hagiographical elements in a broad range of compositional genres, demonstrating the breadth of hagiography, and its literary and social function in Central Asia and the Volga-Ural region. Here we find hagiographical elements in a wide array of compositional genres, including local and regional histories, genealogical charters, travel literature, epic poetry, and others. Finally, in this chapter we discuss the development of hagiography in independent Kazakhstan, tracing its connections to older compositional genres, and the emergence of new ones, and the social function of hagiography in Kazakh society.

Chapter 2 examines Sufi communities and the meaning of miracles, using hagiographical works as sources for the social history of sacred lineages (*khojas* and others) in Kazakhstan. First, we identify and outline four of the sacred lineages whose members appear repeatedly in our study. These lineages claim descent from Shāh-i Aḥmad as-Ṣābawī (1812–1878), Maral Ishan Qŭrmanŭlï (1782–1841), Isabek Ishan Mŭratŭlï (1792–1871), and Ayqozha Ishan (1773–1856), looking at their biographies, and the dynasties they established in various regions of the country. The chapter also discusses how these sacred lineages are treated in Soviet and "Sovietological" sources. The discussion then shifts to the Sufi dimensions of these sacred lineages, their social functions in Kazakhstan, and the basis of religious authority for these sacred descent groups. These 19th and early 20th century communities are discussed in the context of Devin DeWeese's theory of the "disordering" of Sufism, while at the same time, acknowledging the social and religious significance of the master-disciple metaphor in social relations between sacred and "non-sacred" lineages. The next part of the chapter is devoted to the role of miracle stories in these hagiographies, and their meaning in the Kazakh social context. This discussion is above all informed by the writings of Devin DeWeese on the rhetorical and social significance of miracles. Here examples from Kazakh hagiographical literature reveal miracles to be central narrative elements in defining the creation of a religious community. Anticipating the Stalin era, the final portion of the chapter looks at the relationship between sacred lineages and the state, and the depiction of saintly ancestors in their relations with Muslim and infidel rulers before the Soviet era.

Chapter 3 examines how the historical relationship – between Sufis and Sufi communities on the one hand, and the various states on the other that ruled the Kazakh steppe from the 18th century down to the Soviet era – is reflected in the hagiographical sources. The sources depict relations with the Russian authorities as generally hostile, and the anti-religious campaigns of the Stalin era are described as part of a continuum with the Imperial Russia era. The sources also describe the strategies undertaken by the holy lineages to resist persecution, and continue their task of serving as religious examples to their communities.

Chapter 4 is devoted to the depiction of Stalinist collectivization, famine, and repression in Kazakh hagiographies, and the effects of such policies on sacred lineages. First, it provides a timeline of legal and policy measures that lead to the persecution of Muslim religious leaders in general. Then, it examines, based on hagiographical treatises, how Stalinist repression was implemented, how this repression, and the experience of the Second World

War, affected members of sacred lineages, and the strategies they implemented for their survival. The chapter next addresses the significance of the widely encountered phenomenon of "Gulag miracles" – accounts of miracles that saints were said to have performed in the Stalinist prison system. It also looks at the role of sacred relics in these accounts, in conjunction with the "Gulag miracles," and their way these stories of miracles assert the relevance and holiness of these lineages.

The final chapter looks at how, following the Second World War, these lineages accommodated Soviet rule, and how this accommodation was reflected in these hagiographies. It examines the Soviet career paths favored by members of these lineages, parallel with the maintenance of their sacred authority, and their continued relationship with Kazakh kinship groups. In this period, we see new miracles emerge, showing saints using their miraculous powers to intercede with Soviet industrial technology, such as tractors, to benefit their communities, and maintain their status. It also notes the role of sacred lineages in the official Soviet Islamic religious bureaucracy – the Tashkent Muftiate, and as "official" Soviet Muslim clerics. Finally, it examines appraisals of the Stalin era found in these hagiographies.

CHAPTER 1. MUSLIM HAGIOGRAPHIES AND THE SOCIAL HISTORY OF CENTRAL ASIA

CENTRAL ASIAN HAGIOGRAPHIES AS HISTORICAL SOURCES

The hagiographies that are the chief sources for this study belong to a compositional genre found throughout the Islamic world. As a compositional genre, Islamic hagiography traces back to the biographies of Sufis that emerged in Khorasan in the 11th century CE. An enduring purpose of hagiographies, as Jürgen Paul reminds us, is to defend Sufism against its critics by demonstrating that the actions of the biographical subject were in conformity with Muslim revelations, and that the subjects and their descendants constituted at least a spiritual chain of transmission, if not outright genealogical bonds, with the Prophet Muhammad. Their structure changed over time emphasizing, for example, a specific *shaykh*, or moving from a chronological structure to a collection of anecdotes, and after the 11th century CE, including descriptions of miracles. During and after the Mongol era, Persian and Central Asian hagiography began emphasizing the founding saints of Sufi lineages, but they also functioned as platforms for addressing doctrinal disputes. During the 15th and 16th centuries many hagiographies began emphasizing local shrines. This emphasis remains a leitmotif in sacred histories in Central Asia down to the present.[1] In fact, all of the elements Jürgen Paul identifies to characterize medieval Persian and Central Asian hagiography over time are still evident in 20th and 21st century Kazakh hagiographies, where we commonly see the same anticipation of critics who would denounce Sufi practices as un-Islamic, the same emphasis on miracles, shrines, ritual settings, and the same documentation of Sufi lineages, infancy

[1] For a brief survey of hagiographical literature from Central Asia, see Devin DeWeese, "Re-Envisioning the History of Sufi Communities in Central Asia: Continuity and Adaptation in Sources and Social Frameworks," *Sufism in Central Asia: New Perspectives on Sufi Traditions, 15th-21st* Centuries, Devin DeWeese and Jo-Ann Gross, eds. (Leiden: Brill, 2018), 21–74; Jürgen Paul, "Hagiographic Literature," *Encyclopedia Iranica* XI, fasc. 5, 536–539; for a very broad survey of Turkic hagiographical literature, see Thierry Zarcone, "L'Hagiographie dans le monde turc," *Saints orienteaux,* Denis Aigle ed., (Paris: De Boccard, 1995), 55–67.

narratives, public virtue and host of other elements that characterize Islamic hagiographic writing in general.[2]

Another characteristic feature of Sufi hagiographies is their demotic character, which makes them especially worthwhile sources for social history. Some of the earliest works were written in Persian, one of the vernacular languages of Central Asia, and later, in Chaghatay, the literary Turkic language of Islamic Central Asia. In addition to addressing doctrinal issues, which were often of political significance at the time they were composed, medieval and modern hagiographies frequently describe popular piety and practices, and place sacred stories and events in real social contexts, revealing Muslim cultural life as experienced by differing social strata, and most importantly, at the popular level.[3] The modern Kazakh hagiographies used in this study are exclusively written in more-or-less colloquial Kazakh. While it has taken some time for students of Islamic history to appreciate and use hagiographies as sources for social history, and to apply critical approaches for these at times difficult and ambiguous sources, it can no longer be said that hagiographies are neglected as sources for social history, especially for the history of Persia and Central Asia. Soviet historians, despite their ideological constraints in dealing with religion as a historical phenomenon, made extensive and productive use of hagiographies to examine the social, political and economic history of Central Asia,[4] and today scholars make wide use of

---

[2] For a full survey of major thematic elements in Islamic hagiography, and miracle stories in particular, see John Renard, *Friends of God: Islamic Images of Piety, Commitment, and Servanthood,* (Berkeley: University of California Press, 2008); Richard Gramlich, *Die Wunder der Freunde Gottes: Theologien und Erscheinungsformen des islamischen Heiligenwunders* (Wiesbaden: Steiner, 1986).

[3] For a discussion of some of the issues surrounding the use of hagiographies as historical sources, see, Jürgen Paul, "Hagiographische Texte als historische Quelle," *Saeculum,* 41/1 (1990), 17–43; Rian Thum, *Sacred Routes of Uyghur History*, (Cambridge, Massachusetts: Harvard University Press, 2014), 41–51; for a discussion of the rhetorical and social significance of miracle stories, see Jo-Ann Gross, "Multiple Roles and Perceptions of a Sufi Shaikh: Symbolic Statements of Political and Religious Authority," in *Naqshbandîs: cheminements et situation actuelle d'un ordre mystique musulman* (Actes de la Table Ronde de Sèvres, 2–4 mai 1985), ed. Marc Gaborieau, Alexandre Popovic, and Thierry Zarcone (Istanbul/Paris: Éditions Isis, 1990; Varia Turcica, v. 18), pp. 109–121.

[4] Soviet historians also recognized the potential of hagiographies as sources for social history; see P. P. Ivanov, *Khoziaistvo dzhuibarskikh sheikhov (K Istorii feodal'nogo zemlevladeniia v Srednei Azii),* (Moscow-Leningrad: Izdatel'stvo Akademii Nauk SSSR, 1954); B. Suleimenov ed., *Materialy po istorii kazakhskikh khanstv XV-XVIII vekov,* (Alma-Ata: Nauka, 1969), 232–236; V. A. Romodin ed. *Materialy po istorii kirgizov i Kirgizii,* (Moscow: Nauka, Glavnaia Redaktsiia Vostochnoi Literatury, 1973), 177–189; I.

Muslim hagiography for similar purposes, as well as for history of religion more broadly.[5]

Finally, and perhaps obviously, the Kazakh historiogriographies focus on a lineage that includes central holy figure, either as part of an existing lineage or as a founder of a prominent saint withing an existing lineage. These figures are described as saints, having to man of the same holy qualities, and using the same literary devices, that define Islamic in hagiographic literature at large.[6]

Hagiographical elements in Muslim compositional genres

When speaking of Muslim hagiographies, we can expand the definition to include other sacred compositional genres that embed hagiographic elements within them.[7] Often, genres thought of as distinct are inextricably intertwined. This interpenetration is particularly evident in works labeled by their authors as "histories" (*tārīkh*). City histories, for example were often compiled to include extensive discussions of local shrines and saints, including accounts of their miracles, thereby establishing a specific locale's sacred geography, linked to locally prominent Sufis. In his discussion of the sacred histories of Sayram, a town today located in southern Kazakhstan, Devin DeWeese has shown that this sort of historiography/hagiography became quite popular in

A. Saidakhmedov, M. Iu. Iunuskhodzhaeva, G. Iu. Astanova, "Agiograficheskie sochineniia kak istochnik dlia izucheniia dukhovnoi i politicheskoi zhizni Vostochnogo Turkestana," *Iz Istorii Srednei Azii i Vostochnogo Turkestana XV-XIX vv,* (Tashkent: Fan, 1987), 149–162.

5 See, Devin DeWeese, *Islamization and Native Religion in the Golden Horde: Baba Tükles and the Conversion to Islam in Historical and Epic Tradition*, (University Park, Pennsylvania: Pennsylvania State University Press, 1994); Bakhtiyar Babadzhanov ed., *Manaqib-i Dukchi Ishan*, (Almaty: Daik Press, 2004). Thum, *Sacred Routes of Uyghur History*; Jeff Eden, *The Life of Muḥammad Sharīf: A Central Asian Sufi Hagiography in Chaghatay,* (Vienna: Verlag der Österreichischen Akademie der Wissenschaften, 2015); Jeff Eden, *Warrior Saints of the Silk Road: Legends of the Qarakhanids*, (Leiden: Brill, 2018). This list is by no means exhaustive.

6 On definitions and hagiographic treatments of Islamic saints, see Frederick Denny, "Prophet and *Walī*: Sainthood in Islam," *Sainthood and its Manifestations in World Religions,* Richard Kieckhefer and George D. Bond eds., (Berkeley: University of Californa Press, 1988), 69–97; Shahzad Bashir, *Sufi Bodies: Religion and Society in Medieval Islam*, (New York: Columbia University Press, 2011).

7 For a discussion of the major literary genres comprising medieval Islamic hagiography, see Renard, *Friends of God,* 240–246; Marcia K. Hermansen, "Interdisciplinary Approaches to Islamic Biographical Materials," *Religion*, 18 (1988), pp. 163–182.

the 18th and 19th centuries, but nevertheless had a long pedigree. As antecedents for this genre, he has identified similarly structured urban histories of Samarqand, Balkh, Kashgar, and Nishapur.[8] The 19th century histories of Sayram show quite clearly the way older "city histories" could be adapted to created sacred histories and "shrine guides" that addressed changing social and political circumstances in Muslim communities.[9] The continued publication of such works in Kazakhstan testifies to their enduring relevance.

The adaptation to hagiographic ends of older compositional genres occurred not only in Central Asia, but in the Volga-Ural region and Siberia as well, where in the 19th and 20th centuries we find similar descriptions of local shrines and sacred histories embedded within historical works, such as for the city of Astrakhan, which includes defenses of hagiolatry against reformist critiques.[10] Sacred histories emphasizing broader geographic regions, and including Islamization narratives, emerged in the 18th and 19th century among Muslims under Russian rule, in both the Volga-Ural region and Siberia.[11] In the Volga-Ural region in particular, these sacred histories were often associated with, and recited at, shrines. For example, in the 1870s an imam in the village of Adaevo in Viatka Province recited the *Tawārīkh-i Bulghārīya* to a Russian ethnographer, to connect the shrine in his village with this sacred history.[12] In the 21st century, Bashkirs in the Ural Mountains recite the same

---

[8] Devin DeWeese, "Sacred History for a Central Asian Town: Saints, Shrines, and Legends of Origin in Histories of Sayrām, 18th-19th Centuries," *Revue des mondes musulmans et de la Méditerranée* 89–90 (2000), 245–295.

[9] Such shrine catalogs are quite evident in Eastern Turkistan; for the case of the city of Qumul, see Jun Sugawara and Yayoi Kawahara (eds.), *Mazar Documents from Xinjiang and Ferghana* 1, (Tokyo, Research Institute for Languages and Cultures of Asia and Africa, 2006), 116–147.

[10] Allen J. Frank, "Muslim Sacred History and the 1905 Revolution in a Sufi History of Astrakhan," *Studies on Central Asian History in Honor of Yuri Bregel*, Devin DeWeese ed., (Bloomington, Indiana: Research Institute for Inner Asian Studies, 2001), 297–317.

[11] Alfrid Bustanov, "The Narrative of Ishaq Bab and the Lore of Holy Families in Western Siberia: a Preliminary Discussion," in, *Islamizatsiia i sakral'nye rodoslovnye v Tsentral'noi Azii* I, eds. Devin DeWeese and Ashirbek Muminov, (Almaty: Daik Press, 2013), 496–533; Allen J. Frank, "Islamic Shrine Catalogues and Communal Geography in the Volga-Ural Region: 1788–1917" *Journal of Islamic Studies*, VII/2 (July, 1996), 265–286."

[12] S. K. Kuznetsov, "Otryvki iz dorozhnykh zametok co vremia etnograficheskoi ekskursii po viatskoi gubernii v 1880 godu," *Uchenye Zapiski Kazanskago Universiteta* 1882 (2–3), 314–315.

work at a tomb associated with the three *saḥābas* featured in the history's miracle narrative.[13]

Hagiographic elements can be seen in written works originating among nomadic communities. The best studied example in this category is the Islamization narrative of Özbek Khan, and miracles of the saint Baba Tükles, featured in the 16th century Chaghatay work *Chīngīz-nāma* of Ötemish Hājjī.[14] Miraculous conversion narratives were retold in Bashkir genealogical works, most notably, in the *Tārīkh Nāma-yi Bulghār*, an early 19th century history/hagiography/genealogical treatise written by Tāj ad-Dīn b. Yālchīghūl (d. 1838).[15] Similar elements are even evident in more "modern" compositional genres, such as Tatar "village histories." The *Tārīkh-i Barāngawī*, by Aḥmad b. Ḥāfiẓ ad-Dīn al-Barāngawī, is devoted to the history of the imams and mosques in a village in Viatka Province in the Volga-Ural region, and contains miracle narratives of 19th century Bukharan Naqshbandi *shaykhs* with whom some of the local imams studied.[16] Stéphane Dudoignon has shown that sacred elements stressing local shrines are found in in local histories produced in late 20th century Tajikistan that simultaneously reflect the influence of Soviet nationalities ideology.[17]

Regional and Thematic Aspects of Hagiographic Traditions

Local peculiarities, reflecting specific historical, political, doctrinal, and geographic conditions are discernable in broader examinations of regional hagiographic traditions. An appreciation of such peculiarities allows us to better understand how hagiographies themselves functioned socially, especially as documents of collective self-definition. Over the past 25 years, scholars have demonstrated the significance of hagiographies featuring saints and miracle stories that demarcate communal, and even political, boundaries

---

13 S. Kildin et al. eds., *Bashqortostan – äüliälär ile,* (Ufa: Kitap, 2012), 28–31.

14 DeWeese, *Islam and Native Religion,* Chapters 3 and 4.

15 Allen J. Frank, *Islamic Historiography and 'Bulghar' Identity among the Tatars and Bashkirs of Russia* (Leiden: Brill, 1998), 92–122; I. G. Gaiautdinov, *'Tarikh Nama-i Bulgar' Tadzhetina Ialsygulova,* (Ufa: Kitap, 1998).

16 Allen J. Frank, *Bukhara and the Muslims of Russia: Sufism, Education, and the Paradox of Islamic Prestige,* (Leiden: Brill, 2012), 113–119.

17 Stéphane A. Dudoignon, "Local Lore, the Transmission of Learning, and Communal Identity in Late 20th Century Tajikistan, The *Khujand-Nāma* of 'Ārifjān Yakhyāzād Khujandī," *Devout Societies vs. Impious States? Transmitting Islamic Learning in Russia, Central Asia, and China through the Twentieth Century*, (Berlin: Klaus Schwarz Verlag, 2004), 213–241.

for Muslim communities, featuring shrines and conversion narratives. Such narratives are strongly evident among Muslim communities on the "frontiers" of Islam, including among communities under Russian or Chinese rule, in the Volga-Ural region, Western Siberia, and Eastern Turkestan. In these contexts, the shrine catalog's miracle stories and exposition of sacred geography is crucial to imparting Islamic meaning to these communities and their sacred locales.

In the Volga-Ural region miraculous conversion narratives set in the city of Bulghar explained the sacred history of Volga-Ural Muslims at a time when they were under Russian rule. They did so by enumerating the shrines of saints in well-known villages and along prominent rivers, and created for Muslims a sort of mental map featuring shrines villages, and rivers corresponding to the jurisdiction of the Russian-established Orenburg Muftiate in 1788.[18] We see similar conversion narratives popularized in Western Siberia, depicting the conversion of Western Siberia at the hands of Naqshbandi *shaykhs*, and the "uncovering" of saints' tombs. The sacred boundaries established in the Siberian accounts do not correspond to Russian administrative boundaries, but instead emphasize the role of Central Asian *khojas*, whose descendants remained in Siberia, in establishing the Muslim community.[19]

Among the regional hagiographic traditions, scholars have been the most thorough in examining Eastern Turkestan. Their contributions permit us to discern with considerable clarity the social and religious functions of hagiography – and the Sufi ideas it transmits. In his study of historical thought among Muslims in Eastern Turkestan, Rian Thum has demonstrated the complex and profound role of Turkic hagiographies in framing for local Muslims regional boundaries that separated them from non-Muslims, or from Muslims belonging to other communities. Among the aspects he examines are the manuscripts themselves, and the significance of pilgrimage in the creation of a shared historical vision among Uyghurs. To accomplish this, Thum provides an insightful analysis of the recitation of hagiographies at shrines. He observes that hagiographic traditions in the broader sense could differ in terms of certain points of emphasis, reflecting differences in purpose for its compilers and audiences. For example, the rich East Turkestani *tazkira* tradition, with its close relationship to local shrines, and its emphasis on conversion narratives, coexisted with the clearly Naqshbandi orientation of

---

18 Frank, "Islamic Shrine Catalogues," 265–286.

19 See, A. G. Seleznev et al. *Kul't sviatykh v sibirskom islame: spetsifika universal'nogo,* (Kazan: Izdatel'skii Dom Mardzhani, 2009); Bustanov, "The Narrative of Ishaq Bab."

the work *Taẕkira-yi ʿAzīzān*, which emphasizes genealogy, focusing on the descendants of the 16th Century Central Asian Naqshbandi figure Makhdūm-i Aʿẓam.[20]

Thum's identification of two separate doctrinal, or perhaps rather thematic, aspects in East Turkestani hagiography does not signify any sort of impermeable division, however. In Central Asia, *khoja* conversion narratives, which certainly had a strong influence on the Siberian conversion narratives mentioned above, contained both conversion narratives, and genealogical charters of *khoja* families.[21] The melding of local shrine catalogs and "city histories," similar to those Thum and others have described for East Turkestan, as we have seen, is also evident for Sayram, and other cities. Of course, this discussion only touches upon written works. Hagiography as a compositional genre is also transmitted orally. It is oral accounts of saints lives and miracles that typically serve as the sources for the written hagiographies.[22]

Kazakh Hagiographies

The modern Kazakh hagiographies and genealogical treatises used in this study make up the current manifestation of an long tradition of Muslim sacred literature from medieval to modern Central Asia. This continuity is immediately evident in Central Asian sacred compositional genres, and its survival should encourage us to rethink the assertions of scholars that the Soviet era necessarily represented a break in "learned" Muslim cultural traditions, or that Islamic tradition was relegated to "the family."[23] Clearly, for Kazakhs (and other Central Asians) kinship and "family" could be understood more broadly than Khalid suggests. It also should encourage us to qualify what is understood as "learned" tradition, to include Sufi conceptions and literary activity, and beyond simply Islamic jurisprudence and *madrasa* training.

---

20 Thum, *Sacred Routes of Uyghur History*, 114–120; on Muḥammad-Ṣādiq Kashghārī's *Taẕkira-yi ʿazīzān,* the main hagiography and genealogical treatise addressing the lineage of Makhdūm-i Aʿẓam in East Turkestan; see Mŭkhammed-Sadïq Qashghari, *Tazkira-yi ʻazizan,* Aytzghan Nurmanova ed., Qazaqstan tarikhï turalï derektemelerï IV, (Almaty: Daik Press, 2006).

21 Devin DeWeese and Ashirbek Muminov eds. *Izlamizatsiia i sakral'nye rodoslovnye v Tsentral'noi Azii* I-II, (Almaty: Daik Press, 2008–2013).

22 The Soviet ethnographer Gleb Snesarev published some important research on this little-studied aspect of hagiography; see G. P. Snesarev, *Khorezmskie legendy kak istochnik po istorii religioznykh kul'tov Srednei Azii*, (Moscow: Nauka, 1983).

23 Adeeb Khalid, *Islam after Communism: Religion and Politics in Central Asia* (Berkeley and Los Angeles, University of California Press, 2007), 82, 104.

Islamic historical literature is a good starting point for broadening our definition of what comprises Islamic "learned tradition" in Central Asia. Biographical dictionaries and hagiographies, are of considerable antiquity on the territory of modern Kazakhstan. They were well established in the Syr Darya Valley already in the pre-Mongol era.[24] Two major biographical dictionaries, focusing mainly on the *ʿulamāʾ* of the Kazakh steppe, date from the 20th century, and the larger of the two was composed in the Brezhnev era. Parallel to the biographical dictionaries, the most enduring and influential hagiographic compositional genres are the Islamization narratives and genealogical treatises associated with Kazakhstan's *khoja* communities, originally concentrated along the Syr Darya, particularly in and around the city of Turkistan, but in fact located throughout Kazakhstan. Many Kazakh *khoja* narratives are linked to shrines associated with the Yasavi Sufi tradition, such as the shrines of Ahmad Yasavi in Turkistan, of Arïstanbap near Otrar, and others. Much like the East Turkestani hagiographies described by Rian Thum, Jeff Eden, and others, these *khoja* treatises are often affiliated with specific shrines, and explain in sacred terms the Islamization of Central Asia. The Central Asian *khoja* materials, associated with important shrine centers such as Turkistan, Sayram, and Awliya-Ata appear to be, at least to some degree, reflected in East Turkestani and Siberian Islamization narratives and shrine catalogs. In Kazakhstan, modern *khoja* treatises are certainly part of this older, and still thriving, tradition.[25]

Kazakh hagiographies do not have to be shrine-centered, or even lineage-centered. A case in point is the *Manāqib-i pīrān-i ʿazīzān* by ʿAqid b. ʿUlūmchī Qarmāṣāqōf, from a community inhabiting the Chinese Altay. This pre-Revolutionary Kazakh-language work combines history, hagiography, and genealogy. It was published in 1909, structured as a *silsila* of a Khoqandi *pir* named Muḥammad-Mūʾmin, known as Kerey Ishan or Īshān-i Pīr. The *silsila* begins with the Prophet Muhammad, via the Naqshbandīya-Mujaddīdīya *silsila*. This particular hagiography does not describe Kerey Ishan's miracles, even though, we are repeatedly assured, he was able to perform them; rather, it focuses on his role in saving the Kereys from

---

[24] For a discussion of the pre-Mongol historical and geographic literature on Jand and the lower Syr Darya region, see Devin DeWeese, "Baba Kamal Jandi and the Kubravi Tradition among the Turks of Central Asia," *Der Islam*, 71/1 (1994), 61–65; *Istoriia Kazakhstana v persidskikh istochnikakh* I, Ashirbek Muminov, ed. (Almaty: Daik Press, 2005), 156.

[25] See, DeWeese and Muminov, *Izlamizatsiia i sakral'nye rodoslovnye* I-II; for an extensive collection of modern sacred genealogical treatises, see Seyt-Omar Sattarŭlï, *Qozhalar shezhïresï,* (Almaty: n.p., 2016).

ignorance (*nādānlïq*) and educating the entire community to live according to Muslim law. The work is very much a religious history of this Kerey community in the 19th century, where the *ishan* is depicted as the community leader.[26]

Following the collapse of the Soviet Union prohibitions on the publication of Kazakh hagiographic literature vanished in Kazakhstan. Written hagiography reemerged within three primary (and sometimes overlapping) compositional genres. Certainly, the most popular and widespread genre was the genealogical treatise, or *shezhīre*. Publishing Kazakh genealogies and genealogical treatises became a lucrative and praiseworthy activity after 1991, and genealogical treatises devoted to Kazakh society as a whole, and to specific descent groups, including the three *zhüzes*, the individual tribes associated with each of the three *zhüzes*, and the non-*zhüz* descent groups (*khojas, töres, tölengīts*, and others) appeared in profusion. These treatises vary in focus, but often include extensive biographical information on saints, as well as on the *ʿulamāʾ*, political leaders, poets, and similarly prominent historical and cultural figures.[27] Kazakh genealogical treatises can be geographically oriented, or focus on genealogical subdivisions with larger lineages, or even families. The genealogical treatise constitutes the most common compositional genre for historical reference among Kazakh and *khoja* communities. They are important sources not only for the biographical information they contain, but also for their chronological breadth, which typically covers the Soviet era. This study makes use of several such genealogical treatises that contain hagiographical elements and are discussed in more detail below.

The second compositional genre in which we find extensive hagiographic information is the shrine catalog. In Kazakhstan, the authors of these works often structure them as a biographical dictionary of saints. In Islamic societies, the biographical dictionary is usually associated with legal scholars, and this

---

[26] ʿAqid b. ʿUlūmchī Qarmāṣāqōf, *Manāqib-i pīrān-i ʿazīzān* (Kazan: Tipografiia Imperatorskago Universiteta, 1909); Qurbān-ʿAlī Khālidī includes Kerey Ishan in his biographical dictionary but identifies him by the name Muḥammad-Manṣūr; see Qurbān-ʿAlī Khālidī, *An Islamic Biographical Dictionary of the Eastern Kazakh Steppe, 1770–1912*, Allen J. Frank and Mirkasyim Usmanov eds., (Leiden: Brill, 2005), fol. 87a.

[27] Kazakh genealogies in this category include, Khamit Madanov, *Kīshī zhüzdīng shezhīresī*, (Atamŭra-Qazaqstan, 1994); M. S. Mukanov, *Iz istoricheskogo proshlogo (rodoslovnaia plemen kerei i uak)*, (Almaty: Qazaqstan, 1998); T. A. Engsebayev, *Qanzhïghalï shezhīresī*, (Pavlodar: EKO, 2004); Tengīzbay Üsenbayev, *Alshïn shezhīresī*, (Qïzïlorda: Tŭmar, 2003); Sotsial Zhŭmabayev and Kärīm Zhalmaqanov, *Bīrzhannïng belgīsīz ghŭmïrï – Nŭralï shezhīresī* (Petropavl: n.p., 2009).

characterization applies to some of the major Islamic biographical dictionaries compiled in Kazakhstan. Hagiographical elements are essentially absent in Qurbān-ʿAlī Khālidī's untitled biographical dictionary, composed in 1912. Similarly, Sadwaqas Ghïlmani's larger work, *Zamanïmizda bolghan ghŭlamalardïng ghŭmïr tarikhtarï* (Biographies of the Islamic Scholars of Our Times) completed in 1972, mentions saints only in order to denounce pilgrims for violating SADUM's fatwas on the topic.[28]

Biographical dictionaries often appear in Kazakh publishing as reference works, especially embedded within genealogical treatises, where they are included to list prominent individuals within the descent group. Other biographical dictionaries focus on luminaries from specific jurisdictions, literati, historical figures, and so on.[29] However, biographical dictionaries containing hagiographical information on saints appear to be modeled more on the older shrine catalog genre. In addition to listing ancient saints from the medieval era, the hagiographical works used in this study also include accounts of saints who lived in the Soviet era. All of these works were composed and published in Kazakh, and while they share structural features with biographical dictionaries of Islamic legal scholars, or with secular biographical dictionaries, in terms of content, they fit squarely within the older shrine catalog genre, albeit with more extensive versions of biographies devoted to individual saints and their shrines. These shrine catalogs are sometimes published as small pamphlets containing an individual biography, or as local urban histories. Biographies in this category include pamphlets devoted to Baba Tükles and Ükasha Ata, as well as a pamphlet devoted to the history of city of Sayram and its shrines.[30]

Shrine catalogs structured as biographical dictionaries of saints, including saints from the Soviet era, include several substantial works devoted to the Syr Darya Valley, that contain extensive hagiographic material. These include two works by Shaydarbek Qazhï Äshĭmŭlï, and an extensive six-volume set

---

[28] Qurbān-ʿAlī Khālidī, A*n Islamic Biographical Dictionary of the Eastern Kazakh Steppe, 1770–1912,* Allen J. Frank and Mirqasym Usmanov eds. (Leiden: Brill, 2005); Saduaqas Ghïlmani, *Biographies of the Islamic Scholars of Our Times* II, Ashirbek Muminov et al. eds. (Istanbul: IRCICA, 2018), 189–190.

[29] Tĭlegen qazhï Moldabayŭlï Dütpayev, *Sarïköl qazhïlarï men taqualarï* (Qostanay: Qostanay baspa üyĭ, 2012); Tangat Sügĭrbayev, *Qïzïlzhar öngĭrĭnĭng ziyalï qauïmï,* (Petropavl: n.p., 2010).

[30] Absattar Qŭttïqozhaŭlï, *Ükasha Ata tarikhi*, (n.p., n.d.); Dulat Tŭrantegĭ and Zharïlqasïn Boranbap, *Baba Tüktĭ Shashlï Äzĭz*, (Shymkent: Zhĭbek zholï, 1996); Mirahmad Mirkholdor öghli, *Sayram tarikhi,* (Shymkent: Chimkent shahar bosmakhonasi, 1991).

by Qazïbek Täzhiyev devoted to the saints and shrines of South Kazakhstan *oblast*.[31] Äshïmülï identifies himself as a *khoja*, and as a descendants of Baba Tükles via the lineage of Müsïräli (Sopï Äziz), a major figure in the traditions of the Junior Zhüz. He reveals that since 1981 he had served as caretaker (*shïraqshï*) of the tomb of one of his ancestors, Äbzhel Baba, and his work contains hagiographies of dozens of *khoja* saints along the Syr Darya, based on accounts that he heard beginning before the Second World War, or else that his father had collected and recorded. Äshïmülï's two books are our richest sources for saints during the Stalin era.[32] Täzhiyev's geographically-organized work is structurally quite similar to Äshïmülï's two books. His work contains particularly extensive hagiographical accounts devoted to Baba Tükles, and for our purposes, miracle stories associated with Appaq Ishan, an important *khoja* and *ishan* who was a victim of Stalinist repression.[33] Seyt-Omar Sattarülï's voluminous treatise on *khoja* genealogies contains some hagiographical materials, too.[34] Briefer works include a shrine catalog for the Qaratau, a region of the Syr Darya Valley,[35] and a biographical dictionary of saints in Qïzïlorda oblast', embedded in a larger reference work devoted to the cultural heritage of that province.[36] Accounts of saints and their miracles appear in other genres as well, most notably contributions of local journalists and historians. Journalism and local history are self-consciously secular genres and, strictly speaking, fall outside of the realm of Kazakh sacred literature. But, they often transmit accounts of miracles and saints obtained from local oral tradition, and more importantly, the journalists are often strongly invested in the religious foundations of their subjects.[37]

---

31 Shaydarbek Äshïmülï, *Sïr boyïndaghï äuliyeler*, (Almaty: Atamüra, 2000); Shaydarbek-qazhï Äshïmülï, *Sïrgha tolï Sïr boyï: tarikhi-tanïmdïq zhazbalar* (Almaty: Foliant, 2009); Qazïbek Täzhiyev and S. Ömïrzaqov eds. *Äz äuliyeler* I-VI, *Qazïnalï ongtüstïk* vol. 22. (Almaty: Nürlï älem, 2011).

32 Äshïmülï, *Sïrgha tolï Sïr boyï.* 323–324.

33 Appaq Ishan is the subject of a chapter of a monograph, based on NKVD archival sources; see, M. K. Koigeldiev, *Stalinizm i repressii v Kazakhstane v 1920–1940-kh godakh*, (Almaty: n.p, 2009).

34 Sattarülï, *Qozhalar shezhïresï.*

35 Eskermes Zhaqsïmbetov, *Äzïretï Qaratau, äuliyening kenï edï*, (Shymkent: Zhïbek zholï, 2000).

36 Zh. A. Zhontayeva and Sh. Sh. Äbdïbayev, *Sïr elïnïng mädeni müralarï*, (Qïzïlorda: n.p., 2005).

37 Some of these works contain important accounts of saints and their miracles; see Shaytürsïn Äbdïbayev, *Sïr elïnïng mädeni müralarï*, (Qïzïlorda: Qïzïlordapoligrafiya, 2005); for a similar work devoted to Aqtöbe oblast, see Rïszhan Iliyasova, *Dalam tünghan shezhïre*, (Almaty: Zerde, 2007).

In addition to the shrine catalogs mentioned above, another important body of sources are genealogical treatises devoted to holy lineages, including both *khojas* and non-*khojas*. These works share many of the features of classical Islamic hagiography defined by Jürgen Paul and others. They can be structured as a single narrative, moving from generation to generation, and enumerating saints, their miracles, and tracing the lineage's family tree. At other times these works appear as collections of articles by multiple contributors, that nevertheless fulfill the same purpose: tracing the family tree and documenting the lineage's holiness by the transmission of miracle stories. In addition to the biographical dictionaries of saints, we have hagiographies, or hagiographic collections for three holy lineages in Kazakhstan.

Hagiographies devoted to Maral Baba Ishan Qŭrmanŭlï

There are three book-length works devoted to Maral Baba Ishan Qŭrmanŭlï (1783–1841), two of which fall into the category of hagiographies. The first of these is titled *Islam zhäne Maral Baba* (Maral Baba and Islam). The book is undated, without indicating a publisher or place of publication, but it likely appeared in Qïzïlorda in 1996. Its author, Säden Nŭrtayŭlï, is not a member of the lineage. Rather, he is from a family that associated with the lineage, and that obtained its own religious power from it.[38] The work is structured in many respects as a classical Islamic hagiography. It begins by emphasizing the Islamic credentials of his subject, then presents a biography of Maral Ishan, with his travels, deeds, and miracles, depicting him as an ideal Muslim. He discusses the sons of Maral Ishan and their descendants, with an emphasis on their shrines, miracles and ancestral spirits (*äruaqtar*). Nŭrtayŭlï devotes particular attention to explaining the basis of the lineage's religious authority. Maral was an *ishan*, but he was not a *khoja*. He was a member of the Ashaymalï Kerey lineage, of the Middle *Zhüz*. Nŭrtayŭlï emphasizes Maral Ishan's relationship with his Sufi master, his ability to perform miracles (passed on to his descendants), and above all his relationship with his ancestral spirits.

Certainly, Nŭrtayŭlï's purpose in emphasizing these elements is to counter anticipated criticisms from *khoja* lineages. Nŭrtayŭlï relies almost entirely on oral accounts, which includes not only stories and interviews, but also hitherto unpublished songs and poetry composed during the Soviet era. An important

---

[38] Nŭrtayŭlï, *Islam zhäne Maral Baba*, 83; the work is reprinted in a collected volume of Nŭrtayŭlï's writings; see Säden Nŭrtayŭlï, *Keng dalanïng ŭlïlïghï*, (Almaty: n.p., 2018).

source for Nŭrtayŭlï's treatise is poetry by the *aqïn* Seyĭtzhan Bekshentayŭlï (1874–1938), who was arrested and shot during the Great Purges.[39]

The second work devoted to Maral Baba and his descendants is Sïrlïbay Bürkĭtbayŭlï's, *Maral ishannïng nŭr shapaghatï* (Maral Ishan's Divine Intercession), published in Qostanay in 1998. Like Nŭrtayŭlï, Bürkĭtbayŭlï is not a descendant of Maral Ishan, but is from a separate family with close religious ties to the lineage. The author structured this work as a biographical treatise, including a hagiographical biography of Maral Ishan, and similar biographical outlines of his descendants in Qostanay and North Kazakhstan oblasts. In addition to oral traditions, Bürkĭtbayŭlï appears to have used archival materials, particularly related to the trials in the 1920s and 30s of members of the lineage.

The third book devoted to Maral Ishan is *Qasiyettĭ Maral Ishan* (Holy Maral Ishan), published in Qïzïlorda in 2005, and edited by Änĭs Öteuŭlï. The book defies categorization as a hagiographical work. Consisting of a collection articles by differing authors, it does comprise hagiographical and genealogical materials, but appears conceived as a work of popular local history, containing archival documents, testimonials from descendants and local officials, etc. A feature that all of these works share, however, is the promotion of local (and genealogical) pride, and Kazakh patriotism, in addition to the promotion of the religious authority of Maral Ishan and his lineage. Stories about Maral Baba are frequently repeated in the biographical and hagiographical works about the Syr Darya Valley, Aqtöbe *oblast,* and, separately, in treatises devoted to the Kerey tribe, of which Maral Baba was a member.[40]

One of our most extensive sources for this study is a hagiography and genealogical treatise devoted to a prominent *khoja* lineage in South Kazakhstan *oblast'*. This work, titled *Äziz äulet: Shakhiakhmed Khazret pen onïng ĭnĭsĭ Fatikh imamnïng häm olardïng ŭrpaqtarïnïng shezhĭresĭ* (The Honored Lineage: His Holiness Shakhiakhmad, His Younger Brother Fatikh Imam, and the Genealogy of their Descendants), is by Asqar Mangabay (Uäli)ŭlï, who is a member of the lineage. It contains family stories, oral literature, reminiscences, and accounts of miracles of a lineage descended

---

39 For Bekshentayŭlï's collected works, see Dayrabay Tïnïshbek et al. eds., *Bekshentayŭlï Seyĭtzhan, Dabïlŭlï Moldakhmet, Bäykenov Älibek: shïgharmalar,* (Astana: Foliant, 2009).

40 Iliyasova, *Dalam tŭnghan shezhĭre,* 65–68 Zhontayeva and Äbdĭbayev, *Sïr elĭnĭng mädeni mŭralarï,* 69–70, 81–82; Äshĭmŭlï, *Sïr boyïndaghï äuliyeler,* 94–97; Zhŭmabayev and Zhalmaqanov, *Bĭrzhannïng belgĭsĭz ghŭmïrï,* 150–157; Sotsial Zhŭmabayev, *Ŭlïlar tughan ölke* (Petropavl: n.p., 2006), 361–366.

from a Tatar *khoja* named Shāh-i Aḥmad aṣ-Ṣābawī (1812–1878). Although structured as a single narrative, it lacks the focused and integrated structure of Säden Nŭrtayŭlï's work on Maral Ishan. *Äziz äulet* contains verbatim contributions from various sources who corresponded with the author, and can be at times repetitive. Nevertheless, the *Äziz äulet* is one of the finest examples of post-Soviet hagiographic literature in Kazakhstan and provides us with detailed information on the social relations of *khojas* with non-*khojas*, and on the experiences of a rather extensive lineage during the Stalin years. Another important source on Shāh-i Aḥmad and his descendants, sontaining considerable original information, is found in the second volume of the shrine catalogs devoted to South Kazakhstan oblast. [41]

Isabek Ishan

Isabek Ishan Mŭratŭlï (1792–1871) was a *khoja* who lived in Pavlodar oblast', among the Arghïns of the Middle Zhüz. He is the subject of a collected volume, titled *Isabek Ishan*, published in Pavlodar in 2011. The publication coincided with the restoration of Isabek Ishan's tomb in in the settlement of Aqköl, and the Governor of Pavlodar oblast', Erlan Arïn, is credited as the volume's Chief Editor. As Ulan Bigozhin explains in his extensive anthropological study of Isabek Ishan's shrine and lineage, political figures such as Arïn, had an interest in emphasizing their credentials as patrons of Islam and Kazakhstani patriotism by promoting Isabek's shrine. [42] This patronage also involved the promotion of local hagiography devoted to the lineage associated with the shrine. In this regard, the volume contains a section devoted to the *khoja* lineage in general, and locally, three sections devoted to Isabek Ishan's descendants and their genealogies, comprising biographical and hagiographic testimonials from numerous people, and a final section collecting scholarly articles on *khojas* and their significance in Kazakh society. While not a clear-cut hagiography in the manner of *Äziz äulet* or *Islam zhäne Maral Baba*, the publication of *Isabek Ishan* demonstrates that hagiography retains a place in discussions of saints, shrines, and genealogy, and remains socially and politically relevant.

---

[41] Asqar Mangabay (Uäli)ŭlï, *Äziz äulet: Shakhiakhmed Khazret pen onïng ïnïsï Fatikh imamnïng häm olardïng ŭrpaqtarïnïng shezhïresï*, (Almaty: Öner, 2001); S. Ömïrzaqov et al. eds. *Äz äuliyeler* II, *Qazïnalï Ongtüstïk* 22, 6–40.

[42] Ulan Bigozhin, *Shrine, State, and Sacred Lineage in Post-Soviet Kazakhstan*, Unpublished Ph.D. Dissertation, Indiana University, Bloomington, 2017, 142–144.

SOURCES FOR MODERN KAZAKH HAGIOGRAPHIES AND SHRINE CATALOGS

Modern Kazakh hagiographies and shrine catalogs are based in large measure on oral sources. They share this feature with much of the Islamic historiography composed in Russia and Central Asia in the 20th century. Before the emergence of Soviet academic historiography, Kazakhs' historical knowledge was collected and diffused orally or through manuscripts based on oral tradition.[43] Historical themes were, of course, important elements in Kazakh oral epics, and these works form the foundation of much of Kazakh secular historical consciousness (and historical mythology) today. Yet, even this literature, presented today in nationalist terms, was originally composed and circulated within contexts of genealogical recitation, in which descent groups related stories of their ancestors, whose biographies were placed in a broader political context. A particularly clear example of this is a manuscript verse history of Abïlay Khan (1711–1781), titled *Tarikhat*, by the Chingisid poet Shädĭ-töre Aqïn. It is structured as a history of the Kazakh steppe in the 18th century, but also as Shädĭ-töre's own Chingisid genealogy, here centered around his ancestor Abïlay Khan.[44]

In Kazakh oral historiography, the line between the oral and the written could be blurred. Along the Syr Darya River, genealogical treatises were probably retained as manuscripts, to be recited at shrines. The profusion of manuscript hagiographies in East Turkestan, and their use for public recitations to some degree demonstrates that the division of a unified discursive tradition into oral and written aspects can be arbitrary. Kazakh genealogical treatises, too, were sometimes preserved as manuscripts. Maral Baba's Kerey ancestors in northern Kazakhstan traced the written recording of their genealogy to a 17th century figure.[45] At the same time, genealogy was

[43] K. Zhünĭsbayev's useful discussion of 17th and 18th century Kazakh historical sources is actually based in 19th and early 20th century publications of Kazakh genealogical treatises, and collections derived from oral historical accounts of specific lineages, that often are included within genealogical treatises; see K. Zhünĭsbayev, "Qazaqstannïng XVII-XVIII ghasïrlardaghï tarikhïna baylanïstï qazaq tĭlĭndegĭ keybĭr tarikhi derekter turalï," *Voprosy istorii Kazakhstana i Vostochnogo Turkestana*, Trudy Instituta Istorii, Arkheologii i Etnografii imeni Ch. Ch. Valikhanova, tom 15, (Alma-Ata: Izdatel'stvo Akademii Nauk Kazakhskoi SSR, 1962, 154–170. The methodological problems of using Kazakh historical epics as historical sources remains to be thoroughly explored.

[44] For the publication of this work, see Zarïlqasïn Boranbayev, *Shïghïs shayïrlarïnïng songï – Shädĭ Aqïn,* (Almaty: Bĭlĭm, 2014), 139–249. In Shädĭ-aqïn's genealogy Abïlay Khan is descended from the Janid khans of Bukhara.

[45] Zhŭmabayev and Zhalmaqanov, *Bĭrzhannïng belgĭsĭz ghŭmïrï,* 116.

above all a public endeavor, and the specific historical events involving ancestors were known through public recitations. These poems appear not to have been widely committed to writing until the 20th century, and their publication in Cyrillic-script transcription became widespread only following Kazakhstan's independence.[46]

To the degree that the hagiographies consulted for this study conform to the genre of the genealogical treatise, their authors clearly wrote for the same public realm as the genealogical histories described above. For example, the works devoted to Maral Baba and Shāh-i Aḥmad Ishan rely on both unpublished poetry and collective genealogical traditions. At the same time, they make use of numerous informants for stories, and especially for miracle stories. The authors apply a degree of methodological discipline in documenting their oral sources, generally identifying them by name, and recording their relationship to the events, including when necessary, the chain of transmission leading them to the event.[47] Such a method is well known from hadith studies; but hadith criticism is not necessarily at the root of this method, which is widely encountered in both written historiography and hagiography. Such an approach is also evident in the shrine catalogs, although there it appears less uniformly applied, possibly because they often transmitted widely known legends of medieval saints.[48]

[46] The function of genealogies (*shäzhärä*) among Bashkirs as political charters of collective (tribal) landholding rights is well attested in the Bashkir milieu, where they were public documents in every sense of the term; see R. G. Kuzeev, *Bashkirskie shezhere*, (Ufa: Bashkirskoe knizhnoe izdatel'stvo, 1960).

[47] Asqar Mangabay (Uäli)ŭlï, *Äziz äulet,* 52, 80, 83, 96, 136, 177, 209; Nŭrtayŭlï, *Islam zhäne Maral Baba,* 13,44, 46–47, 53, 55–56, 58, 71, 73, 82.

[48] Äshĭmŭlï, *Sïr boyïndaghï äuliyeler*, 111, 114; Äshĭmŭlï, *Sïrgha tolï Sïr boyï*; 196, 300; Zhontayeva and Sh. Sh. Äbdĭbayev, *Sïr elĭnĭng mädeni mŭralarï*, 83, 85; Täzhiyev, *Äz äuliyeler* V, 111.

CHAPTER 2. SUFI COMMUNITIES AND THE SIGNIFICANCE OF MIRACLES

SUFI COMMUNITIES IN CENTRAL ASIA

Stalinist repression was directed against individuals, social classes, and social categories. At the same time, it targeted communities, and in particular, religious communities. Repression fell especially heavily on societies structured on a religious basis, including Kazakh society, where holy lineages constituted a prominent feature of social organization. These holy lineages, which were, and are, found throughout Central Asia, can be defined as Sufi communities, because they derived their holiness and prestige through their Sufi family genealogies. Additionally, their bonds with the communities in which they resided were rooted in Sufi conceptions and metaphors. The Soviet assault on religious communities was, of course, part of a much larger project of cultural revolution, aiming at the absolute secularization of Muslims. In practical terms, the repression of Sufi communities meant that as a targeted social category, they were objects of repressive measures. Of course, they could also be swept up in broader waves of state-organized social and economic disruption, such as mass famine; they could be singled out for retaliation following uprisings, which were numerous in Kazakhstan between 1929 and 1931; or they could be accused of political crimes individually or collectively.

Sufi communities in Central Asia, including in Kazakhstan, were organized as kinship-based lineages; typically, they were *khoja* communities claiming descent ultimately from the family of the Prophet Muhammad (or from the first four Caliphs), but no less importantly, through local saints. Not all holy lineages were *khoja* lineages. They could also come from among "commoner" (*qara*) lineages, descended from saints belonging to a specific tribe. One of the features of these holy lineages, especially in Kazakhstan, was the maintenance of multi-generational relationships with "non-holy" lineages. These bonds were usually expressed using Sufi terminology, with senior members of the holy lineage referred to as the Sufi master, usually by the term "*ishan*," or "*pir*," and the non-holy lineage as disciples, or "*murids*." As a social metaphor, the master-disciple relationship was not restricted to kinship communities. In sedentary Central Asia, such a metaphor was applied in craft guilds.[1]

The founders and senior religious figures in the lineages discussed in this study are called "*ishans*" in the sources. Turkic sources refer to the phenomenon, and more specifically to the activities associated with *ishan* lineages, as *ishanlïq* or, in modern Kazakh, *ishandïq*. In Russian sources this term is translated as *ishanizm*, which in tsarist and Soviet sources often bore a politically pejorative implication.[2] The nature and practices of *ishans* in Central Asia and the Volga-Ural region, and the significance of the term, vary. The term derives from an honorific, derived from the Persian third person plural pronoun, "they." It originated in medieval Sufi brotherhoods and retains strong Sufi associations.[3] Since *ishans* usually belonged to *khoja* lineages, by the end of the 19th century, if not earlier, the terms could be synonymous, especially in Central Asia.[4] In sedentary regions of Central Asia, including

---

1 E. M. Peshchereva, "Organization of Craftsmen in Central Asia in the Late XIXth and Early XXth Centuries, *XXV Mezhdunarodnyi kongress vostokovedov,* III, (Moscow, 1963), 519–522; M. Gavrilov, *Risolia sartovskikh remeslennikov: izsledovanie predanii musul'manskikh tsekhov*, (Tashkent, 1912); pamphlets containing stories linking specific crafts or occupations with *pirs* were circulating in Uzbekistan and Turkmenistan in the 1990s and 2000s.

2 In Soviet sources "*ishanizm*" is often synonymous with "*sheikhizm*," and "*miuridizm*;" for examples of how these terms were used in Soviet sources, see, N. A. Smirnov, *Musul'manskoe sektanstvo*, (Moscow: Bezbozhnik, 1930), 15–22; Z. A. Ishmukhametov, *Sotsial'naia rol' i evoliutsiia islama v Tatarii*, (Kazan: Tatarskoe knizhnoe izdatel'stvo, 1979), 43–58; A. A. Rosliakov, "K voprosu o miuridizme v Turkmenii," Izvestiia Akademii Nauk Turkmenskoi SSR, No. 5, 1962, 21–25. However, the same terms also appear more or less pejoratively in the works Tatar nationalists and of pre-Revolutionary Russian authors; see Gaiaz Iskhaki, *Idel-Ural,* (Kazan: Tatarskoe knizhnoe izdatel'stvo, 1991), 37; "O musul'mankom dukhovenstve, sufiiakh, i ishanakh," *Tserkovnye vedomosti,* 22 October 1898, 1454–1455. For the North Caucasus this concept seems to have been particularly politicized, and as in Central Asia and the Volga-Ural region, used rather imprecisely; for a critical evaluation of the term for the North Caucasus, see, Vladimir Bobrovnikov and Michael Kemper, "Miuridizm," *Islam na territorii byvshei Rossiiskoi imperii* 5, (Moscow: Vostochnaia Literatura," 2013), 98–99.

3 On the origins of the term *ishan* see, Sergei Abashin, "Ishan," *Islam na territorii byvshei Rossiiskoi imperiia: entsiklopedcheskii slovari* I, (Moscow: Vostochnaia Literatura, 2006), 164–166; Sergei Abashin, *Sovetskii kishlak*, (Moscow: Novoe literaturnoe obozrenie, 2015), 501–507.

4 B. Kh. Karmysheva, *Ocherki etnicheskoi istorii iuzhnykh raionov Tadzhikistana i Uzbekistana*, (Moscow: Glavnaia Redaktsiia Vostochnoi Literatury, 1976), 150–153; Abashin, *Sovetskii kishlak*, 501–507.

Tashkent, *ishans* from *khoja* lineages also bore the honorific *töre*, which signified a member of a prestigious lineage.[5]

Historically, *ishan* status grew out of Sufi authority, based on membership in holy lineages claiming descent from both the family of the Prophet Muhammad and through Sufic chains of initiation (*silsilas*).[6] *Ishan* status did not necessarily require practicing the Sufi discipline or training *murids*, although, to be sure, many Central Asian *ishans*, including Kazakh *ishans*, were Sufi masters. Nevertheless, the institution of *ishanlïq* in Central Asia differed in some respects from the Volga-Ural region, where, *ishans* were exclusively associated with the Sufi discipline, and where, for all practical purposes, *ishans* were rarely, if ever, *khojas*. By contrast, in Central Asia most *ishans* came from *khoja* lineages, and *ishans* did not always practice the Sufi discipline. [7] A Russian observer of *ishan* communities in Samarqand distinguished practicing *ishans* from "hereditary *ishans*," who did not necessarily practice the Sufi discipline, but fulfilled the social and economic roles of *ishans,* demonstrating that this phenomenon was not specific to nomads.[8] The disassociation between *ishans* and training in the Sufi discipline per se is well-documented among nomadic and semi-nomadic groups. In those environments, *ishans* could function as religious patrons (*pirs*) to entire nomadic descent groups, and these relationships evolved into relationships between lineages, although there certainly were *ishans* among the steppe nomads who, we know, did train adepts in the Sufi discipline. In any case, with or without the actual practice of the Sufi discipline, these relationships were expressed through the metaphor of the Sufi master-disciple relationship (*pir-murid* or *murid-murshid*). Such collective relationships were already documented among the Turkmen nomads of the Mangghïstau region in the

---

5 Sergei Abashin, "Tura," *Islam na territorii byvshei Rossiiskoi imperiia,* 387–388; among Kazakhs, the title *töre* was used exclusively for the Chingisid nobility.

6 In discussing his father's Sufi master in 19th century Bukhara, the Tatar historian Aḥmad Barāngawī includes Jalāl ad-Dīn Khiyābānī's Ḥusaynī genealogy, as well as his Naqshbandi *silsila,* in his treatise; see Aḥmad b. Ḥāfiẓ al-Dīn al-Barāngawī, *Tārīkh al-Barāngawī*, Manuscript Institute of Tatarstan, 39/34, fol. 141ab.

7 Russian pre-Revolutionary descriptions of *ishans* in Central Asia emphasize their role in training adepts in the Sufi discipline, while lamenting the "ignorance" of *ishans* who did not, particularly among the Kazakhs; see N. S. Lykoshin, *Pol zhizni v Turkestane*, (Petrograd: Berezovskii, 1916), 147–148; Abdulsattar, *K Voprosu o mususl'manskikh ishanakh*, (Kazan: Lito-tipografiia Imperatorskago Universiteta, 1895), 4–5.

8 "Kratkii obzor sovremennago sostoianiia i deiatel'nosti musul'manskago dukhovenstva," *Sbornik materialov po musul'manstvu* I, V. I. Iarovyi-Ravskii ed., (St. Peterburg: Topgrafiia Rozenoer, 1899), 26.

16th century, where an entire Turkmen lineage is identified as "companions" (*aṣḥāb*) of an *ishan*. Such a relationships also appear in 18th century sources in the Kazakh context. We can find a similar relationship among tribal Uzbeks in southern Uzbekistan, where during the Soviet era kinship within a lineage was viewed as synonymous with sharing a common *pir*.[9] Under these circumstances, *ishans* did not have to emphasize their Sufi *silsilas* to establish their authority. The disassociation of *ishans* with *silsilas* is evident among many nomadic and semi-nomadic groups.[10] Based on Kazakh hagiographies in the 19th and 20th centuries a *pir-murid* relationship was seen as a kinship connection binding not only the living, but the dead as well, through each community's ancestral spirits (*äruaqtar*). There could be individuals in these communities who were actual Sufi adepts, learning the Sufi discipline from a master. Sometimes Sufi adepts appear in the sources under the term *pĭradär* (from the Persian word for "brother"), or *duana*. However, the Kazakh sources – at least the post-Soviet sources – can be ambiguous on that point.[11]

Yuri Bregel observed in 1961 that the reason for the development of these sorts of kinship relations between entire descent groups and individual *ishans* was not fully understood.[12] Taking into account more recent work on the history of Sufism in Central Asia and the Volga-Ural region, one possible explanation is that these sorts of kinship relations are manifestations of the decline of the *silsila*, particularly in Central Asia. Devin DeWeese has commented on this phenomenon, describing it as the "disordering of Sufism," which was, in part, made evident by the increased "bundling" of *silsilas*, where Sufi *shaykhs* moved away from identifying with specific Sufi orders,

---

9 Yuri Bregel, *Khorezmskie turkmeny v XIX veke*," (Moscow: Izdatel'stvo Vostochnoi literatury, 1961), 170–171; Karmysheva, *Ocherki etnicheskoi istorii,* 151–152; *Materialy po istorii Kazakhskoi SSR* IV (Moscow:-Leningrad: Izdatel'stvo Akademii Nauk SSSR, 1940), 54.

10 Bregel, *Khorezmskie turkmeny,* 171; Karmysheva, *Ocherki etnicheskoi istorii,* 151–152; S. K. Kamalov, *Karakalpaki v XVIII-XIX vekakh*, (Tashkent: Fan, 1968), 148–149; V. N. Basilov, "Honour Groups in Traditional Turkmenian Society," in: *Islam in Tribal Societies: From the Atlas to the Indus*, edited by Akbar S. Ahmed and David M. Hart, London: Routledge & Kegan Paul, 1984), 229–230; V. N. Basilov and Dzh. Kh. Karmysheva, *Islam u kazakhov*, (Moscow: Institut Etnologii i antropologii im. N. N. Miklukho-Maklai, 1997), 30–33.

11 Asqar Mangabay (Uäli)ŭlĭ, *Äziz äulet: Shakhiakhmed Khazret pen onïng ĭnĭsĭ Fatikh imamnïng häm olardïng ŭrpaqtarïnïng shezhĭresĭ*, (Almaty: Öner, 2001), 91; Basilov and Karmysheva, *Islam u kazakhov*, 31.

12 Bregel, *Khorezmskie turkmeny,* 171.

and sought to accumulate multiple affiliations.[13] It seems likely that integral kinship associations between nomads and *ishan* lineages may have accelerated this phenomenon in the 19th and 20th centuries, when it became commonplace for *ishans*, even if they claimed connections with specific Sufis, to dispense with exclusively associating themselves with specific Sufi orders. Remarkably, it was in the Volga-Ural region, an area commonly (if superficially) associated with Islamic reformism and modernism, that *ishans* seemed to have revealed a strong degree of conservatism by exclusively emphasizing their *silsila* affiliation. It is from Tatar sources – and not Kazakh hagiographies – that we know the *silsila* affiliations of several *ishans* in Kazakhstan mentioned in this study. Furthermore, it was precisely the collective kinship-based relationships of nomads with Sufi masters, described above, that came under strong criticism among Tatar Sufis in the 20th century.[14] Even the most influential Sufi *shaykh* from the Volga-Ural region, the Bashkir Naqshbandi Zaynullāh Rasulev, who trained hundreds of Kazakh *murids* from throughout Kazakhstan, does not appear to have become a *pir* to any Kazakh or Bashkir descent groups.[15] Still, some members of Kazakh lineages who had a collective *pir-murid* relationship with an *ishan* did engage in Sufi disciplinary practice. In his descriptions of *ishans* in Northern Kazakhstan in the middle and late 19th century, Mäshhür-Zhüsīp Köpeyŭlï is unambiguous in describing these *ishans* as Sufi masters.[16] Whatever the causes for the disassociation of the Sufi discipline with the collective *pir-murid* relationship (if it was indeed a disassociation, rather than just a matter of leaving out *silsila* affiliations for other reasons), it is clear that Sufi *silsilas*, and attention to the Sufi discipline, are almost entirely absent from nearly all of the post-Soviet Kazakh

---

13 Devin DeWeese, "Disordering' Sufism in Early Modern Central Asia: Suggestions for Rethinking the Sources and Social Structures of Sufi History in the 18th and 19th Centuries," *History and Culture of Central Asia*, Bakhtiyar Babadzhanov and Yayoi Kawahara eds. (Tokyo: TIAS: Department of Islamic Area Studies, 2012), 259–279.

14 Īshān Muḥammad-Ḥarrāṣ Āydārōf al-Qārghālī, *Īshānlargha khiṭāb!* (Sterlitamak: Nur, 1911), 8.

15 This conclusion is based on the biographical dictionary of a reformist scholar, Saduaqas Ghïlmani, who identified numerous murids of Zaynullāh Rasulev among the Arghïns of the Middle Zhüz. Zaynullah does, however, appear to have taken on this role among Bashkirs since the fall of the Soviet Union; see Z. G. Aminev and L. A. Iamaeva, *Regional'nye osobennosti islama u bashkir*, (Ufa: Dizain PoligrafServis, 2009), 136–147; S. Kildin et al. eds., *Bashqortostan – äüliälär ile,* (Ufa: Kitap, 2012), 223–226.

16 Allen J. Frank, "Sufis, Scholars and Divanas of the Qazaq Middle Horde in the Works of Mäshhür-Zhüsip Köpeyulï," *Islam, Society and States across the Qazaq Steppe,* Niccolo Pianciola and Paolo Sartori, eds. (Vienna: Austrian Academy of Sciences, 2013), 223–227.

hagiographies and genealogical treatises. The disassociation between *ishans* (and especially *ishan* lineages) and the transmission of the Sufi disciplinary practice remains poorly understood, especially in terms of its chronology.

The religious significance of *ishans* for Muslim communities in Central Asia is ultimately connected to ancestral spirits who could intercede for both the *ishans* themselves, and for the kinship lineages the *ishans* were connected with. Although the official Soviet Islamic establishment, including the *qazi* of the Kazakh SSR, Saduaqas Ghïlmani, in the 1960s denounced the idea of *äruaqs*, and the rituals surrounding them, as un-Islamic, they continued to be addressed in Islamic debates in Kazakhstan, and remained central features of Kazakh Islamic practice.[17] The significance of ancestral spirits (*äruaqs*) for the authority of *ishan* lineages is evident from the emphasis placed on them in several of the hagiographies. Bruce Privratsky had demonstrated that the role of *äruaqs* in Kazakh religious belief and practice fits firmly within the boundaries of normative Islam, and had particular relevance in a wide range of Kazakh rituals and practices.[18] However, the significance of these ancestral spirits is appears even more elevated in certain types of holy lineages, to include *khoja* and *ishan* lineages, but also *baqsï*s (commonly, if not quite accurately, referred to as shamans). In the case of *khoja* lineages, their power derived ultimately from the family of the Prophet Muhammad or the first four Caliphs, as well as from local saints in the lineage. In the case of non-*khoja ishans*, their power was derived from other powerful Sufi spirits, such as, in the case of Maral Qŭrmanŭlï, from the "men of the unseen world" (*rijāl al-ghayb*), a class of Sufi tutelary spirits.

Members of *ishan* and *baqsï* lineages, could claim such a connection with ancestral spirits through membership in the lineage. But what made an individual a powerful saint was the quality of his relationship with the spirits. In the hagiographies, such people are referred to by the adjective "*aruaqtï*," meaning "in possession of ancestral spirits" or "having access to ancestral spirits." This quality was not held by all members of a lineage and is in fact passed down from one individual to another, to both men and women.[19]

Complementing their connection with powerful ancestral spirits, and in keeping with the tendency of early hagiographies to demonstrate the Islamic credentials of the subjects, *ishans* were also thought to embody Islamic virtues through their behavior. The *khoja* lineages in particular were associated with

---

17 Saduaqas Ghïlmani, *Biographies of the Islamic Scholars of Our Times* II, Ashirbek Muminov et al. eds. (Istanbul: IRCICA, 2018), 189–190.

18 Bruce G. Privratsky, *Muslim Turkistan,* (Richmond, Surrey: Curzon, 2001), 114–123.

19 Säden Nŭrtayŭlï, *Islam zhäne Maral Baba*, 15–16.

Islamization, and Islamization narratives connected with Iṣḥāq Bāb and other saints set in the early years of Islam feature prominently in their genealogical treatises. *Khojas* in particular depict themselves and their ancestors in these account fulfilling the function of Islamizing their communities by imparting to them Islamic norms, ethics, behaviors, and law. In this respect, "Islamization" was understood as not simply conversion to Islam, but rather the constant perfection of Islamic consciousness and above all, behavior. To that end, one of the tasks of the *ishans* in Kazakh society was to preach (*nasikhattau*) in their communities. The emphasis of *khojas* and *ishans* on their role, and its acknowledgement by Kazakhs, may have contributed to the misunderstanding and stereotype among Tatars and later, Russians, that Kazakh nomads were "partially Islamized." Writing in 1900, Ōrāntāy ibn Qūrïmtāy Qïpchāqī appealed in a verse work on Kazakhs to honor *khojas* because "Kazakhs and *khojas* have been together since the beginning." He explained that God merged the *khojas* and Kazakhs, and the two had "mixed together." He went on to say that *khojas* were "*pirs* to our children, and teach them."[20] *Ishans* from non-noble lineages also took on this role, and as a rule *ishans* depicted themselves as embodying Islamic virtues, and as imparting these virtues to their communities. These virtues could be manifested through the performance of miracles, but they were equally evident through the *ishan's* speech, comportment and actions. Naturally, an *ishan* might not live up to the ideals of Islamic virtue, as the writings of Russian observers and Muslim critics of Sufism are often fond of pointing out. Moralistic and *ad hominem* arguments aside, beyond their role as "Islamizers," *ishans* served their communities through a variety of professions. They were especially prominent in the medical field (*ʿilm-i ṭibb*) as healers (*täuĭp*), which combined their ability to perform miracles with empirical medical knowledge. This combination of powers is especially evident in the ubiquitous accounts within hagiographies and in the ethnographic literature, of their ability to treat the mentally ill and alcoholics, both Muslims and non-Muslims.[21]

Among Turkmen and Kazakh agriculturalists, *ishans* often had an additional economic function in managing and mediating water resources. In Turkmen communities, the position of *sïlag-suw* was usually held by a member of an *ishan* lineage. The *sïlag-suw* was responsible to ensure the equitable division of water, to ensure that the poor and *waqfs* for the maintenance of shrines, cemeteries, and mosques, received their share of

---

[20] Ōrāntāy ibn Qūrïmtāy Qïpchāqī, *Naṣīḥat al-qazāqīya*, (Kazan: Karimov, 1900), 9.

[21] N. S. Lykoshin, *Pol zhizni v Turkestane*, (Petrograd: Berezovskii, 1916), 151–152.

water.[22] Similar associations of *ishan* lineages with irrigation and hydraulic engineering are evident among Kazakhs, where certain *ishans*, particularly those located along the lower and middle Syr Darya River, are remembered in hagiographies for moving nomadic communities in the pre-Revolutionary era toward sedentarization and irrigated agriculture.[23] *Ishans* functioned as judges and mediators in disputes between outside descent groups. Among nomads, even though *ishans* maintained bonds with collective kinship groups, they also mediated disputes between nomadic communities. This role is well documented for the Turkmen *öwlat* lineages, and Kazakh *khojas*. The Soviet ethnographer Sergei Demidov downplayed the mediating role of *khojas*, emphasizing that in Turkmenistan the authority of *öwlat* lineages often yielded to the demands of more powerful tribal interests in disputes over pasturelands. At the same time, Kazakhs remember Maral Ishan Qŭrmanŭlï as judge who resolved cases according to the *sharīʿa*. Such a role is also commonly attributed to the Kazakh *ʿulamāʾ*.[24] Similar qualities are documented for the descendants of Isabek Ishan, the founder of another *khoja* lineage in Northern Kazakhstan.[25]

MIRACLES AND SACRED LINEAGES

The inclusion of miracle stories in accounts of the Gulag experience is consistent with the conventions of Islamic hagiography, in which miracle narratives are often placed squarely in a political context to illustrate and dramatize conflict. To understand the significance of their inclusion in 21st century Kazakh writings, beyond literary custom or even questions of Sufi doctrine, it is helpful to consider the social function of miracle narratives, the themes evident in their retelling, and the didactic elements they contain, particularly as they apply to sacred lineages. Although the countless miracle narratives encountered in the oral and written literature of Islamic Inner Asia serve a wide array of literary and social aims, I would argue that Kazakh miracle narratives set during the era of Stalinist repression serve an

---

[22] Sergei Demidov, *Turkmenskie ovliady*, (Ashkhabad: Izdatel'stvo Ylym, 1976), 26–28.

[23] Nŭrtayŭlï, *Islam zhäne Maral Baba*, 34, 44, 69; Zh. A. Zhontayeva and Sh. Sh. Äbdïbayev, *Sïr elïnïng mädeni mŭralarï*, (Qïzïlorda: n.p., 2005), 81, 87.

[24] Demidov, *Turkmenskie ovliady*, 29; Nŭrtayŭlï, *Islam zhäne Maral Baba*, 81; Tïnïshbek Dayrabay and Moldabek Akhmetov eds. *Biler sözï – kiyelï (Sïr elïnïng bilerï khaqïnda)* (Almaty: n.p., 2012), 76

[25] Ädïlqaq Tügelbayev, "Aqköldï äuliyelï atandïrghan," in: *Isabek Ishan* (Pavlodar: Sïtin baspakhanasï, 2011), 17.

unmistakable social and communal purpose. Above all, they challenge Soviet depictions of their holy ancestors, and of Islam in general, they maintain social bonds within and between kinship groups, and they reinforce collective ethical norms. In this regard, the Kazakh Gulag miracle narratives share certain similarities with Hasidic Holocaust tales that are an adaptation of the philosophical and didactic genre of classic Hasidic tales. As Yaffa Eliach has remarked, these tales "assume the dimensions of moral and social reflections and commentary."[26] In the Kazakh context, the miracle narratives serve a similar purpose. But they also serve a specific communal function of illustrating the holy power and authority of the sacred lineage to which the saint in question belonged, thereby affirming the holiness of the lineage for its members, as well as for members of outside groups linked to the holy lineages, that is, Kazakh kinship groups bound to the holy lineage through the metaphor of the *pir-murid* relationship. The 21st century miracle narrative invokes broader Islamic and nationalistic themes, too, making them relevant to the Kazakh Muslim community at large in independent Kazakhstan.

Among Muslims in Central Asia and the Volga-Ural region, the retelling of miracles is a common, and critical, element of conversion narratives that relate how the ancestors of the people to whom the conversion narrative is addressed became Muslims. Here, the miracle illustrates the sacred dimensions of the formation of a Muslim social and political community as a constituent element of the *umma*. In the Kazakh context, we have seen in a previous chapter the way in which miracle narratives were deployed in genealogical treatises establishing the holiness of the lineages' ancestors. Elsewhere, we can see the retelling of miracle narratives that reinforce, and in a sense, reenact conversion narratives, to further define sacred lineages within the same framework. In the Volga-Ural region, Tatars and Bashkirs circulated, and continue to circulate the conversion narrative (first recorded in the 18th century) in which the khan of Bulghar and his people become Muslims at the hands of three companions (*saḥābas*) of the Prophet Muhammad; in this narrative one of the companions cures the daughter of the khan by miraculously making a birch tree sprout from his staff, enabling him to make a birch leaf whisk to use in a bath to cure her of paralysis. The conversion narrative opens a larger narrative, linking the names of followers of the *saḥābas,* the *tābiʿ* and *tābiʿ-i tābiʿīn,* and their graves with existing villages to create a mental map of the "Bulghar" community in Russia. In Siberia and East Turkestan, we see similar geographic delineations of Muslim territory

26 Yaffa Eliach, *Hasidic Tales of the Holocaust*, (New York: Vintage Books, 1988), xix.

through the subsequent miraculous "discovery" of shrines by saints.[27] On the Kazakh steppe, the creation of a similar sacred landscape through Islamization narratives is evident for *khoja* communities.[28]

The case of Baba Tükles, known among Kazakhs as Baba Tüktĭ Shashtï Äzīz, provides us with the most vivid illustration of how Kazakhs used miracle narratives to both reinforce the status of holy lineages, and integrate these lineages into broader definitions of Kazakh Islamic solidarity. Baba Tükles, one of whose tombs is located in the Syr Darya Valley, near Turkistan (he has another tomb in Russia, near Astrakhan, at the mouth of the Volga), is remembered primarily from an Islamization narrative telling of the conversion to Islam of the ruler of the Golden Horde, Özbek Khan (r. 1313–1341 CE). Turkic nomads, from the Noghay Steppe to northern Kazakhstan, assert that their ancestors' conversion to Islam dates precisely to the reign of Özbek Khan. Although Devin DeWeese made the symbolism and meaning of this conversion narrative and its variants, evidently first recorded in the 16th century in the Khorezmian work attributed to Ötemish Ḥājjī, the subject of a deep and extensive study of Islamization in the Golden Horde, for our purposes it suffices to point out that in that narrative, Özbek Khan arranges a contest between Baba Tükles and local "shamans" with whom Baba Tükles agreed to enter a fire pit to show his holiness. After he emerges unscathed, Özbek Khan and his people, here the steppe nomads of the Golden Horde, convert to Islam. As DeWeese demonstrates, the persona of Baba Tükles became integrated into the genealogies of various lineages, including that of the rulers of the Noghay Horde and Bakrid *khoja* lineages in the Volga-Ural region and elsewhere. Baba Tükles and his tomb are also represented in Kazakh hagiographies and shrine catalogs, almost universally, and he emerges

[27] Allen J. Frank, *Islamic Historiography and 'Bulghar' Identity among the Tatars and Bashkirs of Russia*, (Leiden: Brill, 1998), 61–67; N. F. Katanov, "Predaniia Tobol'skikh tatar o pribytii v 1572 g. mukhammedanskikh propovednikov v. g. Isker," *Ezhegodnik Tobol'skago Gubernskago Muzeia*, VII (1897), 51–61; Thum, *The Sacred Routes of Uyghur History*, 139–140.

[28] For publications and English translations of these sorts of Islamization narratives, see Devin DeWeese and Ashirbek Muminov, *Islamizatsiia i sakral'nye rodoslovnye v Tsental'noi Azii* I, (Almaty: Daik Press, 2013); see also Devin DeWeese, "Yasavian Legends on the Islamization of Turkistan," *Aspects of Altaic Civilization III: Proceeding of the Thirtieth Meeting of the Permanent International Altaistic Conference*, (Bloomington, Indiana, 1990), 1–19.

in a wide range of Kazakh religious contexts, including even in the litanies of Kazakh *baqsïs*.[29]

It is precisely among holy lineages whose *khoja* ancestry is unclear, disputed, or absent altogether that we find miracle narratives, or even claims of ancestry, linked to Baba Tükles. In such contexts, the retelling of miracle narratives unambiguously serves to bolster the holy status of these lineages. A case in point is the Kereyt *khojas* of the Middle and Lower Syr Darya Valley, and in the Aqtöbe region. There is little information on the origins of this lineage. In their own accounts Kereyt *khojas* identify themselves as bona fide *khojas*, although, Ashirbek Muminov has commented on their lack of written genealogies, and their tendency to refer to themselves as *khojas* of whichever specific Junior Zhüz lineage with which they associate.[30] The central ancestral figure is Müsĭrälĭ-Qozha, known as Sopï Äzĭz, who is afforded a number of different *khoja* ancestries, including descent from Iskhaq Bab and Baba Tükles.[31]

Genealogical traditions among the Kazakhs of the Junior Zhüz mention a contest between three *pirs* at the same gathering at Qŭltöbe in 1680, convened by the Kazakh ruler Täuke Khan (r. 1680–1718). One of the purposes of the *qurïltay* was to elect a Chief Pir (*bas pĭr*) for the Kazakh Khanate. Each of the *zhüzes* brought their own *pir*. These included the *khoja* Maghzam from the Senior Zhüz, another *khoja*, Sayd-qozha, from the Middle Zhüz, and Müsĭräli. In these accounts, by performing a series of miracles, Müsĭrälĭ prevails and becomes the Chief Pir of the Kazakh Khanate. Müsĭrälĭ's genealogy is a matter of some contention. The descendants of Müsĭrälĭ Aqsaqalŭlï consider themselves to be *khojas*, and this descent group are known as the Kereyt Khojas, since Müsĭrälĭ was closely associated with the Kereyt people of the Junior Zhüz. The Kereyt *khojas* claim descent from the saint Baba Shashtï Äziz, that is, Baba Tükles, who in Tatar, Bashkir, and Noghay tradition is of

---

29 Devin DeWeese, *Islamization and Native Religion in the Golden Horde: Baba Tükles and the Conversion to Islam in Historical and Epic Tradition*, (University Park, Pennsylvania: Pennsylvania State University Press, 1994), 460–461.

30 Ashirbek Muminov, "Die Qožas – Arabische Genealogien in Kasachstan," *Muslim Culture in Russia and Central Asia Vol. 2: Inter-Regional and Inter-Ethnic Relations*, Anke von Kügelgen et al. eds., (Berlin: Klaus Schwarz Verlag, 1998), 200.

31 Seyt-Omar Sattarŭlï *Qozhalar shezhĭresĭ,* (Almaty: Atamŭra, 2015), 489–490; Rïszhan Iliyasova, *Dalam tŭnghan shezhĭre*, (Almaty: Zerde, 2007), 72; Tölepbergen Tĭleuqabïlŭlï, *Kĭshĭ zhüz Älĭm atalïghïnïng shezhĭresĭ,* 2-nshĭ basïlïm, (Almaty: Shapaghat-Nŭr, 2006), 91–97.

Bakrid descent.[32] However, Müsïrälï's status as a *khoja* (and that of his descendants) is disputed by some genealogists among the Alshïn people, a branch of the Junior Zhüz. According to their version, Müsïrälï was emphatically a Kereyt, and not a *khoja*.[33]

Regardless of Müsïrälï's genealogy, the accounts relate essentially the same story about how he prevailed in the contests to select a Chief Pir for the three *zhüzes* at Qŭltöbe. The story is worth retelling, because it shows us the role of miracle narratives in establishing the religious authority of holy lineages in the context of political events. According to a number of versions, Täuke Khan instructed the three *biys* from each of the three *zhüzes* to bring people they considered to be saints, and to present them for the contest in order to elect the winner as the *pir* of all three *zhüzes*. Tele-biy from the Senior Zhüz brought the *khoja* Maghzam, Qazïbek-biy of the Middle Horde brought the *khoja* Sayd-qozha. However, Äyteke-biy of the Junior Zhüz did not bring anyone from his own people and searching for the proper person to be Chief Pir, went to the Chief Imam of the mosque in Turkistan, Akhtan Sopï, and said, "Your Grace, I am in need of someone worthy of becoming Chief Pir. I need your help." When Akhtan-Sopï asked what kind of boy was needed, Äyteke-biy replied:

> Your grace, he cannot be mute, he must have a tongue. I need a *pir* who is not mute, but has speech, who is not blind, but has sight, and who is not lame, but can walk." Akhtan said, "Äyteke, do not be angry, but I have 1,001 students. Pick the one out yourself. I will bring the students out." Äyteke sat on his horse among the 1,001 students. He said, "Please, give me that boy who has the topknot." That was Müsïrälï. The imam said, "Müsïrälï, come here. Today, you are going to a great gathering and you will compete." He blessed him, saying "May God light your way, may your ancestors' spirits support you, and may you do well." The imam asked, "Äyteke, how did you pick him out?" "Your Grace, there was a lamp burning above his head, and there were two tigers on his shoulders." Akhtan gave him a blessing, saying, "It seems you will not be empty-handed. No other people know what you know. Like your friends, your enemies won't be few. Be able to protect the good fortune that has come to all Kazakhs, and to your people." With that the imam reminded Äyteke that those who went against this especially holy and sacred person Müsïrälï would

[32] Alpïsbay Musayev, *Äyteke bi aymaghïnïng etnomädeni mŭrasï*, (Aqtöbe, 2006), 66–67; Iliyasova, *Dalam tŭnghan shezhïre*, 70–72.

[33] Tengïzbay Üsenbayev, *Alshïn shezhïresï*, (Qïzïlorda: Tŭmar, 2003), 39, 43; for a discussion of Müsïrälï's genealogy, see Musayev, *Äyteke bi*, 66–68.

> not correct themselves in the end. With 30 young men all together, Äyteke placed Müsïrälï on a white piece of felt[34] and raised him up, and brought him to his camp.[35]

The story then describes the three ensuing contests among the *pirs* for the position of Chief Pir. In the first contest, each man was given white batting, and he was supposed to blow on it and set it on fire. The batting that Maghzam-qozha from the Senior Horde blew on half burned, and soot remained. The batting that Sayd-qozha from the Middle Horde blew on burned halfway, and embers remained. But the batting that Müsïrälï blew on burned completely and turned into ash.[36]

In the second contest a pregnant black cow was brought before the saints and they had to predict the sex and color of the calf inside of it. Maghzam-qozha from the Senior Horde said, "Inside the cow is a male calf with red patches." Sayd-qozha from the Middle Horde said, "Inside the cow is a female calf with red patches." But Müsïrälï from the Junior Horde said, "Inside the cow is a pure red female calf with no patches. The end of its tail is white, and its tail falls as far as its forehead." When they slaughtered the cow to find out, like Müsïrälï had said, it was a solid red female calf with a white tail.[37]

In the third contest the three were to enter into a flaming fire, stay in a while, and then come out without being burned or scorched. Then, Müsïrälï said,

> "I'll go into the fire. If I go in and come out without being burned or scorched, then these [two] will be able to go in. I know that *khojas* come out without being burned. Let my elder brothers' beards not be burned." He then went into the fire, stayed a while, and, it is said, came out unburned. But they said that after coming out of the flames, the fire had touched three spots on the hem of the right side of his robe. [Müsïrälï said] "There was a defect in my thoughts when a urinating camel passed by upwind, and some urine must have sprinkled on it." After Müsïrälï the two *khojas* would not go into the fire.[38]

---

34 Raising the saint on a white piece of felt clearly invoked the imagery of the inauguration ceremony of Chingisid khans.

35 Üsenbayev, *Alshïn shezhïresï*, 38–39; Iliyasova, *Dalam tŭnghan shezhïre*, 70–72.

36 This miracle bears strong similarities to similar miracles attributed to Aḥmad Yasavī in which he sends to a rival a box containing water, a glowing coal and a wad of cotton, demonstrating his saintly power by preventing the water from extinguishing the coal and the coal from igniting the cotton; see Devin DeWeese, "A Khwarazmian Saint in the Golden Horde: Közlük Ata (Gözli Ata) and the Social Vectors of Islamization," *Revue des Études des mondes Musulmans et Méditerrané* 143, 113.

37 A similar miracle in which the saint foretells the color of an unborn calf, appears in hagiographical accounts of the Turkmen saint Gözli Ata; see DeWeese, "A Khwarazmian Saint in the Golden Horde," 121.

38 Üsenbayev, *Alshïn shezhïresï*, 39–40.

This account evidently circulated among the descendants of Müsïrälï. His son Qosïm-qozha (b. 1685) was known as the *pir* of the Junior Zhüz and founded his own *khoja* dynasty in the vicinity of Qazalï and in Uzbekistan. According to one account, the Qalmaq ruler Galdan Tseren gave his daughter Maryam to Müsïrälï, and from that union Qosïm-qozha was born.[39]

Another prominent saint from the Kereyt lineage was Seytpenbet-qozha, who was from Khorezm, and lived toward the end of the 18th century. One of the miracle narratives mentions the tests Seypenbet-qozha (also known as Er Seytpenbet) undertook to be accepted as a *pir* among the Shömekey people of the Junior Zhüz. As the story goes,

> When Seytbembet-qozha came to our people, the [Shömekeys'] leaders gathered and said to the *khoja*, "You are a saint. If you can perform miracles, show us your miracle." The *khoja* said, "If that's the case, tell me the conditions you stipulate." Their condition was as follows: "We will cut 90 camel-loads of *saksaul* [a type of desert brush]. We will sit you on top of it and light the brush. If you are not burned in the fire, and you come out unharmed, then we will know you are a saint." The *khoja* accepted that condition. The people cut the brush as if it were for 90 camel-loads. Inside they placed two camel-loads worth of dry kindling made from the *bayalïsh* plant. They sat the *khoja* on top of what had been cut, and they set it alight from underneath. The fire suddenly started roaring, and the flames leapt up toward the sky, and gradually it died down. The people who were standing in a circle stared at the fire. With time the red flames ebbed and the *khoja* was visible sitting inside of the fire, which started smoking. The people were staring. The flames died down, and when the red embers grew dark, the *khoja* said "Yes, my Grandfather," stepped out of the fire, safe and sound, with his staff in his hand. The people said, "O God!" They wrung their hands, fell at the *khoja's* feet, and were satisfied [with his sanctity]. They sacrificed livestock and raised Seytbembet-qozha up as their *pir*.[40]

A similar miracle narrative was recorded in one of the hagiographies devoted to Maral Ishan, whose lineage is unambiguously non-khoja. In this account, when Maral Ishan arrives home after completing his studies in the Emirate of Bukhara, accompanied by several students (*qalpe*), his sanctity was challenged by local notables, who said:

> "We have our own saint. You aren't a saint. You're a sorcerer. If you are a saint, show us your miracle. Let's see it. Otherwise, you'll leave here." Maral asked, "Then what do I need to do to demonstrate it?" [The notable's] people puffed up and replied "We'll lie you down under forty camel-loads of brush. Then if you come out safely, we'll bow to you as a saint." The *qalpes* of Maral-ishan, who was ready to lie down under 40 camel-loads of brush that

---

[39] Musayev, *Äyteke bi,* 67; Iliyasova, *Dalam tŭnghan shezhïre,* 72; in another account, Maryam is identified as Galdan Tseren's sister-in-law; see Shaydarbek-qazhï Äshïmŭlï, *Sïrgha tolï Sïr boyï: tarikhi-tanïmdïq zhazbalar* (Almaty: Foliant, 2009) 323.

[40] Madanov, *Kïshï zhüzdïng shezhïresï,* 134–136.

> were piled up like a small hill, raised a hubbub and said, "Your Grace, no, let us lie under it. If the worst happens, nothing will come of our efforts. But if something happens to us, you will help." With that he lay his *qalpes* named Tŭrghanbay and Törtqara, who had followed him, under the pile. When they were setting fire to it Maral and his horse stayed above the burning flames at a height of 40 *arshins*. When the forty camel-loads of brush finished burning the saint called out the *qalpes'* names and said, "You are alive." Both came out of the ashes safe and sound. The notables of the three *zhüzes* – the *khojas*, mullahs, *töres*, and *biys* held their sides and said, "Astaghfiriallah![41]

Although in this story Maral Ishan sends his students into the fire, he nevertheless displays to the community's religious and especially political leadership, which demanded the test, his sanctity and religious power. Moreover, the fact that the names of his two *qalpes*, Tŭrghanbay and Törtqara, correspond to the names of lineages within the Junior Zhüz with which Maral Ishan's descendants maintained a *pir-murid* relationship was doubtlessly not lost on the audience.

Miracle narratives were important elements in framing and demonstrating the sanctity of *ishan* lineages, and in cases where *ishan* lineages felt compelled to establish the religious credentials of their ancestors in the face of actual or anticipated critiques from *khojas* or other skeptics, the sacredness of the lineage could be documented through the telling of a miracle narrative. In the examples above, the saints proving their holiness do so in miracles reminiscent of Baba Tükles' trial by fire before Özbek Khan. In hagiographies depicting the Soviet era, we can see miracles used in similar ways. Let us now examine the individual lineages featured in such hagiographies.

Five Ishan Lineages in Kazakhstan

The hagiographical material and genealogical treatises that form the basis of this study belong to five separate *ishan* lineages in Kazakhstan. Not only do these sources discuss their fates during the Soviet era, but they also relate their history before 1917. This longer view allows the reader to better understand the social functions of these lineages, and gauge the changes that Soviet rule brought about. The founders of these lineages were historical figures whose lives bridge the period between 1822 and 1867 when, in varying stages, Imperial Russia established more or less direct administration of nomadic Kazakh communities. As such, these central figures transcend major historical periods, and their genealogies present the ancestors, the lineages themselves, and their religious authority, as social and religious constants, against a

[41] Nŭrtayŭlï, *Islam zhäne Maral Baba*, 27.

background of shifting Imperial Russian and Soviet policies targeting these sacred lineages.

The lineage of Maral Ishan Qŭrmanŭlï

Among the exceptional aspects of the lineage deriving from Maral Ishan is that it is a non-*khoja* lineage belonging to the Kerey tribe, one of the major divisions of the Middle Zhüz. The founder of this lineage was Maral-Ishan Qŭrmanŭlï (1781–1841), who appears both in Russian documentary sources, and in Kazakh hagiographies, as a saint. In Russian sources, he appears as the leader of an armed insurrection in northern Kazakhstan against the advance of the Russian frontier line in the region between Qïzïlzhar (Petropavlovsk) and Qostanay (Kustanai) in the 1820s. A Russian report from 1821 identifies him as a Kerey saint who had come to the region from Bukhara, where he had studied under a Sufi named "Kulmagmet." On the steppe, he was accused of preaching to Kazakhs, Tatars and Bashkirs that as Muslims they should live separately from the Russians, and he likewise preached social reforms among the Kazakhs, calling for an end to theft and wife-stealing (*barïmta*).[42] The Russian documents from 1821 are based on second-hand or even third-hand information, and not surprisingly, appear confused in identifying him. Nevertheless, they do indicate he studied in Bukhara and Shahr-i Sabz with a Sufi master, and link him with the Kerey tribe.[43] Maral Ishan is remembered in other Russian sources as an insurgent, who was forced to flee his home territories in the vicinity of Qïzïlzhar and Qostanay, and who eventually settled in the lower Syr Darya.[44] Among the Kereys of northern Kazakhstan, he is still remembered for his to resistance Russian colonialism.[45] Kerey

---

[42] *Kazakhsko-Russkie otnosheniia* II, (Alma-Ata: Akademiia Nauk Kazakhskoi SSR, 1964), 197–199.

[43] The Russian officials identify, or rather misidentify, his father as a certain Kultaba, and they mention two of his sons, Isa and Alchibei, although in one of the documents, the identities of Isa and Maral appear conflated. In any case, neither Kultaba, Isa, nor Alchibei appear in any of the genealogical traditions of the Kereys, or of Maral Ishan's descendants.

[44] For a summary of the Russian accounts on Maral Ishan, see N. N. Kraft, "Vdokhovennyi kirgiz Maral Kurmanov," *Iz kirgizskoi stariny*, (Orenburg: Lito-tipografiia Sachkova, 1900), 83–90.

[45] A. Abil', "Maral-Ishan: kharakter i ideinye osnovy natsional'no-osvboditel'nogo dvizheniia," and Zh. Süleymenov, "Maral-Ishan: Ŭlt-azattïq küresïnïng rukhani köshbasshïsï," in: *Soltüstïk Qazaqstan öngïrïndegï täuelsïzdïk üshïn küres tarikhï – Istoriia bor'by za nezavisimosti v Severnom Kazakhstane*, (Almaty: Atamŭra, 2011), 215–221, 309–315.

genealogical treatises mention a number of figures, including religious scholars, who fought by his side from 1821 until his defeat in 1825. Most notable among these was Eseney Estemĭsŭlï (1798–1867), a Kerey religious, military and political leader who served Maral Ishan during his uprising, and was reputedly one of his *murids*, but later held a number of position as a tribal leader under the Russians.[46] In the tumultuous and tortuous Soviet historiography on Kazakh rebellions, the decision to exclude Maral Ishan appears to reveal a degree of scholarly consensus, undoubtedly because of his connection with Sufism, both in the Russian sources, and in Kerey tradition.[47]

Hagiographical tradition provides few details of his activities as an insurgent, but instead emphasizes his career as a Sufi, and his connection with political events on the steppe in the 18th century. We learn that his father, Qŭrman, was an associate of Abïlay Khan (1711–1781), and was that ruler's favorite healer. His mother, Fatima, is said to have been the daughter of the Qalmaq ruler Galdan Tseren (r. 1727–1745). According to the accounts, Fatima's mother was a Kazakh who predicted that this daughter would give birth to a saint, while her other daughter from Galdan Tseren would give birth to a hero (*batïr*). In the story, Abïlay marries one of the daughters, who would give birth to Kenesarï Khan, the leader of an anti-Russian rebellion in the 1840s, and Qŭrman marries Fatima, who would give birth to Maral Ishan.

The hagiography tells us that Maral was born in 1780, in a place called Qayranköl, later renamed Äuliyeköl (Saint's Lake), in what is today Lenin *raion* in North Kazakhstan *oblast*. His father died in 1789, and in 1793 he travelled with his mother to the vicinity of Aqmeshĭt, on the Syr Darya River, to seek learning. The hagiography at this point emphasizes the evidence, revealed through a series of miracles, that the young Maral was a holy figure, destined to become a great saint. This documentation of his holiness is necessary to the narrative because Maral was from a non-*khoja* lineage, and

---

46 Sotsial Zhŭmabayev and Kärĭm Zhalmaqanov, *Bĭrzhannïng belgĭsĭz ghŭmïrï – Nŭralï shezheresĭ* (Petropavl: n.p., 2009), 372–373; Sotsial Zhŭmabayev, *Eseney estelĭgĭ,* (Petropavl: n.p., 2010), 11.

47 Maral Ishan's insurgency was consistently ignored in the major Soviet surveys of Kazakh history published before, during, and after the Second World War; for a discussion of Soviet historiographic policy surrounding the Kazakh rebellions, see Lowell Tillett, *The Great Friendship*, (Chapel Hill: University of North Carolina Press, 1969), 110–129,171–193; see also, Zifa-Alua Auezova, "Conceiving a People's History: the 1920–1936 Discourse on the Kazakh Past," in: *The Heritage of Soviet Oriental Studies*, Michael Kemper and Stephan Conermann eds., (New York: Routledge, 2011), 241–261.

therefore the authors perhaps felt compelled to explain how he came to possess the holy qualities he later passed down to his descendants.

Maral and his mother travelled to the vicinity of Aqmeshĭt, where they spend the night at the home of a rich man (*bay*) named Qŭlanbay-Ishan. Qŭlanbay, we learn, was a *murid* of a saint named Zhalangayaq-Ishan, and himself had holy powers of prescience [*közĭ-zharïq*]. He immediately sensed Maral's saintliness when he saw light coming out from under the door of the yurt Maral was sleeping in, and when he approached to investigate, he saw a bright light emanating from Maral's navel. When Qŭlanbay employed Maral and his mother, and had Maral tend his livestock, Maral was able to protect the herds from predators, reduce their mortality, and generally bring blessings [*baraka*] to the household.

Qŭlanbay-Ishan sent Maral to study with his *pir*, Zhalangayaq-Ishan, who lived in a cave between Bukhara and Kattakurgan, in modern-day Uzbekistan. [48] The master accepts Maral, who distinguished himself by performing miracles that increased his standing and discredited his spiritually weaker classmates. These qualities caused Zhalangayaq-Ishan to prophecy, tellingly, that Maral would have many descendants. One day a visitor arrived, riding a horse that walked on its hind legs. After Maral performed a series of miracles that revealed him as a holy personage, the visitor announced that he was the leader of the forty *shilten*.[49] He announced to Zhalangayaq-Ishan that one of the *shilten* has died, and that he had chosen Maral as a suitable replacement. However, Zhalangayaq refused to let him take Maral, because then Maral would create no lineage.

Maral eventually concluded his studies with Zhalangayaq-Ishan, mastering the *sharīʿa* and medicine (*tabibtĭk*). He came back to Aqmeshĭt with seven Kazakh followers [*khalpe*], four of whom were from the Törtqara lineage, a division of the Junior Zhüz's Älĭm people, thereby establishing the *pir* relationship between Maral Ishan's lineage and the Törtqaras. Finally, we learn that after leaving Zhalangayaq (who tells Maral before he departs, "My

---

[48] Zhalangayaq-Ishan is not known from extant *silsilas*, and it is unclear if he can be identified with another saint, known as Äzder Zhalangayaq-Äuliye, whose tomb is located in the vicinity of Sozaq, and appears in Kazakh historical tradition as the *pir* of Abïlay Khan. In those accounts, he accompanies Abïlay in person or in spirit on his campaigns against the Qalmaqs and Kyrgyz.

[49] This is a reference to theunseen embodied forces, known as the "Forty Men of the Unseen World," that are known in Arabic sources as *rijāl al-ghayb* and in Kazakh as *ghayb erenner* and *qïrïq shilten*; see R. M. Mustafina, *Predstavleniia, kul'ty, obriady u kazakhov*, (Almaty: Qazaq universitetĭ, 1992), 152–153.

son, I have nothing left"), Maral was followed by the Forty *Shilten*. Additionally, he was followed by the 40,000 *qara äruaq*, that is, a host (*qosïn*) of 40,000 spirits of the "common," non-*khoja*, ancestral spirits, who, as we shall see, would later intervene to help Maral's descendants during the Soviet era.[50]

Four of Maral's eight sons, Qalmŭkhamed (Qalqay), Qalïbay, Elïbay, and Esmŭkhamed (Esey), founded their own lineages. In the 1990s their descendants were located in Qïzïlorda, Qostanay, Torghay, Astana, Taraz, and South Kazakhstan oblasts in Kazakhstan, and in Uzbekistan. However, the center of the lineage was, and is, the tomb of Maral Baba near the winter encampment of Zhosalï, in Qïzïlorda *oblast'*. Qalqay was himself a prominent *ishan*, who studied in Baghdad, and is remembered for his efforts in encouraging the Kazakh community away from nomadism and toward irrigated agriculture. His tomb is next to Maral's, and is a pilgrimage site in its own right. He had four sons and several grandsons who were significant religious figures during the Soviet era, most prominently his grandson, Abdulkhamit (Ämit) Ishan, who was the heir to the 40,000 *qara äruaq*.[51]

The lineage of Shāh-i Aḥmad aṣ-Ṣabāwī

The lineage of Shāh-i Aḥmad as-Ṣābawī (1812–1878), who is known among Kazakhs as Shayakhmat Ishan or Noghay Ishan (the Tatar *ishan*), features prominently in this study. The genealogical treatises devoted to this lineage is rich in hagiographical elements that illuminate in particularly vivid terms the manner in which the *pir-murid* relationship functioned between *khoja* and Kazakh lineages, the geographic extent of these relationships, and the ways in which miracle stories were used to illustrate these sacred relationships. The accounts of Shāh-i Aḥmad's lineage differs substantially from the narratives surrounding Maral Ishan, foregoing an explicit emphasis on the *aruaqs*, and instead emphasizing the lineage's specifically *khoja* ancestry, which is traced to the Caliph ʿAlī via Zayn al-ʿĀbidīn b. al-Ḥusayn. Most importantly, for our purposes, the treatises emphasizes above all the relationships of this noble (*aq süyek*) lineage with various non-noble (*qara süyek*) lineages throughout the Kazakh steppe, including in China.[52]

---

[50] Nŭrtayŭlï, *Islam zhäne Maral Baba*, 17–25.

[51] Nŭrtayŭlï, *Islam zhäne Maral Baba*, 27, 34, 42.

[52] The main treatment this lineage is found in Asqar Mangabay (Uäli)ŭlï, Äziz äulet: *Shakhiakhmed Khazret pen onïng ïnïsï Fatikh imamnïng häm olardïng ŭrpaqtarïnïng shezhïresï*, (Almaty: Öner, 2001); there is also an extensive entry on Shāh-i Aḥmad included

Shāh-i Aḥmad was born in the village of Ulugh Saba (Bogatye Saby, in Russian sources), which is today located in the Republic of Tatarstan, in the Volga-Ural region. We possess parallel accounts of his family's religious history. The *Äziz äulet* relates that while Shāh-i Aḥmad came to Kazakhstan from Russia only in the 1830s, he came from a family of *khojas* with roots in the city of Turkistan. It is affirmed that his ancestor, ʿAbd al-Ḥamīd, was from Turkistan, and had become a *pir* to a Nayman chieftain named Bayghara-Biy (1699–1775) in the vicinity of Ayagöz. He trained Bayghara-Biy in Sufism, and became a *pir* to that lineage. During the Qalmaq invasions in the 1720s, to protect him from those infidels, the Naymans sent ʿAbd al-Ḥamīd to the Volga-Ural region.

In Tatar biographical sources, specifically, in the biographical dictionaries of Ḥusayn b. Amīrkhān, Shihāb ad-Dīn Marjānī, and Riżāʾ ad-Dīn b. Fakhr ad-Dīn, this lineage is depicted not as a *khoja* dynasty, but rather as a family of great scholars, based in Ulugh Saba. According to Tatar genealogies, the family is traced back to figures from era of the Kazan Khanate. While thee Tatar accounts appear to have been unknown to the compiler of the *Äziz äulet,* they complement and support the Kazakh accounts by confirming that ʿAbd al-Ḥamīd had gone and lived "many years" among the Kazakhs. The *Äziz äulet* tells us that Shāh-i Aḥmad's father, Jamāl ad-Dīn (1784–1866) left Russia and moved to Tashkent, because the Russian authorities were persecuting *khojas* and *ishans.* He returned to Russia, and instructed Shāh-i Aḥmad to go to the Kazakh steppe and find a people there "called Bayghara-biy." After spending time there, he should go to Sozaq, near Turkistan, to be close to his *khoja* kinsmen.[53]

Shāh-i Aḥmad does not appear in the Tatar biographical dictionaries, and the *Äziz äulet* tells us nothing of his life before coming to the Kazakh steppe. He is identified in one other Tatar source, a compilation of *silsilas* entitled *Qaṭrat min biḥār al-ḥaqāʾiq,* by ʿAbdullāh al-Muʿāẕī. There he appears as Shāh-i Aḥmad b. Jamāl ad-Dīn as-Ṣābawī and as a *murīd* of the Bukharan shaykh Jalāl ad-Dīn Bukhārī, better known as Jalāl ad-Dīn al-Khiyābānī (1785/86–1870/71). Khiyābānī was himself a Ḥusaynī, and according to one account, his Sufi lineage went back to Aḥmad Sirhindī via Mūsā Khān

---

in a shrine guide for the city of Sozaq; see S. Ömīrzaqov, et al. eds. *Äz äuliyeler,* VI, *Qazïnalï Ongtüstïk* 22, (Almaty: Nŭrlï Älem, 2011), 6–40.

[53] Jamāl ad-Dīn appears in the Tatar biographical dictionaries as a prominent scholar and imam in Ulugh Saba. However, those sources make no mention of his travel to Central Asia.

Dahbidī and Muḥammad-Ṣiddiq as-Samarqandī. The *Qaṭrat* also identifies one of Shāh-i Aḥmad's *murids*, a certain ʿAbd al-Majīd as-Sibirī.[54]

The Nayman sources that the *Äziz äulet* draws from describe the reestablishment of the religious bond between Shāh-i Aḥmad and the descendants of Bayghara-Biy through a series of miracles and revelations (*ayan*) credited to both Shāh-i Aḥmad and Bayghara-Biy, who himself was revered as a saint among his descendants. In conjunction with Jamāl ad-Dīn's advice to Shāh-i Aḥmad that he reestablish contact with the Bayghara people, we are told that toward the end of his life, Bayghara-Biy instructs his youngest son, Samed, to "find the *pir* I had once found." Samed decided to honor that request, but before he set out, Shāh-i Aḥmad appeared in Samed's dream, and instructed him, "Don't look for me, I will come and find you." Samed accepted the revelation and waits for Shāh-i Aḥmad in Ayagöz. In April when the Ayagöz River was flooding, "his *pir*" Shāh-i Aḥmad revealed to Samed in a dream that he was coming. The next day Shāh-i Aḥmad arrived, crossed the flooded river without incident, and came to the mosque of Muḥammad-Ṣādiq b. Ismāʿīl al-Ayāgūzī, the Bashkir imam in that city, who was also awaiting Shāh-i Aḥmad.[55] After his arrival, Muḥammad-Ṣādiq (Sadïq-molda in Kazakh sources) gave him his daughter, Shäripzhamal. Then Samed took Shāh-i Aḥmad to the encampments of his people, who in the account are called the Zhanköbek people, after the name of Bayghara-biy's great grandfather.[56] Shāh-i Aḥmad's arrival among the Zhanköbek people, which took place in 1838, is confirmed in a Tatar source as well. Qurbān-ʿAlī Khālidī writes in his history of the town of Ayagöz that "Shāh-i Aḥmad Ṣābawī came to the town" and the imam there, Damullā Muḥammad-Ṣādiq b. Ismāʿīl gave the *ishan* his daughter, and both the Kazakhs on the steppe and the Tatar and Bashkir townsmen became his *murīds*, and the "entire Bayqara [Bayghara] people [*īl*] became his *murids*."[57] The Nayman sources show how Shāh-i Aḥmad's status

[54] ʿAbdullāh al-Muʿāẓī *al-Qaṭrat min biḥār al-ḥaqāʾiq fī tarjuma aḥwāl mashāʾikh aṭ-ṭarāʾiq*, (Orenburg: Dīn wa maʿīshat maṭbuʿasī, n.d.); 28–29; on Khiyābānī, see Frank, *Bukhara and the Muslims of Russia*, 113–117.

[55] On Muḥammad-Ṣādiq, see Qurbān-ʿAlī Khālidī, *Tawārīkh-i khamsa-yi sharqī*, (Kazan, Kazakov, 1910), 409; Qurbān-ʿAlī Khālidī, *An Islamic Biographical Dictionary of the Eastern Kazakh Steppe, 1770–1912*, Allen J. Frank and Mirkasiym Usmanov eds. (Leiden-Boston: Brill, 2005), fol. 78a.

[56] Mangabay (Uäli)ŭlï, *Äziz äwlet,* 52–53; Shāh-i Aḥmad had evidently come from Russia to Sozaq first, and from Sozaq traveled to the Ayagöz region; Mangabay (Uäli)ŭlï, *Äziz äulet,* 58.

[57] Qurbān-ʿAlī Khālidī, *Tawārīkh-i khamsa-yi sharqī*, 409.

as a *pir* to their lineage was cemented through marriages of their daughters to Shāh-i Aḥmad and his sons.

Following problems with a local Chingisid chieftain, who secretly denounced Shāh-i Aḥmad as being a *sayyid* and a saint, the Russian authorities exiled him to Irkutsk, in Siberia. However, the Zhanköbeks pledged a substantial quality of livestock to send a delegation to Irkutsk and bring him back. After his return, Shāh-i Aḥmad left the Zhanköbeks and moved to Sozaq. Shāh-i Aḥmad's sons and their descendants substantially expanded his authority, originally based among the Naymans in the Ayagöz region, and in Sozaq, to southern and eastern Kazakhstan, as well as to China's Xinjiang Province. Shāh-i Aḥmad had five sons, who carried on the tradition of serving as *ishans*. These were, 1) Mukhammed Kamal-maghzŭm (1845–1905) known as Kamal; 2) Shärip; 3) Wali-maghzŭm (1855–1904); 4) Safar-maghzŭm (1861–1921); 5) Khasen-magzŭm; 6) Shäker-maghzŭm (1855–1904); and 7) Zhollïqozha-maghzŭm (d. 1931).

The accounts of Shāh-i Aḥmad and his sons explain in some detail and consistency the ways in which the *pir-murid* relationship between *khojas* and Kazakhs functioned as a system of mutual obligation. We see that the relationship between Bayghara-biy's lineage, variously called the Sïban-Naymans or Zhanköbek-Naymans, and Shāh-i Aḥmad's lineage was established in the early 18th century. This account is based not on *khoja* accounts, but on the poetry of one of Bayghara-biy's descendants, the poet Ärip Tängïrbergenŭlï (1856–1924). To protect Shāh-i Aḥmad's ancestor ʿAbd al- Ḥamīd, the Naymans sent their *pir* away to Russia, to save him from the Qalmaqs. After Shāh-i Aḥmad's return to the Naymans in 1838, his relationship with that lineage is cemented by his acceptance of brides from among the local Naymans. His son Kamal, we learn, traveled to Qulja, in China, and became a *pir* to the local Middle Zhüz lineages, the Naymans, Kereys, and Qïzays, as well to the Albans, a Senior Zhüz lineage.

The biography of Shāh-i Aḥmad's son Safar-maghzŭm demonstrates in especially clear terms the collective aspect of the *pir-murid* relationship between *khojas* and Kazakh descent groups. Safar studied in Tashkent, and after completing his studies, the elders of the Nökïs people in Kökbŭlaq became his *murids*, and brought him to live amongst them as their *pir*. "The Nökïs in Kökbŭlaq gave him a house, built him a mosque, and gave him their daughters Äshirkül and Shïnar as an offering for his blessing [*näzïrge batagha beredï*]. He also had *murids* among the Sätek people, a branch of the Senior Zhüz's Ïstï tribe, who had lived around Sholaqqorghan, near Sozaq, but moved to Oyïq, in the Talas region, near Awliye-Ata (modern-day Taraz). He then left his children in Kökbŭlaq and moved to Oyïq. Although he had a particularly close relation with the Nökïs and Säteks, we are told that the Oyïq, Oshaqtï, Botpay, Shïmïr, Siqïm, and Zhanïs lineages [*ru*] also held him to be their pir, "and gave their livestock to him and their daughters to his sons." [58] Shāh-i Aḥmad sent another of his sons, Khasen-maghzŭm, outside of the Sozaq region, to the Zhezqazghan area "to spread Islam," where the chiefs of the Nayman and Tama people took him in and made him their *pir*. He married there and had several children. [59] Finally, Shāh-i Aḥmad's son Shäker-magzŭm[60] reestablished the family's bonds with the Sïbans in the Ayagöz region and went to a place called Engrekey.

In the accounts of Shāh-i Aḥmad and his sons, we have perhaps the clearest indication of the role of Sufi disciplinary practice in these relationships. While the *Äziz äulet* provides no concrete evidence on the *silsila* affiliations of Shāh-i Aḥmad and his sons, it is clear that this *khoja* lineage was also involved in transmitting the Sufi disciplinary practice. Shāh-i Aḥmad's affiliation as a Naqshbandi, and his activity as a Sufi master among the Tatars and Bashkirs in Ayagöz is clearly established. His son Kamal-Ishan is identified as a *pir* not only to Kazakhs, but to Taranchis (these would today be known as Uyghurs) in Qulja. Similarly, Shäker-maghzŭm is identified as having 60 adepts (*duana*).

The Lineage of Isabek Ishan Mŭratŭlï

Unlike the other holy lineages, we have so far examined, which are based primarily in the Syr Darya Valley, the *khoja* lineage of Isabek Ishan Mŭratŭlï is based far to the north, in Pavlodar *oblast*, among the Kazakhs of the Arghïn tribe, a major subdivision of the Middle Zhüz. Our sources for this lineage include a collection of genealogies, oral traditions, and historical articles published in 2011 under the sponsorship of the oblast administration and the Governor of Pavlodar oblast, commemorating the tomb of Isabek Ishan, in the vicinity of Aqköl. In his doctoral dissertation, the anthropologist Ulan Bigozhin collected additional information on this saint, his shrine, and his lineage. By comparison, this lineage is highly localized, primarily centered on the territory of the Qanzhïghalï branch of the Arghïn lineage.

---

[58] Mangabay (Uäli)ŭlï, *Äziz äulet,* 197–199.

[59] Mangabay (Uäli)ŭlï, *Äziz äulet,* 209.

[60] His name appears elsewhere as Mŭkhammedshäkir and Shäkizhan-äuliye.

Isabek Ishan is identified as an ʿAlīd descended from ʿAlī's son Muḥammad b. al-Ḥanafīya. His great-grandfather is identified as Aqqu Ishan (White Swan Ishan), a descendent of Sahid Qozha. Aqqu Ishan's son was Nazar Ishan. Nazar's Ishan's son was Isabek's father, Mŭrat Ishan.[61] Seyt-Omar Sattarŭlï includes Isabek-Ishan's genealogy within the Duana-Qozha lineage, which goes back to ʿAlī via Muḥammad b. al-Ḥanafīya. He identifies Aqqu Ishan's father as Qozha Kälän, the son Qozhzhan-Qozha, the founder of the Duana *khoja* lineage.[62]

Our chief biographical source on Isabek Ishan is an extensive praise poem devoted to him, written by Mashhür-Zhüsĭp Köpeyŭlï, composed in 1871, the year of Isabek's death.[63] In this elegy, Mashhür-Zhüsĭp remarks on Isabek Ishan's relationships with various Arghïn lineages, including the Qanzhïghalï, Qarzhas, and Aydabol people. The elegy reveals that Isabek was involved in the Sufi disciplinary practice as well, training *murids* among the Bauïr and Qanzhïghalï people, from the Aqköl-Zhayïlma region as far as Omsk. The Qarabŭzhïr and Tentek lineages, from the among the Qanzhïghalï, were said to be particularly zealous. Elsewhere, Mäshhür-Zhüsĭp related that in the Aqköl-Zhayïlma area Isabek also trained *murids* from among the Aqtĭles, Sïrïm, and Küshĭk Bäsentiyin people. Isabek's chief patron was a member of the Aydabol lineage named Qïsatabay Abïz, who married his daughter to Isabek.[64]

There are varying dates for Isabek's death. Since Mäshhür-Zhüsĭp wrote his praise poem in 1871, that year is commonly accepted as the year of his death. But the editors of Mäshhür-Zhüsĭp's collected works suggest that the poem was written while Isabek was alive, and that he may have died in 1883. In any case, Isabek's tomb became an important pilgrimage site, and he was credited with performing miracles during and after his life. Saduaqas Ghïlmani, the *qazi* of Kazakhstan from 1954 until 1972, and a member of the Qanzhïghalï tribe, included Isabek Ishan his biographical dictionary, primarily as a platform to denounce pilgrimage and the veneration of saints. Ghïlmani nevertheless reveals that he lived mainly among the Tentek people, a branch of the Qarabŭzhïr-Qanzhïghalï. Among his many miracles was the curing of a

---

61 Nïghi Akhmetqaliŭlï, "Isabek Ishan kĭm?" in: *Isabek Ishan*, 69.

62 Sattarŭlï, *Qozhalar shezhĭresĭ*, 277–278, 391, 398.

63 Mashhür-Zhüsĭp Köpeyŭlï, *Shïgharmalarï* I, (Pavlodar: Pavlodar University, 2003), 229–238. The poem was reprinted in *Isabek Ishan*, 87–98, and in Sattarŭlï, *Qozhalar shezhĭresĭ*, 391–396.

64 Mashhür-Zhüsĭp Köpeyŭlï, *Shïgharmalarï* IX, 265–266.

mentally ill Russian who was brought to him for treatment.[65] His mausoleum was evidently destroyed, probably in the 1930s, rebuilt in 1946, and was completely renovated in 2011 with the support of local patrons and government officials.[66]

While Isabek had many descendants, those who remained close to the shrine and carried out the religious duties of *ishans* and sustained the lineage's holy powers were relatively few, unlike the lineages of Maral Ishan and Shāh-i Aḥmad aṣ-Ṣābawī discussed above. His three grandsons are remembered as saints who maintained the lineage's religious power. These included Mŭkhamedsoltan, known as Sŭltan Ata (1896–1962), Äshĭm Qozha (1903–1971), and Zhandarbek Qozha (1907–1996), all of whom lived in the vicinity of Ekĭbastŭz in Pavlodar *oblast*.

The Lineage of Ayqozha Ishan

The lineage of Ayqozha Ishan is one of the larger *khoja* lineages in in southern Kazakhstan, estimated as comprising over 300 families on the territory of Kazakhstan and Uzbekistan. While there is, so far, no integral genealogical treatise or hagiographic compilation devoted to this lineage, similar to those for Maral Ishan, Isabek Ishan, and Shāh-i Aḥmad, many members of this lineage are included in the shrine catalogs and biographical dictionaries of saints devoted to the Syr Darya Valley.

Ayqozha Ishan (1773–1855) was a member of the Duana Khoja lineage, the same lineage as Isabek Ishan, but descended from a figure named Mädĭ Qozha.[67] A story of Ayqozha's early studies shows he possessed unmistakable religious power. He initially went to Tashkent to study in a madrasa, where, so the story goes, he stayed at the home of a local notable (*bek*). The *bek* had a wife who was pregnant, and who herself possessed religious powers (*äruaqtï*). Ayqozha had entered her dreams, and one day, when she awoke, she predicted he would be someone with great religious powers, and this was described as his first step on the path of religion. When his master in Tashkent wanted to go to Bukhara, to be with his *pir*, Ayqozha accompanied him there. Later, he left Bukhara and went to Afghanistan, where he studied with the holy

---

65 Ghĭlmani, *Biographies of the Islamic Scholars of Our Times*, 189–190.

66 V. D. Boltina and L. V. Shevelëva eds. *Iz istorii islama v Pavlodarskom Priirtysh'e, 1919–1990*, (Pavlodar: Department arkhivov Pavlodarskoi oblasti, 2001), 177, Ulan Bigozhin, *Shrine, State, and Sacred Lineage in Post-Soviet Kazakhstan*, Unpublished Ph.D. Dissertation, Indiana University, Bloomington, 2017, 55–56.

67 Muminov, "Die Qožas," 198.

(*aruaqtï*) Islam Shaykh.[68] There, Ayqozha studied four years, and before graduating his students, Islam Shaykh devised a test for them. He hid a Qur'an by the threshold of his house, and bade his students come in. Ayqozha was the only one of them who held back, who asked that a holy person pass the threshold, before he entered. When it was time to graduate, Islam Shaykh gave his four students, who included, besides Ayqozha, Maral,[69] Qŭlboldï, and Qasïm, their diplomas (*shatïrkhat*), and also travel funds and valuable gifts. But Ayqozha refused this largesse, telling Islam Shaykh that his blessing was sufficient. On his way home from Afghanistan, Ayqozha stopped to visit the *bek* at his home in Tashkent. The *bek*'s wife had given birth to a daughter, and the *bek* gave the daughter to Ayqozha as a wife. He returned to his people with his bride, and "they made him their *pir*."[70] Another story about Ayqozha demonstrates both his ability to perform miracles, and his authority as a scholar. Once, when Ayqozha was preparing for the noon prayer (*besĭn namaz*) in a place called Kökĭbay, he became very angry and upset. At that time, a scholar from Khoqand was preaching at the mosque in Turkistan, and was mocking the local scholars, saying "This place is a desert. It makes me laugh when you say there are scholars here." Ayqozha called for his camel, and in an instant, was in Turkistan where the arrogant Khoqandi was preaching. When Ayqozha asked, "What kind of skill is that? It would be something if his mouth didn't start bleeding." At that moment, the scholar's mouth began bleeding, and he crawled to Ayqozha and fell before him.[71]

Other accounts relate that Ayqozha studied in Bukhara with a companion named Qarasopï, described as a saint and a *pir*. Upon returning home, Qarasopï and Ayqozha lived in the same vicinity, in a settlement subsequently named Qarasopï after the saint's mausoleum. The lineages of Ayqozha and Qarasopï retained a close relationship through the Soviet period. At the beginning of the 21st century, the descendants of Ayqozha and Qarasopï would still come and perform prayers at Qarasopï's mausoleum.[72] Furthermore, the

[68] Evidently a reference to a prominent figure also known as Ṣūfī Islām (d. 1807); see Devin DeWeese, "Shamanization in Central Asia," *Journal of the Economic and Social History of the Orient* 57 (2014), 351.

[69] This is evidently a reference to Maral Ishan Qŭrmanŭlï, who did, by all accounts, study in the Emirate of Bukhara; see Shaydarbek-qazhï Äshĭmŭlï, *Sïrgha tolï Sïr boyï: tarikhi-tanïmdïq zhazbalar* (Almaty: Foliant, 2009), 277.

[70] Shaydarbek Äshĭmŭlï, *Sïr boyïndaghï äuliyeler*, (Almaty: Atamŭra, 2000), 92–93; Zh. A. Zhontayeva and Sh. Sh. Äbdĭbayev, *Sïr elĭnĭng mädeni mŭralarï*, (Qïzïlorda: n.p., 2005), 89.

[71] Äshĭmŭlï, *Sïrgha tolï Sïr boyï*, 276.

[72] Äshĭmŭlï, *Sïr boyïndaghï äuliyeler*, 97.

nearby settlement named after Qarasopï appears to have been a center for the Ayqozha *khojas*.

Like other holy lineages, Ayqozha Ishan and his descendants maintained *pir-murid* relationships with Kazakh clans. Ayqozha sent each of his sons to a different branch of the Qongïrat tribe, a major division of the Middle Zhüz, to be their "fathers" (*ata*).[73] Ayqozha had eleven sons, named Ibadulla, Zhumadĭlla, Mamïrayim-shayïq, Ïbïrayim-shayïq, Ïsmayil, Ïsqaq, Pĭrshe, Rämet, Mŭsakhan, Sapar, and Ĭskendĭr. Among these, Ibadulla carried on his father's legacy. In one account, we are told how Ibadulla identified a boy named Mïrzakeldĭ as a healer (*täuip*) and formalized his status as a healer by changing his name to Tänĭ-Päk.[74] It was primarily his grandsons and great-grandsons who lived during the Stalin era.

The lineage of Appaq Ishan

Appaq Ishan Seydakhmetŭlï (1864–1931) was a *khoja* based in the village of Shayan, in South Kazakhstan oblast. This was a village of Shayan, in South Kazakhstan oblast. He belonged to the Sablut lineage of *khojas*, an Ḥusaynī lineage which included Zayn al-ʿĀbidīn and the 16th century Central Asian Naqshbandi figure Makhdūm-i Aʿẓam.[75] Although the lineage continues to exist in Kazakhstan, its members do not seem to have compiled a hagiography or genealogical treatise; nevertheless, thanks to the publication of a detailed overview of the prosecution of Appaq Ishan and his sons, we have a particularly clear insights into the legal framework for the persecution of this lineage between 1929 and 1931.[76]

Ishan communities in Kazakhstan were in most respects typical of analogous sacred communities among the Kazakhs' sedentary and nomadic neighbors. The prestige and holiness of the communities were based on genealogical lineages linking the community usually to the family of the Prophet Muhammad, and to local saints. In Kazakhstan, the social function of *ishan* lineages was characterized by the existence of formal religious bonds between specific holy lineages and Kazakh "tribes" and clans." As we shall see in the next chapter, during the Soviet era, "*ishans*" became a watchword

---

73 Äshĭmŭlï, *Sïrgha tolï Sïr boyï*, 295.

74 Äshĭmŭlï, *Sïr boyïndaghï äuliyeler*, 102–103.

75 Sattarŭlï, *Qozhalar shezhĭresĭ*, 177–178.

76 M. K. Koigeldiev, *Stalinizm i repressii v Kazakhstane 1920–1940-kh godov,* (Almaty: n.p., 2009), 194–311; Much of Koigeldiev's information on Appaq Ishan was reprinted in: Sattarŭlï, *Qozhalar shezhĭresĭ*, 177–187.

in Soviet political discourse for the exploiter class, and during the Stalin era, these lineages became the targets of repression.

CHAPTER 3. CONFISCATION, COLLECTIVIZATION, AND REPRESSION

Just as their ancestors Baba Tükles, Müsīralī-Qozha, Er Seytpenbet, and Maral Baba proved their sanctity by undergoing fiery trials, the *ishans* of the Soviet era led their lineages through their own ordeals. By recounting their miracles, their descendants and followers bore witness to their sanctity, and to the survival of their lineages. The experiences of the *ishan* lineages in the Stalin years took place within a larger human tragedy of famine, disruption and social breakdown that was the direct result of Soviet policies, if these were not the policies themselves. The human catastrophes experienced by the Kazakhs during the Stalin years affected a historically nomadic society that had been experiencing major socio-economic dislocation and had been the targets of state-organized violence, already in the tsarist period. The 18th and early 19th centuries saw social and political disruption, but also was a period of increases – albeit uneven – in standards of living among Kazakh nomads. This period saw the integration of Kazakh nomads into the expanding Russian economy, by providing markets on a large scale for Kazakh livestock and animal products, and by providing Kazakhs access to Russian grain and cheap manufactured goods produced by Russian industry.[1] This economic expansion contributed to the growth in Islamic education and institutions such as mosques, madrasas, and scholarly networks among Kazakhs.[2] By the late 19th century, however, the intensification of capitalist economic relations, as well as growing peasant colonization of the steppe, was causing land shortages among Kazakh nomads, and intensifying social differentiation and wealth inequality in Kazakh society.[3] These conflicts within Kazakh society came to a head in 1916, when the Imperial authorities sought to implement conscription of Kazakhs into the Russian Army, ostensibly into labor units. The new policy, which overturned a policy dating from the early 19th century exempting Kazakhs from military conscription, precipitated an armed revolt

---

[1] Allen J. Frank, "The Qazaqs and Russia," *The Cambridge History of Inner Asia: the Chingisid Era,* Nicola Di Cosmo et al. eds. (Cambridge: Cambridge University Press, 2009), 371–379.

[2] In his biographical dictionary of the Kazakh *'ulamā'*, Saduaqas Ghïlmani takes the 1830s as his starting point for the development of Islamic scholarship among Arghïns of the northern Kazakh steppe. This period corresponds to the establishment of Russian authority in the region; see Saduaqas Ghïlmani, *Biographies of the Islamic Scholars of Our Times* II, Ashirbek Muminov et al. eds. (Istanbul: IRCICA, 2018), 117.

[3] Niccolò Pianciola, *Stalinismo di Frontera,* (Vicenza: Viella, 2009), 77–80.

not only on the Kazakh Steppe, but elsewhere Central Asia, which the Imperial authorities violently suppressed. The voluminous Soviet studies of this revolt generally depicted it as a "progressive" revolt that foreshadowed the 1917 revolutions, and strongly emphasize not only on the anti-tsarist currents among the insurgents, but also the conflicts between the "democratic" insurgents on the one hand, and the wealthier pro-government elements Kazakh society on the other.[4]

While presenting evidence of class conflict was *de rigeur* in Soviet historiography, class-based social tensions are also reflected in the private writings of Kazakh religious scholars. Saduaqas Ghïlmani, who was a participant in the 1916 events in the Aqmola region, during which his brother was killed by Russian troops, emphasized the conflicts of poorer nomads with wealthy Kazakh district leaders who assisted in suppressing the revolt, and supporting Imperial policy.[5] In poem written in 1933, Momaqan Äliyev, Deputy Qazi for Kazakhstan in the Central Asian Muslim Religious Administration (SADUM), and the imam in the city of Kökshetau in the 1950s and 1960s, directly linked the sedentarization and collectivization of his tribe, the Qarauïl, a branch of the Middle Zhüz, with rampant wealth concentration (and poverty) in the pre-Revolutionary era, and he viewed the Soviet-era forced sedentarization of his people, during which his infant son died, as divine punishment for the sin of greed:

We have entered such an unhappy time.
For every perfection, there is a time of collapse,
The ancients left us such a tale.
People could not live with gratitude,
When they had so much wealth.
Not everyone could be satisfied with little,
The only rich one is God.
And before, the rich were not satisfied with little
They wanted to be like the rich man Aydos,
With 3,000 animals.

---

4 There is an enormous body of Soviet historiography devoted to the 1916 Revolution, and historians in independent Kazakhstan continue to publish on the revolt; for a bibliography of the Soviet literature, see Yuri Bregel, *Bibliography of Islamic Central Asia* I, (Bloomington, Indiana: Research Institute for Inner Asian Studies, 1995), 621–630; for recent studies from Kazakhstan, see B. R. Amangel'diev, *Vosstanie 1916 goda v Turgaiskom uezde i Amangel'dy Imanov,* (Almaty: Alatau, 2015); S. Tänekeyev, *1916. Qarqara-Alban köterĭlĭsĭ,* (Almaty: An Arïs, 2016); R. E. Orazov, *Qarqara qŭzhatï,* (Almaty: An Arïs, 2016).

5 Ghïlmani, *Biographies of the Islamic Scholars of Our Times* II, 467–468.

One could not see a sense of satisfaction with Aydos,
If he wanted to become like Khan Jänggïr in Aqmola,
Jänggïr had 17,000,
Even when he wanted to be like the rich man Kelden.
Kelden alone had 18,000.
Even then he wanted to be richer than Kelden.
The rich stole from the poor,
There's never enough for these seven-headed demons.
Swallowing so much, their desire had no limits,
They all wanted to become pharaohs.
They did not value blessings,
God Himself grew angry with his servant.
This is precisely the punishment for unbelief.[6]

The experiences of the Russian Civil War, and of the 1919–1922 famine in western Kazakhstan that affected both nomadic and peasant communities, as well as the 1918 famine in the Syr Darya Valley, did not mitigate the social pressures within Kazakh society, and they were certainly exacerbated by external political forces and Bolshevik policies in the Civil War.[7] Among Kazakh religious leaders who survived the Stalin era, the period from 1922 until 1928, was sometimes viewed nostalgically, since in these years, Muslim religious institutions expanded considerably, and most Kazakhs communities were placed under the authority of the mufti of the Central State Muslim Administration in Ufa (TsDUM), which satisfied a long-standing Kazakh demand. The pressures of Soviet anti-religious policy were nevertheless making themselves felt at that time. Such pressures came not only from the Soviet authorities, but from within Kazakh society, and sometimes from within the *ʿulamāʾ* itself. Saduaqas Ghïlmani tells of an improvised poetry contest (*aytïs*) that took place in May of 1923 between Kazakh intellectuals (*intelligentter*) and Aytqozha Äliasqarŭlï (1887–1937), an imam and *mukhtasib* in Kökshetau. So-called "Red mullahs," who came out in support of Bolshevism, and whom Ghïlmani, an official in the Soviet Islamic establishment, described as careerists, also emerged during the Russian Civil War.[8]

6 Ghïlmani, *Biographies of the Islamic Scholars of Our Times* II, 428.

7 Valeriy Mikhailov, *The Great Disaster: Genocide of the Kazakhs,* (London: Stacey, 2014), 70–75.

8 Ghïlmani, *Biographies of the Islamic Scholars of Our Times* II, 218–219.

ISHANS AND THE STATE TO 1917

The political dimensions of Sufism, including its relationship to the state, is a central aspect of the social, religious and political history of Muslim societies.[9] Historians of Islamic Central Asia have often placed the political aspects of Sufism to the fore, particularly with respect to the Naqshbandi order.[10] The Kazakh hagiographical materials describe – and were written during – an era in which the traditional Sufi lineage was in decline, or at least, when these lineages were undergoing substantial changes in terms of *silsila* affiliation and organization. Given the fate of the lineages during the Soviet era, it is not surprising that the narratives generally depict the relations between *ishans* and the state (and in particular with Imperial Russia and the Soviet Union) as tense. In the narratives recounting the miracles that *ishans* performed in the Gulag, we can see the relationship concisely symbolized, where the saint uses his spiritual power and moral authority to publically resist the impious excesses of the state. The asymmetric confrontation between the sovereign and the Sufi, in which the Sufi master lays bare the moral deficit, if not bankruptcy, of the sovereign, is well established in both Sufi hagiography and in Sufism-inflected folk tales. In the latter category, perhaps the most entertaining examples are the body of Turkish Nasreddin Hoca stories depicting the Hoca squaring off against the mightiest of sovereigns, Amir Timur.[11] In hagiography, one of our most colorful examples is the story of the Sufi Bābā Sangū, who during a feast unexpectedly threw a large piece of meat at the dread king, Amir Timur.[12] In a similar vein, we find Bashkir folktales describing the meetings between Joseph Stalin and the Bashkir scholar and

---

[9] For an overview of some of the major themes on the political dimension of Sufism, see Paul L. Heck, "Introduction," in: *Sufism and Politics*, Paul L. Heck ed. (Princeton: Markus Weiner Publishers, 2007), 1–22; see also Milad Milani, *Sufi Political Thought*, (Routledge: New York, 2018).

[10] A list of some of the important works on the political dimensions of Central Asian Sufi orders includes: P. P. Ivanov, *Khoziaistvo Dzhuibarskikh sheikhov,* (Moscow-Leningrad: Izdatel'stvo Akademii Nauk SSSR, 1964); B. M. Babadzhanov ed. *Sobranie fetv po obosnovaniiu zikra dzhakhr i sama',* (Almaty: Daik Press, 2008); Anke von Kügelgen, "Die Entfaltung de Naqšbadīya muğaddidīya im mitteleren Transoxanien vom 18. Bis zum Beginn des 19. Jahrhunderts," and Thierry Zarcone, "Political Sufism and the Emirate of Kashgaria (End of the 19th Century): The Role of the Ambassador Yaʿqūb Xān Tūra," in: *Muslim Culture in Russia and Central Asia from the 18th to the Early 20th Centuries Vol. 2,* Berlin: Klaus Schwarz Verlag, 1998), 101–151; 153–165.

[11] Jean-Louis Manmoury, ed. *Sublimes paroles et idioties de Nasr Eddin Hodja*, (Paris: Phébus, 2002), 331–335 and *passim*.

[12] Hamid Algar, "Bābā Sankū," *Encyclopedia Iranica* III Fasc. 3, 295.

Sufi Gabrakhman Rasulev during the Second World War, in which Rasulev advises Stalin to leverage divine power to defeat the fascist invaders.[13] There is no question that such accounts can be deeply satisfying for listeners and readers at varying levels. For the pre-Soviet period, the Kazakh hagiographies provide numerous examples of conflicts with state power, and in the case of Russia, with the *ishans'* victimization and oppression at the hands of the Imperial authorities and their Kazakh representatives.

Ishans and the Qalmaq Khanate

Curiously, the relationship between some of the lineages' ancestral figures and the Qalmaq khans in the 18th century is perhaps the most ambiguous. The Qalmaqs, that is, Tibetan Buddhist Mongols, are usually depicted in Kazakh epic tradition and Kazakh folklore as the infidel enemies of Islam and Muslims *par excellence*, and indeed, we are told how the Sïban Naymans sent their *pir* to Russia in the 1720s to save him from the Qalmaq invasions.[14] The depiction of the Qalmaqs as inveterate enemy of Muslims is tempered, nevertheless, by the presence of Qalmaq ancestors in three *ishan* lineages in Kazakhstan, and by stories relating how women connected to the Qalmaqs prophesied the birth of saints who emerge as ancestral figures in the lineage. For example, one of the genealogical narratives of Isabek Ishan's lineages, we are told how a Qalmaq woman predicts that her daughter would give birth to a saint. Her prophecy, in fact, turns out to be incorrect, but close: it is the captive girl's daughter who gives birth to Mūrat Ishan, the father of Isabek Ishan.[15] In two other lineages, we find important ancestral figures descended on their mothers' sides from the Qalmaq khan Galdan Tseren, a powerful political leader of the Qalmaq Khanate, and a recurring figure in Kazakh historical verse epics. The Kereyt *khojas* relate that Galdan Tseren gave his daughter

13 S. Kildin et al. eds., *Bashqortostan – äüliälär ile,* (Ufa: Kitap, 2012), 225–226; similar stories, involving the Rabbi of Gur and Winston Churchill, also circulated among the Hasidim; see Yaffa Eliach, *Hasidic Tales of the Holocaust*, (New York: Vintage Books, 1982), 79.

14 For a discussion of the religious aspects in depictions of Qalmaqs in Kyrgyz oral epics, see Devin DeWeese, *Islamization and Native Religion in the Golden Horde: Baba Tükles and the Conversion to Islam in Historical and Epic Tradition*, (University Park, Pennsylvania: Pennsylvania State University Press, 1994), 59–66.

15 Erbol Aytbayev, "Qalmaq äyelïnïng säueleyïlïgï," in: *Isabek Ishan* (Pavlodar: Sïtin baspakhanasï, 2011), 22–24.

Maryam to Müsïräli, and from that union Qosïm-qozha, who became *pir* of the Junior Zhüz, was born in 1685.[16]

The presence of Qalmaq ancestors in three separate lineages suggests the narrators may have had a purpose in mind. Qalmaq mothers are commonly mentioned in many Qazaq genealogies, not least in Chingisid genealogies, including that of Abïlay Khan's descendants. While the accounts of the Kereyt *khojas* and of Maral Baba are chronologically problematic regarding Galdan Tseren and his daughters, the point of the insertions seems clear enough: to buttress the genealogical credentials of the lineages by associating them with "white bone" (*aq süyek*) nobility, which comprised both Chingisid and *khoja* lineages. It is perhaps for this reason that the relationship with Galdan Tseren appears in two lineages where *khoja* status is either disputed (in the case of the Kereyt Ishans) or entirely absent in the case of Maral Ishan's non-noble descendants (although Maral Baba and Kenesarï Khan are made cousins through the Qalmaq khan). Ambiguity in depictions of the link between Kazakh Sufis and Qalmaqs may also reflect the historical relationship between the Qalmaq Khanate and competing Naqshbandi *khoja* lineages in Eastern Turkestan in the 17th and 18th centuries. While these are not alluded to in the Kazakh accounts, these East Turkestani *khojas* were descendants of Makhdūm-i Aʿẓam, and thus had kinsmen among the Kazakh *khojas*.[17]

Ishans and Imperial Russia

The hagiographies devoted to the lineages of Maral Baba and Shāh-i Aḥmad are the most explicit in detailing the conflicts between their ancestors and Imperial Russia, In part, this was because these lineages' ancestors had the most contact with Russia, either as a homeland or as a military foe. But at the same time, the accounts of conflict with Imperial Russia serves to foreshadow

[16] Alpïsbay Mūsayev, *Äyteke bi aymaghïnïng etnomädeni mūrasï* (Aqtöbe: n.p., 2006), 67; Iliyasova, *Dalam tūnghan shezhïre,* (Almaty: Zerde, 2007), 72; in another account, Maryam is identified as Galdan Tseren's sister-in-law; see Shaydarbek-qazhï Äshïmūlï, *Sïrgha tolï Sïr boyï: tarikhi-tanïmdïq zhazbalar* (Almaty: Foliant, 2009) 323.

[17] See, Henry G. Schwarz, "The Khwājas of Eastern Turkestan," *Central Asiatic Journal* 20 (1976), 266–296. Several major Kazakh lineages in the Senior Horde, including the Sarïüysïn and Suan, claimed descent from Makhdūm-i Aʿẓam through his daughter Domalaq Ana; see Qūralbek Ergöbekov, *Bäydïbek Baba men Domalaq Ana,* (Shymkent: Zhïbek zholï, 1999); Daniyarbek Düysenbayev, *Domalaq Ana*, (Almaty: Mūrattas, 1991), 19–25; Sūltanbek Eshmūkhambetov, *Suan shezhïresï*, (Almaty: Zhalïn, 1993), 29.

the more impactful events of the Soviet era, and of the Stalin years in particular.

The hagiographic accounts comment on the actions of saints in opposing Russian expansion in the Kazakh steppe and Central Asia. For example, the 18th century saint and *pir* of the Shömekey people, Er Seytpenbet is remembered for opposing the decision of the khan of the Junior Zhüz Abū'l-Khayr, to submit to Russia in 1731.[18] A descendent of Ayqozha Ishan, Äbdïuayt Ishan, is said to have served in the palace of the Emir of Bukhara, and was present when, according to the account, the Soviets (here called "the Russians") were besieging the palace in Bukhara:

> When the Soviet government came to power, the Russians surrounded Bukhara and fired at it with cannons, but were unable to take it. When they fired artillery shells at the fort, the shells did no damage. The Russian commander looked through his binoculars and saw that someone with a white turban, who was tall and wearing white had caught the shells with his hand several times, and put them to the breast in his robe. So, the Russians decided to set fire to the city with kerosene, and brought a train. Hiding weapons and cannon, the soldiers were able to surround the emir's residence. He was forced to flee with his family to Afghanistan.[19]

Maral Ishan's credentials as an opponent of Russia are well documented, especially in pre-Revolutionary Russian official sources. In the Kerey materials he is also remembered as the leader of a holy war (*ghazauat soghïsï*) against the Russians from 1819 to 1822. Unlike the Kerey genealogical materials, which focus particularly on his resistance to Russia, the numerous hagiographies devoted to him provide little information on his military confrontations with Tsarism. However, his flight, first to the Qostanay region, and later to the Syr Darya Valley, was certainly a result of Russian military pressure. He ceased his armed resistance once he settled in the vicinity of Qarmaqshï, but, according to one hagiography, turned to resisting, and later coopting, a pro-Russian Kazakh leader. The notable he came into conflict with was named Shaghïray-batïr, a powerful leader in the area between Qarmaqshï and the Aral Sea. We are told Shaghïray-batïr was favored by the Russians and received awards from the Tsar. The chieftain became envious of Maral, and began insulting him and disrespecting his ancestral spirits. Maral sent one of his *qalpes* to convince him to change his attitude, and failing that, instructed the *qalpe* to be out of the *batïr's* yurt by midnight on the third day of his visit.

---

18 Tïnïshbek Dayrabay and Moldabek Akhmetov eds. *Biler sözï – kiyelï (Sïr elïnïng bilerï khaqïnda)* (Almaty: n.p., 2012), 74. Admittedly, such a story serves the modern purpose of affirming Kazakh nationhood.

19 Äshïmülï, *Sïr boyïndaghï äwliyeler*, 121–122.

At precisely that time, a bullet struck Shaghïray-batïr's leg, and he repented, pledging to sacrifice a horse for Maral, and offering him his daughter to take as a wife. Maral then predicted the girl would give birth to four sons "like the Four Righteous Caliphs (*char-i yar*)," and he gave her to his son Qalqay to marry.[20] Maral was not the only member of his lineage to take up arms against Imperial Russia. One of Maral's descendants, Omar Ishan, served as the religious leader to Keykĭ-batïr, the leader of the Kazakh insurgency in the Qostanay region in 1916.[21]

Not surprisingly, it was the Tatar *ishan* Shāh-i Aḥmad aṣ-Ṣābawī and his descendants who had the most complex relationship with Tsarism. The genealogical account of Shāh-i Aḥmad's ancestors reveal a lineage that was on the one hand rooted in the Volga-Ural region, and on the other, attempting to establish its connection with the steppe and with various Kazakh communities both in the Sozaq region and in the Ayagöz region, in eastern Kazakhstan. We are told, for example, that the Naymans had sent Shāh-i Aḥmad's ancestor ʿAbd al-Ḥamīd to "the Ufa-Kazan region," to protect him from the Qalmaq onslaught. Later, ʿAbd al-Ḥamīd's grandson Jamāl ad-Dīn (Zhamali) was forced to leave Russia and move to Tashkent because the Tsarist government was persecuting "shaykhs and *khojas*" for spreading Islam. Shāh-i Aḥmad later suffered from the anti-*khoja* policies of the Tsarist authorities when a Senior Sultan (*sŭltan-agha*), that is, a Russian-appointed tribal leader, denounced him to the Russian authorities as a "*khoja* and a *sayyid*." Consequently, he was exiled to Irkutsk, and was only brought back thanks to the nomadic community for whom he was a *pir*, who donated sufficient livestock to be able to go to Irkutsk to bring him back. Whether Shāh-i Aḥmad was tried, and exiled to Siberia, and, if so, under what circumstances, is less important than understanding the significance of the narrative, which serves to foreshadow and contextualize the repression the lineage experienced in the Soviet era.[22] Elsewhere in the hagiography, the author says directly that "in the lands it conquered, the Tsarist government looked for *sayyids* and persecuted them."[23]

---

[20] Säden Nŭrtayŭlï, *Islam zhäne Maral Baba*, 35–36.

[21] Keykĭ-batïr was the nickname of Nŭrmaghambet Kökembayŭlï (1871–1923); according to Nŭrtayŭlï's account, Seyitzhan-aqïn Bekshentayŭlï, the author of an important hagiographical poem about Maral Baba, was Keyki-batïr's chief *aqïn*; see: Nŭrtayŭlï, *Islam zhäne Maral Baba*, 64.

[22] Asqar Mangabay (Uäli)ŭlï, *Äziz äulet: Shakhiakhmed Khazret pen onïng ĭnĭsĭ Fatikh imamnïng häm olardïng ŭrpaqtarïnïng shezhĭresĭ*, (Almaty: Öner, 2001), 57–58.

[23] Mangabay (Uäli)ŭlï, *Äziz äulet*, 134.

Shāh-i Aḥmad's son Kamal experienced similar treatment from the Tsarist authorities. In the account, we learn that Kamal faced his own legal troubles, resulting from a bad marriage that ended in divorce. His ex-wife married a Senior Sultan, that is, a Russian-appointed tribal leader, in Auliye-Ata, who, it is claimed, engineered Kamal's arrest and exile to Astrakhan.[24] He was imprisoned in that city, and was credited with performing miracles while in prison there. According to a subsequent wife named Balïsh-Bibi, he performed several miracles as a prisoner. The greatest of them was as follows: when some fishermen had gone into the Caspian Sea with their boat to fish, a storm came up and the fishermen were drowning. The commandant of the prison beseeched Kamal, "Your Holiness, reveal your sainthood. If you intervene for these unfortunates, and bring them back safely, I promise to release you from prison." Kamal then appealed to God, prayed with all his strength, asked for God's mercy, and brought the ship back safely. After that, we are told, everyone in the prison called Kamal "His Holiness" (*khazïret*). However, a short while later, in 1905, Kamal died, and was buried on an island near Astrakhan.[25]

The lineages' sense that the Tsarist Russia was hostile to *ishans* may reflect the temper of much writing by Russian missionaries and officials in the later 19th and early 20th centuries, when ishans became a rhetorical target during the anti-Muslim *kulturkampf* of that era, and were seen as a cultural and political threat to Russia. Writing in 1910, the missionary M. Mashanov blamed *ishans* for "fanatizing" the "simple Kazakhs," but more significantly, he accused them of opposing the authority of the Russian-appointed tribal leaders, inciting Kazakhs to "disobedience."[26] Those denuncials of *ishans* carried over into the Soviet period, and the arguments and fears of missionaries and Tsarist officials later appeared almost verbatim in the documents of Soviet bureacrats.

Stalinist Repression in Kazakhstan

The persecution of *ishan* lineages during the Stalin era was part of a much broader program of state violence that enveloped every community, social class, and ethnic group in the Soviet Union. Among the early targets of Soviet repression were the religious leaders of virtually all religious communities in the Soviet Union, including Jews, Orthodox Christians, Catholics, Protestants,

24 Mangabay (Uäli)ŭlï, *Äziz äulet,* 79.
25 Mangabay (Uäli)ŭlï, *Äziz äulet,* 81.
26 M. Mashanov, *Sovremennoe sostoianie tatar-mukhammedan i ikh otnoshenie k drugim inovertsam*, (Kazan: Iman, 2002), 47–48.

Old Believers, Muslims, Buddhists, and even Siberian shamans. In the Soviet Union at large, collectivization, "de-kulakization," the forced sedentarization of nomads, and other policies led to massive social disruption, collapses in agricultural production, large scale and deadly famines, and armed revolts. In terms of lives lost as a proportion to the population, nowhere was Stalinism deadlier than in Kazakhstan, where the famine of 1931–1933 cost over a million lives, although the exact number will probably never be known.[27] The number of Kazakhs imprisoned, exiled, and executed by the OGPU and NKVD also remains imprecisely known. In any event, there is no doubt that during the Stalin years, it was virtually impossible for any Kazakh family to escape Stalinist repression or its direct impact in one way or another.

In his monograph on the experience of pre-war Stalinism in Kazakhstan, Niccolò Pianciola provides a chronology of Stalinist policies, which we can use as a backdrop in discussing the experience of the *ishan* lineages.[28] According to this chronology, while a degree of state violence, including large-scale famines (in the Syr Darya Valley in 1918, and in western Kazakhstan from 1920–1922),[29] and localized land reforms that anticipated some of the excesses of the Stalin years took place during the civil war and in the 1920s, during that decade the authorities sometimes advanced policies that seemed to respond to the Kazakh nomads' collective interests, such as maintaining pastoral nomadism as a method of livestock production, maintained the draft exemption for Kazakh males, restricting peasant colonization of Kazakh pasturelands, and the undertaking the "nativization" (*korenizatsiia*) of local cadres. This policy shifted in 1927 and 1928, when the Soviet authorities abandoned "nativization" and "decolonization," and in

[27] Estimates on the number of dead during the 1931–1933 famine are based on Soviet census data showing substantial declines in the country's overall population of Kazakhs; see, Pianciola, *Stalinismo di frontiera,* 463–464; for recent Kazakh studies and document publications on collectivization and the 1931–1933 famine, see K. S. Aldazhumanov, et. al. eds. *Nasil'stvennaia kollektivizatsiia i golod v Kazakhstane 1931–1933 gg.: Sbornik materialov i dokumentov*, (Almaty: Fond XXI vek, 1998; T. Bayqŭlov, *Äuliye-Ata öngĭrĭndegĭ asharshïlïq* (Almaty: Üsh qiyan, 2017); B. Ayaghan et. al. *1932–1933 zhïldardaghï asharshïlïq aqiqatï – Pravda o golode 1932–1933 godov*, (Almaty: Ligera-M, 2012); other studies of famine and collectivization include Isabelle Ohayon, *La sédentarisation des Kazakhs dans l'URSS de Staline : Collectivisation et changement social* (1928–1945), (Paris: Maisonneuve & Larose, 2006); Mikhailov, *The Great Disaster;* Robert Kindler, *Stalins Nomaden: Herrschaft und Hunger in Kasachstan* (Hamburg: Hamburger Edition, 2014).

[28] Pianciola, *Stalinismo di frontiera*, 5–6.

[29] Mikhailov, *The Great Disaster*, 70–75.

addition to denouncing *kulaks*, began publicly attributing Kazakh "backwardness" to its kinship-based social structure ("tribalism") and certain social customs, to include religious institutions and practices. These initiatives were part of Stalin's Cultural Revolution, and included the "de-veiling" of women, the closing of mosques (Islamic education had been banned already in the mid-1920s), and the arrests of some Muslim religious leaders. In 1928, the Soviet state, in Pianciola's words, "went on the offensive," reintroducing forced requisitions of agricultural produce, including livestock, and confiscating the property of wealthy Kazakhs (*bays*) (although the definition of who was or was not "wealthy" was evidently flexible).[30] This program, which reached its peak in 1929, included not only depriving the *bays* and their families of their property, but exiling them to other parts of Kazakhstan. Similar methods were used in the application of "dekulakization" in the Kazakh milieu, where Kazakh families rated as "kulaks" were deprived of all of their property.[31] In general, in the reminiscences of *ishans* and other Kazakhs, these forced requisition campaigns, regardless of their policy and legal specifics, are remembered as the "confiscations" (*kanpeske* or *tärkĭleu*). The reform of territorial-administrative units in Kazakhstan also served to undermine the traditional Kazakh social structure, since the *volost'* (*bolïs*) territorial units that had been established in Tsarist times and were maintained until 1929, were largely organized around Kazakh descent groups and were often led by more or less hereditary tribal leaders.[32] Similarly, in 1928 the authorities began conscripting Kazakhs into the Red Army. The authorities also re-opened formerly Kazakh pasturelands to peasant settlement, as well as to forced resettlements.[33]

In 1930 the authorities stepped up the assault, with the large-scale collectivization and sedentarization of Kazakhs, complemented by further confiscations of livestock. This time, the remaining holdings of the *bays* were liquidated, and the confiscations now targeted "kulaks," which effectively

[30] For a Soviet description of the confiscation campaign against *bays,* see Sadïqbek Saparbekŭlï, *Kanpeske qorïtïndïsï*, (Qïzïl Orda: Qazaghïstan baspasï, 1929); the human dimensions of this program are evident in the biography of the poet and political leader Olzhabay Nŭralïŭlï who was declared a "*bay*," during this period, see Saduaqas Ghïlmani, *Biographies of the Islamic Scholars of Our Times* II, Ashirbek Muminov et al. eds. (Istanbul: IRCICA, 2018), 362–363, 366–367.

[31] Mukhamet Shayakhmetov, *The Silent Steppe: the Memoirs of a Kazakh Nomad under Stalin*, (New York: Overlook/Rookery, 2006), 48–54.

[32] This is the picture Ghïlmani paints for the Arghïns in northern Kazakhstan at the end of the 19th century; see Ghïlmani, *Biographies of the Islamic Scholars of Our Times* II, 117–118.

[33] Pianciola, *Stalinismo di frontiera*, 330, 332–334, 338.

corresponded to the middle layers of nomads.[34] If a chronological recounting of these Soviet policies gives the impression that they were systematically applied, in fact, the confiscations of livestock, and the sedentarization and collectivization of the nomads were marked by chaos and violence carried out by party activists, eventually resulting in a number of armed Kazakh uprisings against the Soviet authorities. The largest of these was the Sozaq uprising in 1931, but other uprisings occurred in the Mangghïstau, Qostanay and Torghay regions, and elsewhere.[35] After a brief respite following the uprisings, the Soviet authorities again aggressively implemented collectivization. The result was a drastic decline in livestock numbers. The collapse of the Kazakh livestock herd was attributable to a number of causes, all directly stemming from Soviet social and agrarian policies: forced requisitions, a steep decline in livestock prices, and Kazakh resistance. The Kazakh livestock census for 1929 counted 35,817,100 animals (this was probably a relatively low number to begin with, since that census was preceded by confiscations and localized natural disasters), and by 1934 the livestock census had fallen to 4,495,820 head, which proved inadequate to feed the Kazakh population.[36]

The ensuing famine caused major displacements of the Kazakh population, with the migration of hundreds of thousands of Kazakhs out of Kazakhstan, primarily to Russia, Turkmenistan, Uzbekistan, Afghanistan, and China. The number of people who perished in the famine is difficult to determine with any precision, but scholars have estimated the losses at between 1 and 1.75 million, making it certainly among the worst famines of the 20th century.[37] Kazakhs were not unaccustomed to great fluctuations in livestock numbers due to natural disasters or wars, and consequently were familiar with periods of hunger.[38] However, in their reminiscences, the survivors of the 1931–1933

---

[34] Pianciola, *Stalinismo di frontiera*, 352–353.

[35] Niccolò Pianciola, "Interpreting an Insurgency in Soviet Kazakhstan: The OGPU, Islam and Qazaq 'Clans' in Suzak, 1930," *Islam, Society and States across the Qazaq Steppe,* Niccolò Pianciola and Paolo Sartori, eds. (Vienna: Austrian Academy of Sciences, 2013), 297–336; Ötesh Qïrghïzbayev, *Sozaq köterĭlĭsĭ,* (Almaty: Arqas, 2003); *Qazaq ŭlt-azattïq qozghalïsï v. 19, Adaiskoe vosstanie 1929–1931 gg.,* (Astana: Astana Poligrafiia AQ, 2001); see also Kindler, *Stalins Nomaden,* 178–199.

[36] Pianciola, *Stalinismo di frontiera*, 392.

[37] Pianciola, *Stalinismo di frontiera*, 463–468.

[38] Historically, Kazakhs had experienced localized famines primarily as a result of ice storms (*zhŭt*) that deprived their livestock of fodder; one such famine, in the vicinity of Öskamen (Ust'-Kamenogorsk) was the subject of a Kazakh appeal for aid (in verse) during the Tsarist era; see, *Sēmey Bōlāṭ ōblāstī ōskāmen uyāzīna qārāghān qazāqlārnïng āshlïqdan zārlïqlārī,* (Orenburg: Waqït, 1912).

famine in Kazakhstan appear to have been particularly affected by the breakdown of social solidarity within Kazakh descent lineages that starvation caused.[39] In a particularly hideous manner, the famine furthered the Stalinist program of cultural revolution aimed against "traditional" Kazakh society by undermining the bedrock principle of kinship solidarity.[40] By 1934 the worst effects of the famine had ended, and much of the surviving Kazakh population returned to Kazakhstan. However, by then the Kazakhs had for the most part returned to collective farms and state farms, and remained sedentarized.

Beyond the massive programs of collectivization and sedentarization, rather more focused campaigns of political repression gained particular intensity in 1937 and 1938 against prominent political figures and religious leaders in Kazakhstan, including many *ishans*. The repression of Muslim religious leaders, among others, continued through to the end of the Stalin era, and well beyond, until the dissolution of the Soviet Union. However, the events of 1937 and 1938 are especially prominent in the hagiographies, as well as in the biographical dictionaries devoted to Muslim religious scholars.

In contrast to examinations of high-level policies, Sïrlïbay Bürkĭtbayŭlï's description of the persecution of Maral Baba's great grandson, Zhünĭskhan Ündemesŭlï, provides a telling "on the ground" chronology of the differing campaigns and waves of repression in the Qostanay and Torghay regions of northwestern Kazakhstan, as they affected Zhünĭskhan's lineage. His account corresponds closely to Pianciola's chronology of Stalinist repression in Soviet Kazakhstan. Bürkĭtbayŭlï describes the catalytic event as the "Great Confiscation" (*ŭlï tärkĭleu*), which arrived in 1928. This campaign targeted the wealthiest members of the community. There followed in 1929 the "Small Confiscation" (*kĭshĭ tärkĭleu*), which affected the middle and even poorer layers of nomads. Then, in 1930, the Soviets introduced collectivization, which was followed by mass famine. Zhünĭskhan and his family managed to survive the famine, which peaked in 1932 and 1933. Bürkĭtbayŭlï credits divine protection for sparing the descendants of Ündemes, but observes that the population fled "in chaos" to Russia and Afghanistan, while others "roamed around," often seeking local protection in vain. Entire families

39 See, for example, Ghïlmani, *Biographies of the Islamic Scholars of Our Times* II, 199–202; Robert Kindler has emphasized the social disintegration that famine caused among Kazakh nomads; see Kindler, *Stalins Nomaden,* 239.

40 Filipp Goloshchekin specifically named "patriarchal-clan survivals," and manifestations of kinship solidarity among Kazakhs as obstacles to collectivization, that Party activists needed to eliminate; see, F. I. Goloshchekin, *O kollektivizatsii v kazakskom aule*, (Alma-Ata: Partizdat, 1932), 11, 17, 19.

perished, or as he puts it, "There were many smoke holes whose flaps were left closed" (*tündĭgĭ zhabïlïp qalghan shangïraqtar köp boldï*). In 1937, a new wave of oppression enveloped his community, during which the Soviet authorities singled out individual "enemies of the people" for arrest and often execution. Zhünïskhan succumbed to this wave in 1938.[41]

The Persecution of Muslim Religious Leaders in Kazakhstan

The persecution of *ishans* and their lineages took place as part of a broader assault on Kazakh religious institutions, such as mosques, *madrasas*, *maktabs*, *waqfs*, shrines, the *ʿulamāʾ*, and *ishan* and *khoja* lineages.[42] As with its agrarian policies, Soviet policies regarding religion and religious institutions were inconsistent, at least before 1928. Islamic education had been banned in 1923, and *madrasas* were effectively closed as of that date. During this period, the Communist Party actively promoted anti-religious propaganda. At the same time, the Kazakh steppe had been placed under the authority of the muftiate in Ufa, thus fulfilling a long-time administrative demand on the part of many Kazakh believers. TsDUM began implementing an expansion of mosque communities (*maḥallas*) in nomadic communities, substantially swelling the number of imams and *mukhtasibs* on the steppe.[43] Beginning in 1928, the authorities began closing mosques and pulling down their minarets, and by 1932 virtually all mosques in Kazakhstan had ceased to function, and had become barns, clubs, schools, and other facilities. Muslim religious leaders were also targeted as class enemies, and later in the 1930s, often on charges of being "pan-Islamists" and supporters of the Alash Party. Some religious leaders escaped arrest. Momaqan Äliyev, an imam in Kökshetau, who was to become Deputy Qazi of Kazakhstan in SADUM, attributed his salvation to his class origins, remarking in his autobiography, written in the 1960s, that it was his origins from a poor nomad family that enabled him to

[41] Sïrlïbay Bürkïtbayŭlï, *Maral ishannïng nŭr shapaghatï*, (Qostanay: n.p., 1998), 50–52.

[42] The persecution of the Kazakh *ʿulamāʾ* in the Stalin era awaits an informed study. For a discussion of the relations between the *ʿulamāʾ* and the Soviet authorities in Tatarstan, see Il'nur Minnullin, *Musul'manskoe dukhovenstvo i vlast' v Tatarstane (1920–1930-e gg.)*, (Kazan: Akademiia Nauk Respubliki Tatarstan, 2006).

[43] For an overview of the integration of Muslim mosque communities into the TsDUM in the 1920s, see Kemel Tokumbaev, "Tatarskii plast v musul'manskoi kul'ture Vostochnogo Kazakhstana," in: *Tatary na vostoke Kazakhstana*, (Ust'-Kamenogorsk: Tatarskii kul'turnyi tsentr VKO, 2008), 28–38; for TsDUM's views on the integration of the Kazakh steppe, see, Kashshāf Tarjumānī, "Dīnī tashkīlātlarïmïznïng älikkī wa ḥazirgī aḥwālī," *Islām majlisī*, February 1925 (5–6), 194–204.

avoid arrest.[44] Nevertheless, Ghïlmani's biographical dictionary, focused on northern Kazakhstan, reveals quite clearly that a substantial portion of the *ʿulamāʾ* suffered from arrests, executions, and deaths in custody.[45]

Ishans as Targets of Soviet Propaganda and Jadid Polemics

Ishan communities in Central Asia, the Kazakh steppe, and the Volga-Ural region experienced Soviet repression unevenly but also repeatedly. They were obvious targets of anti-religious policies, particularly those *ishans* formally registered as imams, mullahs, and *mukhtasibs* within the religious establishment. Similarly, *ishans* whose activities included education, and especially madrasa instruction, were, by the mid-20s, deprived of their livelihood by Soviet law. The income that the *ʿulamāʾ* and many *ishans* received as offerings elicited punitive taxation, and was also addressed in police investigations.[46] We find ishans denounced as a particular threat in both internal government documents and in propaganda. An anonymous report on the Muslim "clergy" from 1927 describes the political threat from ishans in almost identical terms as the tsarist missionary accounts cited above. Kazakhs are described as coming under the fanaticized influence of Uzbek *ishans*, but at the same time, Kazakh *ishans* are described as engaging in anti-Soviet agitation, and of attracting "low-level soviet workers and communists."[47]
Ishans were sometimes singled out in Soviet propaganda, particularly during the Cultural Revolution, when they became incarnations of class oppression, obscurantism, superstition, and violence against women. In a pamphlet from 1930 devoted to the campaign against the face veil (*päränzhi*) in the Auliye-Ata and Sayram regions of Kazakhstan – a region where *khoja* communities were particularly prominent – the author names *ishans*, along with the wealthy, mullahs, and merchants as the inveterate foes of the anti-veil campaign.[48] Another anti-religious pamphlet devoted to "the reactionary role of the Muslim clergy," published in Kazakhstan in 1937, alleged that in 1928,

---

44 Ghïlmani, *Biographies of the Islamic Scholars of Our Times* II, 387,

45 Ashirbek Muminov et al, "Introduction to the English Translation," in: Ghïlmani, *Biographies of the Islamic Scholars of Our Times* II, 50–51.

46 Ghïlmani, *Biographies of the Islamic Scholars of Our Times* II, 220, 386; M. K. Koigeldiev, *Stalinizm i repressii v Kazakhstane 1920–1940-kh godov*, (Almaty: Zerde, 2009), 200.

47 B. A. Tulepbaev et al. ed. *Preodolevaia religioznoe vliianie islama: sbornik dokumentov i materialov*, (Alma-Ata: Kazakhstan, 1990), 132–134.

48 M. Riadnin, *Päränzhige qarsï küres ashïp ädet, ghurïpqa töngkeris kirgizilsin*, (Qïzïl-Orda: Qazaghïstan baspasï, 1930), 31.

ishans and their *murids* in Uzbekistan opposed the emancipation (*raskreposhchenie*) of women by attacking and murdering them. In one case, an *ishan* reportedly killed his former sister-in-law for divorcing his brother using Soviet legal services (ZAGS), and in another, an *ishan's murids* supposedly had murdered a woman near the town of Urgut for violating the *sharīʿa* by having eloped.[49] One of the most extensive Soviet propaganda critique of *ishans* is a monograph published in Tatar in 1930 devoted primarily to the Volga-Ural region, but also including a discussion of *ishans* in the Kazakh Inner Horde. In this account, the author provides all of the labels necessary to marginalize *ishans* and their followers in the Soviet system, equating them with the wealthy, with the Muslim "clergy," and with obscurantism.[50] Whatever the accuracy or inaccuracy of the authors' accusations, in fact these works were designed to discredit the individuals and communities that would become the targets of violent repression, thereby serving as a public justification of repressive measure.

Critiques of *ishans* and Sufism were not restricted to Soviet anti-religious propagandists and atheists, but were also embraced by *jadids*, who in the 1920s staffed the official Soviet Muslim religious administrations in the Volga-Ural region and the Crimea. While the Islamic rationalist critique of Sufism is as old as Sufism itself, and in Russia was strongly evident before 1917, the Soviet *jadid* critique took place in a context of intensifying state repression, which would eventually swallow up the *jadids* themselves. The scholar Żiyāʾ Kamālī and the mufti Riżāʾ ad-Dīn b. Fakhr ad-Dīn were engaged in anti-Sufi polemics in the Central Muslim Religious Administration (TsDUM) in Ufa, which had jurisdiction of the Volga-Ural region and much of the Kazakh steppe. Mozaffari's anti-Sufism pamphlet, while a work of Soviet propaganda, broadly coopted many elements of the pre- and post-revolutionary *jadid* critiques of Sufism, as he cites the TsDUM's anti-Sufi polemics approvingly.[51] Anti-Sufi polemics were not restricted to Volga-Ural *jadids*, but are evident in other state-approved *jadid* publications from 1920's. Bakhtiyar Babajanov has observed these polemics in the short-lived Uzbek

---

[49] F. Oleshchuk, *O reaktsionnoi roli musul'manskogo dukhovenstva*, (Alma-Ata: Partizdat TsK KP(b)K, 1937), 19–20.

[50] Zarif Mozaffari, *Ishannar-Därvishlär*, (Kazan: Janalif, 1931), *passim*.

[51] Iu. N. Guseva, *Ishanizm kak sufiiskaia traditsiia Srednei Volgi v XX veke: formy, smysly, znachenie*, (Moscow: Medina, 2013), 97–98.

jadid journal *Ḥaqīqat*, that appeared in Tashkent in 1922.[52] Similar anti-Sufi polemics are evident in the Crimean *jadid* journal *ʿAṣrī musulmān*.[53] The commitment of the Kazakh reformist *ʿulamāʾ* to its rhetorical assault on Sufis is evident in a poem, titled "Sufis," composed in 1931 by Saduaqas Ghïlmani while he himself was in the Gulag, and during the Great Famine, in which he denounces the ignorance of Sufis and their pretensions to religious leadership.[54]

The Persecution of ishans

The level of repression meted out to *ishans* in the Soviet Union depended on where they were thought to pose the gravest political threat to Soviet authority. Citing an assessment of the Eastern Department of the OGPU (VOOGPU), Iuliia Guseva notes that the Soviet security services considered *ishans* to pose the greatest danger in the Central Asian republics. She concluded that *ishans* in the Volga-Ural region suffered relatively lightly from repression in the 1920s and 30s, compared to *ishans* in Central Asia.[55] The differences in VOOGPU risk assessments between *ishans* in Russia and Central Asia, including Kazakhstan, appear to reflect differences in the social functions of *ishans*, where in the Volga-Ural region, they were usually part of the *ʿulamāʾ* and functioned more as the leaders of Sufi networks, while in Central Asia, they functioned as kinship lineages, and assumed a much broader social and economic role. Still, Soviet officials did not have to invoke "*ishanism*" to justify the repression of *ishans* in Kazakhstan. No "*ishans*" are listed among names and occupations of 30 Muslim religious figures included in a 1934 list of persons in Alma-Ata deprived of electoral rights, although *ishans* and *khojas* could certainly have been included there under varying professional categories. The most common (and quite generic) titles associated with figures in this list are "minister" (*sluzhitel' kul'ta*), and "mullah," although we also find in this list one "parish clerk" (*psalomshchik*), and his wife.[56] While

---

52 Bakhtiiar Babadzhanov, *Zhurnal "Ḥaqīqat" kak zerkalo religioznogo aspekta v ideologii dzhadidov,* TIAS Central Eurasian Research Series No. 1 (Tokyo: University of Tokyo, 2007), 32.

53 Ḥājjī Muṣliḥ ad-Dīn, "Qïrïmda shaykhlïq wa ahl-i taṣawwuf," *ʿAṣrī musulmān* 1924 (1), 5–6.

54 Saduaqas Ghïlmani, *Ölengder, maqalalar, zerteuler*, (Almaty: El-Shezhïre, 2010), 101–104.

55 Guseva, *Ishanizm*, 101–102.

56 *Spisok lits, lishennykh izbiratel'nykh prav po gorodu Alma-Ata i prigorodnomu raionu, noiabr' 1934* (Alma-Ata: Poligrafkniga, 1934).

Guseva's arguments may apply to an overall comparison of the Volga-Ural region and Central Asia, it is clear that the Soviet authorities in the Volga-Ural region continued to view "*ishanism*" as a political concern, or at any rate, used the charge of *ishanism* as sufficient political justification, and as a legal tool, for the persecution of Muslim religious leaders. A case in point is the investigation and trial in 1947 and 1948 of a group of Sufis in Molotov *oblast'* (today Perm' *oblast'*), known as the "Ishanism Anti-Soviet Organization." While the charges and "evidence" against these figures may or may not have corresponded to actual deeds, clearly the Soviet authorities could deploy "*ishanism*" as a serious charge against Sufi leaders anywhere, even after the Second World War.[57]

In the hagiographical accounts of persecution, the members of the lineages generally attribute their persecution to their status as *ishans*, and they assert that the Soviet authorities targeted them for that reason. There is ample reason for such a conclusion. At a speech in 1930 at the Seventh All-Kazakhstan Party Congress in Alma-Ata, Filipp Goloshchekin, the First Secretary of the Communist Party of the Kazakh ASSR who oversaw the sedentarization, collectivization, and consequently, famine, on the Kazakh steppe, accused "semi-feudal elements, *ishans*, and the clergy" as being the leaders of opposition to collectivization.[58] Soviet OGPU documents also name *ishans* as a targeted social category. A report from March 1930 detailing the "liquidation of kulak-White Guard and bandit elements" in the Soviet Union at large, remarks on the continued growth in activity of "bandit *bay-ishan* elements" in Kazakhstan.[59] Hereditary *ishan* status was also sufficient to make one a target of persecution. A *khoja* named Sattabergen related that his lineage began experiencing persecution and confiscations in 1929, when "they were accused of being descendants of *ishans*." Sattarbergen's grandfather Qozhakhmet Ümbetŭlï (1856–1934), known as Sarï Ishan, was a religious scholar in the Irgiz region of western Kazakhstan, and was forced to flee to Nukus, in Karakalpakstan, where he remained until 1933. Sattarbergen's uncle, Äbdilghani Qozhakhmetov, was arrested in 1937, and sentenced to death by an NKVD *troika*.[60]

---

[57] Andrei Starostin, Ol'ga Seniutkina, and Rustam Bikbov, "Antisovetskaia organizatsiia ishanizma v Molotovskoi oblasti," *Islam na Urale: Entsiklopedcheskii slovar'*, (Moscow-Nizhnii Novgorod: Medina, 2009), 37–39.

[58] Mikhailov, *The Great Disaster*, 68.

[59] *Sovetskaia derevnia glazami OGPU-NKVD* III/1 1930–1931, A. Berelovich et al. eds., (Moscow: ROSSPEN, 2003), 277–278.

[60] Iliyasova, *Dalam tŭnghan shezhïre*, 69–71.

In the autumn of 1932 a group trial of 45 members of Maral Baba's lineage was held in Qïzïlorda. Local activists had specifically accused the "*ishan* lineage" (*ishan äuletï*) of deliberately failing to sow 10 or 15 hectares of land with wheat, out of hostility toward the Soviet authorities. Two of the lineage were sentenced to death, and ten were condemned to various periods of imprisonment. The remaining 32 or 33 were released, after one of the *ishans* was able to produce an (evidently falsified) document signed by a member of a local village committee that that swore the 32 or 33 were not descendants of Maral Baba. The account goes on to say that the elders (*aqsaqals*) then convened their own "religious court," where they cursed the activists who identified the family members.[61] Säden Nŭrtayŭlï similarly attributes the persecution of Ämit Ishan (1906–1961), a great-grandson of Maral Baba to the simple fact that he was an *ishan*. Ämit Ishan was forced to flee to Tajikistan, from which he returned in 1946, but continued to endure persecution from the KGB until his death. In fact, we are told he drafted a letter to the KGB on his death bed, bragging that he finally escaped them.[62] The hagiography of the lineage of Shāh-i Aḥmad aṣ-Ṣābawī affirms that the actual reason some of the members of the family were arrested and shot in 1931, following the Sozaq uprising, was also their status as *ishans*. Zholli-maghzŭm, the youngest son of Shāh-i Aḥmad aṣ-Ṣābawī, was arrested and shot in 1931 in Shymkent, "for being the son of an *ishan*." Similarly, Shāh-i Aḥmad's grandson, Qozhakhmet, the son of Mukhay-maghzŭm was declared "the son of an *ishan*, or else a *bay*."[63]

The Soviet authorities categorized many members of *ishan* lineages as *bays*, but ultimately the two categories were interchangeable, at least for the purposes of persecution. The descendants of Shāh-i Aḥmad suffered heavily under the charge of being *bays*, which the authorities applied to entire families, who were exiled from their communities. Before the Revolution, this lineage had established close ties with many wealthy individuals from various tribal lineages. For example, Akhatay-maqzŭm, the son of Kamal-maghzŭm who had died in prison in Astrakhan around 1905, was married to a woman from a wealthy family of the Qanglï tribe, a division of the Senior Zhüz. This made Akhatay the wealthiest descendant of Shāh-i Aḥmad's lineage, owning 3,000 sheep, 1,000 horses, and 300 camels. Following the Sozaq Uprising, Akhatay-maghzŭm, Shāh-i Aḥmad's youngest son, Zholliqozha, and Qozhakhmet, the

---

61 Öteulï Änis Zhaqïpŭlï, "Maral ishan ŭrpaqtarïna qŭrïlghan sot ükïmïnen song," *Qasiyettï Maral Ishan*, Öteulï Änis Zhaqïpŭlï ed. (Qïzïlorda: Tŭmar, 2005), 89–91.

62 Nŭrtayŭlï, *Islam zhäne Maral Baba*, 60–62.

63 Mangabay (Uäli)ŭlï, *Äziz äulet*, 96.

son of Mukhay-maghzŭm, were shot on charges (denied by their descendants) of participating in the uprising. Following Akhatay's execution, virtually all of the family's livestock and household goods were confiscated, and the Party activists threatened to arrest anyone who helped the family. As a result, Akhatay's wife and one of her infant sons starved to death, and Akhatay's two-year-old son was secretly taken in by a Qanglï relative. Some members of Shāh-i Aḥmad's lineage changed their names; small children, including the author of the hagiography, Asqar Mangabayŭlï, were sent to Tashkent to be taken in by strangers. Another child, Nïghmet-agha, was told by a village policeman that "a child of an *ishan* is not allowed to go to school." As a consequence, he was expelled from school and even had his shoes confiscated. The descendants of Kamal-maghzŭm and Shäker-maghzŭm were taken in by the Sïban-Naymans in the Ayagöz region, a lineage with whom they had a *pir-murid* relationship, and their status as *sayyids* was concealed.[64] One of Shäker-maghzŭm's grandsons, Ghabdiakhmet Abuyusŭpŭlï (b. 1914) was expelled from school in in Semey 1929, after his father had been declared a *bay* the previous year. In 1930, he was arrested, charged with being the son of a bay, and was put in a labor camp felling timber, until his release in 1934.[65]

Numerous descendants of Maral Baba owed their salvation from Stalinist repression to the protection of members of local tribes with which the lineage had a historical *pir-murid* relationship with. The descendants of Maral's son Esey obtained protection on a collective farm, where the "unity and zeal" of the Zhappas people protected them.[66] Qazbek Erniyazŭlï, on the same kolkhoz obtained protection through the Üngït people, who were his relatives on his mother's side.[67]

Interrogations and charges

The Soviet authorities, primarily the OGPU, and from 1934, the NKVD, were responsible for the interrogations and investigations of *ishans* and other Muslim religious leaders, leaving in the archives investigation reports and interrogation transcripts. Paolo Sartori cautioned skepticism in the use of such materials to study the Tashkent *ʿulamāʾ* of the 1920s, despite the absence of

---

64 Mangabay (Uäli)ŭlï, *Äziz äulet*, 95–96.

65 Mangabay (Uäli)ŭlï, *Äziz äulet*, 118–120.

66 Öteulï Änis Zhaqïpŭlï, "Maral baba nemeresï, Eseyŭlï Süleyman ishan turalï bïr üzïk sïr," *Qasiyettï Maral Ishan*, Öteulï Änïs Zhaqïpŭlï ed., (Qïzïlorda: Tŭmar, 2005), 92.

67 Tazagül Qazbek-ishanqïzï, "Äkem Qazbek turalï," *Qasiyettï Maral Ishan*, Öteulï Änïs Zhaqïpŭlï ed., (Qïzïlorda: Tŭmar, 2005), 107.

standard Islamic biographical references for the Soviet era, such as hagiographies and biographical dictionaries.[68] Sartori's skepticism is well founded. While the interrogations often appear to contain substantive details about religious institutions, networks, and practices, the purpose of the interrogations appear to be 1) obtaining from the prisoner a confession, if only to substantiate the assumptions of the interrogators regarding the political threat of religious activity, and 2) implicating others. Such "evidence" can only be considered potentially coerced testimony, and must be weighed accordingly. With regard to the 1939 interrogation of Alyautdin, the son of Appaq Ishan, Koigeldiev expresses doubt where the interrogation transcript maintains that Alyautdin between 1937 and 1939 received substantial offerings from the public, while he was a fugitive in Qïzïlorda *oblast'* and Uzbekistan. Koigeldiev observes that the sums, and the claims about the number of *murids* he and his father had, appear inflated to enable these *ishans* to be classified as exploiters.[69]

As further evidence of the dubiousness of OGPU and NKVD documentation, Sïrlïbay Bürkĭtbayŭlï examined in detail the charges and "evidence" used against Zhünĭskhan Ündemesŭlï in the NVKD investigation. One charge, that Zhünĭskhan was an "exploiter," purported that Zhünĭskhan used a holy staff (*asa*) to obtain money from women who would make pilgrimages to his house. Bürkĭtbayŭlï denied that Zhünĭskhan would ever have kept such an incriminating relic at his home, and declared that it was hidden elsewhere for safekeeping. Similarly, Bürkĭtbayŭlï categorically rejected the second charge that Zhünĭskhan was a supporter of the Alash Party and had made anti-Soviet statements to members of the *kolkhoz*. He similarly argued that three other charges against him, including sabotaging the harvest, were manufactured, and concluded that as far as the authorities and their witnesses were concerned, Zhünĭskhan's crime was his *ishan* status as a descendant of Maral Baba.[70]

The hagiographies and other sources discussing the experiences of *ishan* lineages during the Stalin era depict above all a period of more or less constant violence, persecution, and disruption. As we have seen, wealthier *ishan* lineages, such as the lineage of Shāh-i Aḥmad aṣ-Ṣābawī, suffered seriously

---

68 Paolo Sartori, "The Tashkent *'Ulamā'* and the Soviet State (1920–1938): A Preliminary Research Note Based on NKVD Documents," *Patterns of Transformation in and around Uzbekistan*, Paolo Sartori and Tommaso Trevisani eds. (Reggio Emilia: Diabasis, 2007), 162–163.

69 Koigeldiev, *Stalinizm i repressii v Kazakhstane*, 196–200.

70 Bürkĭtbayŭlï, *Maral ishannïng nŭr shapaghatï*, 57–67.

from confiscations. Several senior members of the lineage were executed in 1931 following the Sozaq Uprising. Other members of the lineage, including Sadïq-maghzŭm, were killed by Soviet troops while trying to flee to China. Others, often children, were scattered among the "tribal murids" of the lineage in Uzbekistan and in Kazakhstan, and their identities concealed.[71] In Maral Ishan's lineage, Mŭkhtar, the son of Qalïbay-Ishan was executed without trial by Soviet troops in 1932, in the midst of the famine, during an uprising in the Qara Qŭm region. Batïrkhan Elĭbayŭlï endured "a great deal of repression" and died in the city of Troitsk in 1935.[72] Many members of Ayqozha Ishan's lineage were forced to flee to various cities in Central Asia, where they remained for long periods. Shämshĭ Ishan Remetŭlï, a descendant of Ayqozha Ishan, was forced to go and live among relatives in Samarqand, and eventually was invited by his *murids* to live in Dushanbe, where he remained under an assumed name, where he was nevertheless re-arrested on charges of being the leader of a group that had moved from Kazakhstan to Uzbekistan. He was convicted and sent to a series of camps near Tashkent, where he died in 1938. Shämshĭ Ishan's son, Äbuseyit-qari, was arrested three times. The first time was in 1928, and in the end, he was shot in the Shymkent Prison in 1937.[73] However, some *ishans* avoided persecution entirely. Säruar Ishan Ibadullaŭlï, a grandson of Ayqozha Ishan, was not arrested, but many of his students were shot or exiled to Siberia, mainly in 1937 and 1938. Similarly, Aqlima, the son of Ïsqaq Ishan, a descendant of Maral Baba, managed not only to avoid persecution, but even to survive the Second World War.[74] Süleyman-ishan Eseyŭlï was thought to have escaped repression on the whole, but he too was arrested in 1937, and only released through the assistance of the chief of the Qïzïlorda jail, who arranged his escape.[75] In the Manggïstau region, the Aday *ishan,* Kenzhe Äbdĭrakhman-ishan and his community evidently avoided the persecutions that took place in the region following an uprising there in 1929 and 1930. His survival was credited on his apparent poverty, which allowed him to teach "barefooted children" in the old manner.[76]

---

[71] Mangabay (Uäli)ŭlï, *Äziz äulet*, 83–84, 96.

[72] Nŭrtayŭlï, *Islam zhäne Maral Baba*, 64, 68.

[73] Shaydarbek-qazhï Äshĭmŭlï, *Sïrgha tolï Sïr boyï: tarikhi-tanïmdïq zhazbalar* (Almaty: Foliant, 2009), 299–301.

[74] Äshĭmŭlï, *Sïrgha tolï Sïr boyï*, 299; Nŭrtayŭlï, *Islam zhäne Maral Baba*, 56.

[75] Öteulĭ Änis Zhaqïpŭlï, "Maral baba nemeresĭ, Eseyŭlï Süleyman ishan turalï bĭr üzĭk sïr," 92–93.

[76] Äbĭlqadïr Span, *Aday qasĭretĭ* (Almaty: Nŭrlï Älem, 2011), 111.

In the midst of demonization by the state, famine, persecution, exile, and social isolation, the *ishan* lineages affirmed their holiness, their sacred connection with others Kazakh lineages, and their religious power, by relating stories about the experiences of their ancestors and kinsmen in the Soviet Gulag. These stories, of miracles, and holy relics, are the subject of the next chapter. As we shall see, they challenged, if not indicted, the moral authority of the Soviet system, and became important elements in the survival of these lineages.

CHAPTER 4. GULAG MIRACLES AND SACRED RELICS

The miracle narratives, told against the backdrop of Stalinist repression, continued the tradition of recounting miracles in hagiographic contexts. These narratives, describing incidents in the Gulag, and in the face of Soviet oppression more broadly, should encourage us to rethink the impact of Soviet atheism on Central Asian societies. The narratives refute the assertion that Soviet anti-religious policies somehow altered or degraded the Muslim status of these communities, or that the measure of "Islamic-ness" was restricted to the realm of intellectualized scholarship. These Sufism-inspired accounts of Gulag miracles, which demonstrate the tenacity of collective ideas of historically informed, conceived, and practiced Islamic-ness, in no way can be considered post-Soviet "foreign importations." They also show how Sufi ideas and practices might exist outside the *tariqat* and the Sufi disciplinary practice, surviving in the stories and actions of Muslims under Soviet rule. For those recounting these stories, the survival of the lineages, under circumstances in which so many perished, proves the *ishans'* holiness, through the continuity of their bonds with their ancestral spirits, and by fulfilling the role of the *ishan* lineage in Kazakh society.

GULAG MIRACLES

Within the major Kazakh hagiographical sources consulted for this study, there are fifteen accounts of miracles set in the context of arrest or repression (full translations of these miracle stories appear in Appendix 1). Miracle narratives are standard features of hagiographies; however, in the hagiographies of multiple lineages the repeated and consistent inclusion of miracles set in the Gulag suggests a common narrative purpose and goal. What distinguishes a Gulag miracle from other miracles is that they occur in the context of Soviet custody, such as in prison (most commonly), interrogation, court, or pursuit by the authorities. As such, they must be viewed as *political* statements, not only bearing witness to state oppression, but also containing an implicit religious and moral challenge to the abuse of state power. Gulag miracles fall into three main genres, all of which illustrate in dramatic form the holiness of the saint against the abuse of power by the state. These categories include 1) the locking and unlocking of prison doors by a saint; 2) using miraculous powers to flee, evade, or be concealed from the authorities; and 3) retribution against persecutors. These miracles often involve the intercession of the ancestral spirits (*äruaq*), whose bond with the living members of the community through a particularly holy *ishan* forms the basis of sanctity for the *ishan* lineages.

The most extensively elaborated Gulag miracle narrative describes the fate of Appaq-ishan, who was arrested in 1931 in the town of Shayan, in South Kazakhstan *oblast*. Some of the numerous miracles in this narrative, in fact, do not fit neatly into the three categories listed above, but merit a sustained examination for their detail and their message. Appaq-ishan's miracles are included in a biographical dictionary devoted to the saints of the Syr Darya Valley. They appear under an entry for Qaz Ata, a saint buried in the settlement of Tŭrmïs, near Shayan.[1] Here, the compiler includes Appaq-ishan's miracles in the Gulag to exemplify the holy power of Qaz Ata, who was Appaq-ishan's *pir*. It begins by explaining the political context of his arrest:

> It was the 30s when they raised up the cry of the Soviet state, [they said] "Drive the *khojas*, and mullahs with whips, like sheep." This cry put pressure on the major religious figures and forced them into exile. They persecuted them, accusing them in the following manner: "Appaq Ishan, his son Bakhibulla, and [Appaq's] younger brother Sabïr, these three *ishans* went to the people and tried to foment discord, saying, 'Famine is coming. Think of the coming days. Keep your spare food. Don't give it up.' They came out against the Soviet government's excellent policy." Appaq Ishan, who held the Holy Qaz Ata as his *pir*, was aware through his power [*qŭdĭret*] that bad oppression was coming to the people, and what he did to protect his son, his younger brother, and his people was correct. So, they threw Appaq Ishan in jail.

The first night that Appaq-Ishan was in jail, we are told, he summoned the guard, a young Kazakh, and promising not to escape, he asked him as a Muslim to open the door and let some fresh air into the dark cell. The guard refused. Moreover, he violated Kazakh norms of etiquette by rudely addressing his elder as "old man," and telling him that he was a prisoner, not a guest. He explained that the rules of Kazakh (and Islamic) norms of kinship relations did not apply, and insulted the *ishan*, by telling him, "There are no older brothers or younger brothers here, and no relatives. There are just criminals." Appaq-ishan looked at him disapprovingly, and reminding the young man of his youth (and hence junior status vis-à-vis the *ishan*) told him "My son, you are young. Don't be arrogant. The *äruaqs* will open it themselves," and that night, we are told, the doors of the cell opened and let in fresh air. The guard was disturbed by this, after verifying that the key had

---

[1] Shaydarbek Äshĭmŭlï, *Sïrgha tolï Sïr boyï: tarikhi-tanïmdïq zhazbalar* (Almaty: Foliant, 2009), 121; his full name is said to be Qazï Ata.

not left his belt. The next day, all the senior officials of the jail gathered to watch the door miraculously open after midnight, and let fresh air into the cell. The chief of the prison realized there was a great saint in his jail, and ordered the young guard to place Appaq-ishan in a separate cell with his companions.

Later, the investigation of Appaq Ishan's case was concluded, and he was brought before the court to make a statement before his sentence was read. The *ishan* admitted to the court that he had told the people that famine was coming, and to keep their food, and look to their own future. He explained that his *pir*, Qaz Ata, had revealed that a great and deadly famine would befall Kazakhstan. In the revelation, Qaz Ata ordered Appaq-ishan to save himself and his lineage, and protect the people. So, he instructed the "*ishans*, *khojas* and mullahs" to preach this warning to the people. When the investigator asked who had opened the cell door, Appaq-ishan told him it was his *pir*, Qaz Ata, which elicited laughter from the judge, who sentenced him to exile in Pavlodar *oblast*.

After they were sentenced, Appaq-ishan, Bakhibulla, and Sabïr were ordered to be transported to Almaty, and the three were placed in a special "Red" train car that had come from Moscow. The car contained religious figures who had been tried in Russia and were all gaunt, exhausted, hungry, and dirty. The common people (*qara khalïq*) and the *khojas* of Auliye-Ata had given Appaq-ishan and his companions four sacks of provisions for the trip, including rolls (*toqash*), fried bread (*bauïrsaq*), horse meat, sausage, mutton, and other victuals. When the saint saw the miserable condition of the people in the car, he ordered his son to spread his coat on the floor and pour the bag of rolls out onto it. When the inmates began fighting over the rolls, he found that unacceptable, and so had his son pick is coat up off the floor, and instead laid out his own white robe (*zhamïlghï*), and spread all of the food out onto it. When the train reached Almaty, the inmates in the car placed Appaq-Ishan on two mattresses, and carried him all the way to the prison without letting his feet touch the ground.

In prison, the account continues, the *ishan* worked tirelessly imparting cleanliness, purity, and faith. He called on the prisoners "to study the law of creation and the Holy Qur'an, to take direction from the Prophet Muhammad's hadiths, to hold eternally in the human heart the merciful light of the Islamic faith, and in that way, placing in every heart the law of being human [*adami bolmïs*]." When Appaq-ishan died, the prisoners grieved bitterly, and told the guards standing by the door, "Appaq-ishan is a saint in the true sense of the word. He taught us to live like humans, to exist like humans, and to know the difference between human and animal, between good and bad, and between despoiling and protecting. He established order in the prison. He summoned us onto the path of humanity."[2]

Symbolism in the Narrative of Appaq-Ishan

This very concise narrative is rich in symbolic meaning, and an analysis of some salient features will enable us to better understand its relevance to the author's audience.

1) The account emphasizes the role of the saint, here Appaq-Ishan, as one element in a spiritual chain of transmission. The miracle narrative is not included in an entry for Appaq-Ishan (the work, in fact, contains no entry for him), but rather for his *pir*, Qaz Ata, and therefore illustrates the religious power of Qaz Ata's *äruaqs*. By emphasizing Qaz Ata's status as Appaq-Ishan's *pir*, the author demonstrates both the spiritual authority of Appaq-Ishan's *khoja* lineage, through Appaq-Ishan's ability to perform miracles, alongside the significance of the *pir-murid* relationship, which gives him the ability to perform the miracles, through the tutelary spirits (*äruaqtar*) of his *pir*. Qaz Ata is repeatedly invoked in the account, most notably when Appaq-Ishan is facing the judge who exiles him, and he explains his place in the chain of religious authority.

2) Appaq-Ishan's interaction with the young Kazakh prison guard dramatizes, in very concise form, the Soviet challenge to Kazakh traditionalism, that the authorities pursued most aggressively during the period when this story is set. The chain of generational authority, of which the *pir-murid* relationship is a manifestation, was an aspect of social authority that came under attack during the Stalin era, as part of the assault on "tribalism" and "traditionalism." Generational conflict is a perpetual fault line in the rise of all mass movements, and was certainly exploited in the Kazakh context during that era. When the *ishan's* religious and generational authority is bluntly rebuffed by the prison guard who invokes the prison regimen as representative of the new Soviet order (a telling admission), Appaq-Ishan miraculously opens his cell door, reaffirming his authority (and that of Qaz Ata), enabling him to maintain his dignity as a faithful Muslim.

---

[2] Qazïbek Täzhiyev, *Äz äuliyeler* V, *Qazïnalï ongtüstïk* 22, (Almaty: Nŭrlï älem, 2011), 107–108, 111.

3) The state's charges against the *ishan* are shown to be arbitrary. When he tries to protect his community by using his religious power to warn them of the coming famine, the Soviet authorities cynically, and perversely, charge *him* with fomenting discord. At his trial, he freely admits assisting his community, even though it will cost him his life.

4) The entire community plays a role in his miracles. He feeds the starving prisoners in the railroad car with food donated to him by "the common people and khojas" of Auliye-Ata.

5) The jail car becomes a microcosm of Kazakh society, – another fitting symbol for 1931 – where the prisoners adopt the role of the Kazakh *murids* to their *pir,* the *ishan*. Remarkably, the prisoners are not identified as Muslims, but simply as being "from Russia." Appaq-Ishan teaches the inmates Islamic norms of behavior and fulfills the role of the *khojas*, as bringers of Islamic norms of behavior and etiquette to their communities. He spreads his robe on the ground, as an eating cloth (*dastarqan*), a symbol of Islamic etiquette, and makes the prisoners eat in a proper and dignified way worthy of Muslims. The inmates, like the Kazakh descent groups, recognize that they have been ennobled by the sacred power of the *ishan*, and they raise him up on two mattresses. The act of raising the *ishan* on two mattresses is reminiscent of the nomadic tradition of raising a newly inaugurated political or religious leader on a piece if white felt.[3] As we have seen above, Äyteke-biy had Müsïrälï-Qozha lifted up on a piece of white felt, after he had declared him *pir* of the Junior Horde. Similarly, the fact that they carry him from the car to the prison, "without letting his feet touch the ground" is reminiscent of a similar practice documented by Saduaqas Ghïlmani, who relates how Toqang-khazïret (1851–1916), a prominent religious scholar among Qanzhïghalï people, would be lifted from his horse and carried into the yurt he was visiting, without his feet touching the ground.[4]

---

[3] The practice of raising a newly inaugurated sovereign on a piece of white felt was not restricted to nomads. This ritual is also documented among the *amirs* of Bukhara; see Ron Sela, *Ritual and Authority in Central Asia: the Khan's Inauguration Ceremony,* Papers on Inner Asia, No. 37, (Bloomington Indiana: Research Institute for Inner Asian Studies, 2003), 12.

[4] Saduaqas Ghïlmani, *Biographies of the Islamic Scholars of Our Times* II, Ashirbek Muminov et al. eds. (Istanbul: IRCICA, 2018), 127–128.

6) The prisoners' eulogy of Appaq-Ishan expresses very unambiguously the role of the *ishan* in Kazakh society. He taught the prisoners to live and behave like human beings, to distinguish between good and bad, and between decency and indecency. The eulogy not only reaffirms the social and religious role of the *khoja* and the *ishan*, but, given the context in which it was retold, contains an implied moral challenge to Stalinism.

The miraculous opening of a cell door is the most common type of miracle in the hagiographies, and serves similar narrative and symbolic purposes in other accounts as it does in that of Appaq-Ishan. Äzzam-ishan Baltaqozhaŭlï (1899–1971) was a grandson of Ayqozha-ishan. We are told he fled to Uzbekistan and Tajikistan with his family at some point between 1929 and 1931. According to his Gulag miracle story, Äzzam-ishan was arrested unexpectedly and thrown in jail. When it was time for the daily prayers, the prison door would open on its own accord. Äzzam-ishan went out, and performed his ablutions and prayers. One day, the head of the prison, seeing that Äzzam-ishan had gone out and performed these rituals, cursed at the guard and asked why Äzzam-ishan was going out. The guard replied, "Comrade Chief, when he went out, the locks opened on their own, when he came back, it was [left] like it had been before." So, the chief got rid of that guard and brought another, but the same thing happened. Waiting for him, the prison chief caught him, struck him once or twice with a whip, and said, "Who gave you permission to go out?" Äzzam made a little smile, and went into the cell. At that moment two black snakes wrapped around the jailer's neck. When the jailer said, "Shoot the heads of these snakes! Get [Äzzam-ishan] Baltayev!" the executioner's pistol wouldn't shoot. The jailer then begged Äzzam Ishan forgiveness, and the *ishan* replied, "I will forgive you when you stand on the threshold with water and a pitcher (representing items needed for the ablutions). Once the jailer apologized, Äzzam Ishan went out, recited a Qur'anic verse, and made the two snakes disappear. After that, Äzzam Ishan would walk around the prison freely. The account cites Nŭrdïlla Paluanŭlï, a secretary and translator at the prison – but also a descendant of the saint Bozhban Ata of Zhangaqorghan – as an eye-witness. Nŭrdïlla, we are told, had kept telling the head jailer to free the *ishan*, explaining that had not harmed anyone, and was a scholar. The chief jailer agreed to free the *ishan*, on condition that he answer one question. The executioners brought Äzzam Ishan to the jailer. The jailer greeted him and spread out a map of the world on the table. "If you make the world fit into one point for me, you are free." Äzzam Ishan responded, "When I think about it and ponder it, God Almighty puts an answer in my mind, and that is what I will give. The point that is referred to is the pupil of my eye." When Nŭrdĭlla interpreted the *ishan's* reply for the chief jailer, he was satisfied, and let him out of prison. Äzzam Ishan went back to his home in Kazakhstan and joined his kin.[5]

A saint named Äbduayt-ishan, a descendant of Ïsqaqbab,[6] was forced to flee Kazakhstan for Tajikistan. He was arrested 17 times. On two occasions, he was not locked up for more than 21 days. The other times he was jailed for only three or four days, and then released. At night, the locked doors would open, and he would go out, and perform his ablutions and prayers. After a while he went to Uzbekistan, to Bekobod, and eventually made his way to Afghanistan. Then he saw Ahmad Yasavi in a dream, who told him three times to return home. Äbduayt, the story goes, told Ahmad Yasavi, "If I go back, they'll persecute me." Then Ahmad Yasavi lifted his head and said, "Look at me. The head of your ancestor Ahmad Yasavi is above the clouds, and his feet are on the ground." Äbduayt Ishan grew frightened and looked down. Ahmad Yasavi promised that no one would persecute him, and ordered him to return home. As a result, he waited for Nikita Khrushchev, who was notorious for his anti-religious policies, to be replaced by Leonid Brezhnev, and he returned to Turkistan in 1965.[7]

As with the previous miracle, where an *ishan* received a revelation from an ancestor, in that case, from Ahmad Yasavi, the saint Mŭkhamedzhan-ishan, another grandson of Ayqozha-ishan, known as Mhän-ishan also received a revelation from his ancestors. Mhän-ishan was arrested in 1937, when the village activists (*belsendĭler*) were specifically pursuing *ishans*. When he was in jail, his ancestors made a revelation to him (*babalarï ayan berĭp*) and he said, "go out" three times. The door then opened on its own, and he put on women's clothes and escaped. In the morning, also by a miracle (*keremetpen*) the guard did not notice his absence, and he returned safely to his people, where he died in 1939.[8]

---

[5] Shaydarbek Äshĭmŭlï, *Sïr boyïndaghï äwliyeler*, (Almaty: Atamŭra, 2000), 111–114.

[6] Ïsqaqbab, whose name appears in Arabic-script texts as Isḥāq-bāb, is remembered as a descendant of Muḥammad al-Ḥanafīya, and as an early Islamizer of Central Asia. He is also an important ancestral figure in *khoja* genealogies; see Devin DeWeese and Ashirbek Muminov eds. *Islamizatsiia i sakral'nye rodoslovnye v Tsentral'noi Azii* I-II, (Almaty: Daik Press, 2008–2013); on his shrine, located near Sozaq, and related legends, see Qazïbek Täzhiyev, *Äz äuliyeler* VI, *Qazïnalï ongtüstĭk* 22, (Almaty: Nŭrlï älem, 2011), 57–71.

[7] Äshĭmŭlï, *Sïr boyïndaghï äuliyeler*, 121.

[8] Äshĭmŭlï, *Sïrgha tolï Sïr boyï*, 277.

Another saint with the power to open and closed locked cell doors was Nïghmet-ishan Makhmutŭlï (1894–1982). He was arrested and put in prison, charged with leading a branch of the foreign-based Aral counter-revolutionary organization. When he was in prison, we are told, he would perform the prayers five times a day, and when it was time to perform the prayers, the doors would open on their own, and the chief of the prison became frightened. Nevertheless, he served eight years in prison from 1943 until 1951.[9]

Similar stories exist for the descendants of Maral Baba. His great-grandson Batïrkhan Tobaghabïlŭlï, was arrested during collectivization and put in the Qarmaqshï jail. While he was in jail, Batïrkhan's grandfather, Qalqay-ishan, the eldest son of Maral Baba, appeared to Batïrkhan in a dream, and advised him that there was a nail by the side of the stove, and to use that nail to take a brick out of the side of the window, and get away. He and his companion managed to escape, thanks to the revelation. However, Batïrkhan was arrested again in 1937 as an enemy of the people, and was evidently executed.[10] Zhünïskhan Ündemesŭlï, another member of Maral Baba's lineage, was arrested in 1937 and thrown jail. He would escape from prison repeatedly, greatly annoying the chief jailer. In the end, he stopped escaping, and instead used his powers to help treat sick prisoners in the jail, and as the narrator observes, "Who [else] would protect the 'enemies of the people' in prison?"

Some saints used their powers to perform miracles that concealed them and their family members from the Soviet authorities. Ämit-ishan Äbdïrakhmanŭlï (1906–1961), a great-grandson of Maral Baba, is remembered for inheriting Maral Baba's host of 40,000 "commoner" *äruaqs* (*qïrq mïng qara äruaq qosŭnï*). Ämit-ishan had been forced to flee to Tajikistan, where he remained for many years. Before that, he was living as a fugitive near his relations in Kazakhstan, in a small yurt, in a remote area hidden from his home village:

> Ämit-ishan spent a few months ducking in a yurt that had been pitched in a place hidden from the eyes of the people. He had nobody with him except an old student [*qalpe*] who would be with him. When the people were asleep, the sound of very many cavalrymen was heard on the outskirts of the tent. There was no end to the crowd of rattling soldiers passing by. Ämit-ishan went outside and after it was time to milk the mare, he returned. Even when the dawn was starting to break, the clopping of horses' hooves was audible. In a flash the cavalry was going by the yurt. Based on the sound of the clopping, it was probably thousands. Ämit got out of bed, dressed, and went out. After a while he returned completely unconcerned, as if he were sleeping. Not revealing the secret, [his companion] had woken

---

[9] Äshïmŭlï, *Sïrgha tolï Sïr boyï*, 298.

[10] Another source for the hagiography claims that Batïrkhan died in Troitsk in 1935; see, Nŭrtayŭlï, *Islam zhäne Maral Baba*, 46, 64.

> up and covered himself with the blanket and was shaking, out of his mind with fear. Involuntarily, he was compelled to ask, "What, is this a miracle?" Ämit-ishan said casually, to calm his student, "This is the host of the 40,000. Don't be afraid. It's to protect us from the enemy.[11]

Other saints whose miracles saved them from arrest included Inayat-maghzïm Omarŭlï (d. 1979), a great grandson of Ayqozha-ishan. He was forced to flee his home, first to Tajikistan, and then to a settlement near the town of Kitap, in Uzbekistan. At one time, two officers of the secret police came to his house to arrest him. They gave him permission to perform a prayer (*namaz*) before leaving, and then as they walked past some sand hills, he performed two supplemental prayers (*nafl namazï*). Once he had completed those prayers, the pistols that the officers were holding broke in two. They both sensed why this had happened, and begged Inayat's forgiveness, saying, "You haven't seen us and we haven't seen you," and they went back to where they had come from. On another occasion when an officer of the secret police was going to execute him, he again performed two supplementary prostrations. Then, when he said, "I'll take the pistols of the KGB officers,"[12] they disappeared. They begged him. "We have done wrong! Give us our weapons back. We will let you go safely." Inayat-maghzïm recited a prayer, returned the weapons, and they went back.[13]

Another type of miracle in the accounts is the retribution miracle, where the saint reveals his power by punishing his (and his people's) tormentors. Before Zhünïskhan Ündemesŭlï was arrested in 1937, an official from the district came to the Zhanga Tŭrmïs kolkhoz in Qayïndï and summoned him into the office. He confronted Zhünïskhan with being from an *ishan* lineage and cursed at him. After the meeting, the official became tormented by a swollen abdomen, "and groaned in pain." He pleaded with Zhünïskhan for forgiveness, and the saint "treated that petty tyrant and cured him."[14]

An *ishan* named Babqozha Äbdïmälikŭlï (1890–1976), a descendant of Babazhan, of the Khorasan Ata *khoja* lineage, had decided not to flee during the famine and "separate himself from Khorasan Ata."[15] He helped wash the

---

[11] Nŭrtayŭlï, *Islam zhäne Maral Baba*, 60–61.

[12] "KGB" is an anachronism here, and is used here simply as a term for the secret police.

[13] Äshïmŭlï, *Sïrgha tolï Sïr boyï*, 292; Äshïmŭlï, *Sïr boyïndaghï äuliyeler*, 117–118.

[14] Nŭrtayŭlï, *Islam zhäne Maral Baba*, 67.

[15] Khorasan Ata is the founder of a major Kazakh khoja lineage; see Ashirbek Muminov, "Die Qožas – Arabische Genealogien in Kasachstan," *Muslim Culture in Russia and Central Asia Vol. 2: Inter-Regional and Inter-Ethnic Relations*, Anke von Kügelgen et al. eds., (Berlin: Klaus Schwarz Verlag, 1998), 196–198.

bodies of the dead, and bury them so they would not be eaten by scavengers. The local people took him as their *pir*, because of his good deeds. His reputation for holiness was such that the chairman of the kolkhoz spoke with the village chief (*auïlnay*) and got witnesses to testify that Babqozha had accepted a bride-price (*qalïng*) when the village chief had given the chief's sister in marriage.[16] He was arrested and sentenced in 1936, and imprisoned in Byelorussia for a time. Within a year the judge's wife lost nine of her children. The judge's kin and learned elders gathered, and told the judge to absolve Babqozha; he brought a document absolving him, and they released him.[17]

Shabar Ishan Esenŭlï (b. 1860), was an *ishan*, hajji, and *madrasa* instructor among the Aday people in the Mangghïstau region. According to stories recorded among these Adays, the first wave of migrants left the Mangghïstau region for Turkmenistan in 1928, and a second wave left in 1930. Hoping for a positive outcome, Shabar-ishan stayed behind, and the people who looked to his wishes waited to see what God would bring. Finally, we are told, his patience ran out, and the Red activists came after him. They caught him trying to flee to Khorezm, tied him up, and transported him first to Fort Shevchenko, and then to Üyshĭk (formerly Gur'ev, today Atyrau), where he was put in jail. In prison, he did not neglect a single daily prayer, and once, when he was touching his forehead to the floor in prostration in his cell, a "foolish young guard" insulted him, and Shabar placed a curse on him. When the guard came home, he found he could not urinate, and by morning, we are told, it was like the Torment of the Grave (*qabïr azabï*) His father, an old man, repeatedly queried the son, and found out that a mullah, "bent over with one foot in the grave," had cursed him. The son admitted his mistake, and the father went to see the chief of the prison, to explain the situation. There the father met with the *ishan*, and with tears in his eyes, apologized for his son, who, the father explained, was heedless, and had taken that job without thinking. Shabar-ishan himself admitted his guilt for yielding to human weakness, and from his cell, treated the boy, and allowed him to again urinate. After that, the father brought the *ishan* and his family and hosted them well. He offered to help the *ishan* escape, and to hide him among his relatives in the Inner Horde. However, Shabar-ishan refused, predicting his own death, which came to pass soon after, when he was executed.[18]

---

[16] The payment of bride-price was one of the Kazakh practices denounced during the Cultural Revolution.

[17] Äshĭmŭlï, *Sïr boyïndaghï äuliyeler*, 341.

[18] Äbĭlqadïr Span, *Aday qasĭretĭ* (Almaty: Nŭrlï Älem, 2011), 107–110.

Besides miracles performed by *ishans*, a lineage's *äruaqs* were also credited for exacting retribution on those who would commit transgressions against the tombs and other holy sites of a lineage. Stories about the divine retribution that befell anti-religious activists who demolished a shrine or mosque are extremely numerous in accounts of religion during the Soviet era, and constitute a definite sub-genre of Soviet and post-Soviet folklore.[19] An account collected in 1994 at the tomb of the saint Mullah Hajji Taz in Iske Qazan, in Tatarstan offers a good example:

> The cemetery and the spring were bulldozed under in the time of Khrushchev by three local Komsomol members. The stones were saved, however, by two local young men, who realized that the site was sacred. At night they took the stones away and hid them. Two of the stones were later recovered by [the archeologist] Ravil' Fakhrutdinov, but the third remains lost, since the only man who knew where it was has since died. The fate of the three *komsomols* was as follows: one of them spent a long time in the hospital; the wife of the second one was killed by either a streetcar or trolleybus. After Islam began to become acceptable again, the third *komsomol* continued to deny his involvement. Nevertheless, realizing the severity of his sin, he asked an old woman what he should do. The old woman told him to build a metal enclosure (*chardughan*) on the site of the tomb that he had destroyed.[20]

These sorts of legends were not restricted to Muslims. Eastern Orthodox Maris in Gorkii oblast' relate tales about how all of the men of the village of Mel'nikovo died after they cut down their sacred groves and pulled up the stumps. The fact that their village no longer exists is proof of divine retribution. Similarly, when villagers built a stable on the site of the grove, all of the horses kept at that stable died.[21] The conclusions by villagers that divine retribution could be experienced by persons who destroyed shrines were not a post-Soviet phenomenon, but were a problem that Soviet anti-religious authors were sometimes compelled to address. The Chuvash anti-religious author Georgii Kudriashov, writing during the time of the Khrushchev anti-religious campaigns, relates that

> the kolkhoz activists and atheists struggle ineffectively against such superstitions [sacred groves, known as *keremet* groves], at the same time as false rumors and prejudices do not dissipate. In 1931–32, in order to put an end once and for all to this absurd faith, a chairman of a local kolkhoz, V. A. Kudriaev, ordered the uprooting of a *keremet* grove. At that

---

19 For a discussion of this genre and an informed analysis of its meaning in Soviet Islam, see Paolo Sartori, "Of Saints, Shrines, and Tractors: Untangling the Meaning of Islam in Soviet Central Asia," *Journal of Islamic Studies* (2019), 24.

20 Author's field notes.

21 N. V. Morokhin, *Nizhegorodskie mariitsy*, (Ioshkar-Ola: Ministerstvo kul'tury Respubliki Mari El, 1994), 169–170.

> moment, completely coincidentally, the kolkhoz chairman fell ill. When they heard about his illness, the woodcutters became frightened and left the grove. Obviously, the chairman's illness had nothing to do with cutting down the grove. Two phenomena, completely unconnected with one another, happened to coincide, and this gave ammunition to superstitious interpretations "the *keremet* [spirit] got him."[22]

For our purposes, the significance of this passage is that it reveals how believers in the Soviet era, by attributing divine retribution to those who executed Soviet anti-religious policies, could challenge and criticize the ethical basis of Soviet anti-religious policies, using religious arguments. Kudriashov's reaction to the criticism demonstrates it could be effective. Among the Kazakh *ishans* we find very similar stories, concerning their shrines. For example, we are told how someone who struck the tomb of Safar-maghzŭm, in the Taraz region, with a tractor later died. When the Soviet authorities turned Safar-maghzŭm's mosque into a calf shed, the 90 calves housed in the shed suddenly died.[23]

Such retribution stories, which are ubitquitous in both hagiographies and in Soviet anti-religious "scientific" literature, reveal in effect a subversive challenge only to Soviet authority, but to the very philosophical underpinnings of the entire Soviet project. Clearly, these stories circulated widely; they represent the assertion of an alternative moral universe to the Soviet system; they offer a radically different perception of Soviet realities, and demand that the listener take into account a radically different moral universe. As we have seen, this sort of subversion was not unique to Muslims, but in the Muslim context, the retribution story was also a common feature of pre-Revolutionary Islamic hagiographies, and was a further evidence of how older narrative elements could be deployed in a Soviet context.

Both the miracle narratives and the retribution stories demonstrate in dramatic fashion the ideological conflict between Soviet atheism with the Islamic faith. However, in the Kazakh context, rather than being a contest of intellectualized theological and philosophical positions (evident, for example, in the *aytïs* contests between Muslim scholars and anti-religion activists recorded by Saduaqas Ghïlmani), the Islamic faith as embodied by the miracle-working *ishans* is above all a matter of ethics, behavior, dignity, and justice, juxtaposed against the iniquity, coarseness, humiliation, and cynicism of Stalinism, and the Soviet system more broadly. The miracles reveal, using

---

[22] G. E. Kudriashov, *Perezhitki religioznykh verovanii chuvash i ikh preodolenie,* (Cheboksary: Chuvashskoe Gosudarstvennoe Izdatel'stvo, 1961), 63.

[23] Asqar Mangabay (Uäli)ŭlï, *Äziz äulet: Shakhiakhmed Khazret pen onïng ïnïsï Fatikh imamnïng häm olardïng ŭrpaqtarïnïng shezhïresï,* (Almaty: Öner, 2001), 199, 201.

a variety of backdrops and metaphors, the *ishans'* self-perception of their role in society, a perception doubtlessly shared by the lineages who were their *murids*. *Ishans* fulfilled several crucial roles in Kazakh society, above all at the bringers of Islamic norms, ethics, and behaviors to Kazakh society. Their Islamizing ancestors first took on this role in the early medieval era, and at no time was the maintenance of this role more important than during the Stalin years.

RELICS AND OTHER SACRED OBJECTS

Embedded within the Gulag miracles are stories of a variety of sacred artifacts that as objects possess sacred power, and are mentioned in the narratives to demonstrate the religious power and authority of the lineages. While sacred relics and objects are regular, if not common, features in the religious history of Central Asia and the Volga-Ural region, they appear with unusual frequency in the telling of Gulag miracles, and merit closer investigation.

The definition of a "relic" or sacred object in the Central Asian context can be quite broad. These sacred objects fulfilled different religious and even political roles throughout history. At the upper end were relics typically brought from Turkey or the Hijaz connected with the Prophet Muhammad. The most prestigious relics were beard hairs of the Prophet Muhammad (*mū-yi mubārak*), that were brought back to Central Asia, usually by hajjis, at great expense. They were located in numerous Central Asian cities. Typically, their owners would build small structures to house them, and build mosques around them.[24] Mosques devoted to a *mū-yi mubārak* also existed on the Kazakh steppe. There was one in Semey, brought back by a Hui (Dungan) pilgrim returning from Mecca, and another among the nomadic Kereys in the Chinese Altay, which was brought back from Istanbul by the son of an *ishan* known as Kerey Ishan.[25] Bakhtiyor Babajanov had examined the political context of relics in the Qoqand Khanate, where they became both objects of large-scale

---

[24] "Kratkii obzor sovremennago sostoianiia i deiatel'nosti musul'manskago dukhovenstva," *Sbornik materialov po musul'manstvu* I, V. I. Iarovyi-Ravskii ed., (St. Peterburg: Topgrafiia Rozenoer, 1899), 35.

[25] Allen J. Frank and Mirkasyim Usmanov eds. *Materials for the Islamic History of Semipalatinsk: Two Manuscripts by Aḥmad-Walī al-Qazānī and Qurbān-ʿAlī Khālidī* (Berlin: Das Arabische Buch, 2001), 34; Qurbān-ʿAlī Khālidī, *An Islamic Biographical Dictionary of the Eastern Kazakh Steppe*, (Leiden: Brill, 2005), fol. 87a; ʿAqid b. ʿUlūmchī Qarmāṣāqōf, *Manāqib-i pīrān-i ʿazīzān* (Kazan: Tipografiia Imperatorskago Universiteta, 1909), 16.

pilgrimage, and also matters of critical debate among historians and theologians.[26]

Some sacred objects are also associated with *ishan* and *khoja* lineages. The manufacture of amulets was (and is) a common occupation and source of income for *khojas*. These often included the writing of Qur'anic verses and other formula that themselves were believed to have sacred qualities. Describing the libraries and "sacred inheritance" of *khoja* lineages in Siberia, Alfrid Bustanov has observed that manuscripts, including genealogies, litanies, shrine catalogs and other works constituted a sacred aspect of the Islamic "culture of the book" in that region.[27] Besides manuscripts, Siberian *khojas* also preserved sacred candle holders, usually made of clay, that were believed to have miraculous qualities, and that were cared for by caretakers of shrines.[28]

Two types of relics appear in the Kazakh hagiographies set in the Stalin era. These relics are commonly passed from generation to generation, like the lineages' *äruaqs*. The first is a holy staff (*asa* or *kök asa*), and the second is a dervish cap (*kulah*), which in the Kazakh texts appears as *gülä*. The Kazakh term *asa* is derived from the Qur'anic term *ʿaṣā*ʾ, which denotes the staff used by the prophet Moses to perform a number of miracles. Moses' staff is mentioned consistently in Turkic Sufi literature about the prophets, as well as in folktales. A detailed account of the miraculous qualities of Moses' staff appear one of the most popular Turkic *maktab* texts in the Volga-Ural region and the Kazakh steppe, the *Risāla-yi ʿAzīza*, a late 18th century commentary by the Bashkir scholar Tāj ad-Dīn b. Yālchïghūl on the 17th century Turkic work *Subāt al-ʿājizīn* of Ṣūfī Allāhyār.[29] Accounts of holy staffs miraculously sprouting leaves are also commonly encountered in hagiographies from East Turkestan, and it is likely that the Kazakh term *kök asa* (green staff) derives from the hagiographical tradition linking holy staffs with living vegetation.

---

[26] B. M. Babadzhanov, *Kokandskoe khanstvo: vlast', politika, religiia*, (Tashkent: Yangi Nashr, 2010), 646–649; see also R. D. McChesney, "Reliquary Sufism: Sacred Fiber in Afghanistan," *Sufism in Central Asia: New Perspectives on Sufi Traditions, 15th-21st Centuries*, Devin DeWeese and Jo-Ann Gross eds. (Leiden: Brill, 2018), 191–237.

[27] Al'frid Bustanov, "Rukopis' v kontekste Sibirskogo islama," in: A. G. Seleznev et al., *Kul't sviatykh v Sibirskom islame: spetsifika universal'nogo*, (Moscow: Izdatel'skii dom Mardzhani, 2009), 162–166.

[28] Al'frid Bustanov, *Knizhnaia kul'tura Sibirskikh musul'man,* (Moscow: Izdatel'skii dom Mardzhani, 2013), 74–76.

[29] N. Katanov, "Musul'manskiia skazaniia o zhezle Moiseia," *Izvestiia obshchestva arkheologii, istorii i etnografii pri Kazanskom Universitete*, XVI/1 (1900), 87–93; Tajeddin Yalchïgol, *Risaläi gazizä* I, (Kazan: Iman, 2001), 57–60.

In Kazakh tradition, the *asa* is commonly known by the names *asa-mŭsa, asa-tayaq,* and *kök asa.* Russian, and later, Soviet ethnographers tended to associate this item with *duanas*, highly visible and public itinerant Sufis who, as a rule, carried an *asa.*[30] However, the *asa* was also associated with particularly powerful Sufis masters, and these staffs, which were thought to be holy (*kiyelĭ*) and miracle-working (*keremettĭ*) were regarded as holy relics, and, while objects of pilgrimage, were generally not carried in public. Kazakh hagiographies contain legends telling of miracles saints performed with their staffs. Isabek-ishan struck his staff on the ground to predict where his tomb, those of his brothers, and that of his descendant Zhandarbek-ishan would be located.[31] We also find in the accounts the ubiquitous Sufi motif of a saint using his staff to create a spring. When Shāh-i Aḥmad aṣ-Ṣābawī was crossing the Betpaq Desert, one of his companions had been seriously wounded by bandits. He used his staff to strike the ground, and where it hit, there emerged a spring, which he used to wash and heal the companion's wounds.[32] When they were fleeing the local Soviet authorities and trying to reach Tajikistan, the descendants of Ayqozha-ishan struck his staff into the ground, and from where it struck a spring came forth.[33]

One holy staff that remains an object of pilgrimage is the staff (*kök asa*) of the saint Beket Ata, the *pir* of the Aday tribe, whose tomb in western Kazakhstan is one of the most important pilgrimage sites in the country. The staff is owned by the family of Tŭrsïnghali Latïpŭlï Nakesh in Aqtöbe *oblast*. It is kept in a separate room, and attracts pilgrims, primarily from the Aday tribe. The staff was originally given to Beket Ata in 1813 by his *pir*, Paqïrzhan-shaykh, while Beket was studying in Khorezm. Beket subsequently gave it to his student Shektībay Orazayŭlï, whose sixth-generation descendant is Tŭrsïnghali Nakesh. Tŭrsïnghali received it from one of his uncles, a Sufi, who was arrested in 1937, but managed to give the staff to his nephew before he was detained.[34]

---

30 N. Sarkin, *Chudodeistvennyi zhezl Moiseia po musul'manskim skazaniiam i posokh kirgizskikh dervishei*, (Kazan: Tipo-litografiia Imperatorskago Universiteta, 1904), 6–8.

31 Seyt-Omar Sattarŭlï *Qozhalar shezhĭresĭ,* (Almaty: Atamŭra, 2015), 391.

32 Mangabay (Uäli)ŭlï, *Äziz äulet,* 58.

33 Äshĭmŭlï, *Sïr boyïndaghï äuliyeler*, 111.

34 B. B. Mïrzabay, "Kiyelĭ 'kök asalar' turalï," *Aralo-Kaspiiskii region v istorii kul'tury Evrazii*, (Almaty-Aqtöbe: Arïs, 2011), 212; I. V. Stasevich, "Sovremennye formy kul'ta sviatykh u kazakhov Orenburgskoi oblasti (RF) i Aktiubinskoi oblasti (RK)," *Aralo-Kaspiiskii region v istorii kul'tury Evrazii*, (Almaty-Aqtöbe: Arïs, 2011), 226.

The hagiographies devoted to Maral Baba's lineage provide us with the most detailed account of the religious concepts and functions of the *kök asa* among Kazakh Sufis. Maral received his staff, which is today in the possession of his descendants in Qostanay *oblast*, from his *pir* Zhalangayaq-ishan. It is clear from the accounts that Maral-ishan's staff is thought to be a living thing. When Minuar Sälenŭlï, a descendant of Elïbay Maralŭlï, gave the iron tip of the staff to his relative Aqlima Ïsqaqŭlï, he told him that the tip of the staff would rattle, and was especially audible in Thursdays and Fridays. The metal tip of the staff was also said to moan and growl, making a sound similar to a tiger. The staff itself was in the possession of Ündemes, and then of his son, Zhünïskhan, and it, too, had the properties of a living thing. We are told that when Zhünïskhan was arrested in 1937 as an "enemy of the people," his mother, Mïngghoy, became angry at the staff, and saying, "Is this your intercession?" she angrily threw the case for the green staff into the fire. At that moment she suddenly bent over, and remained hunched. Finally, because of the staff's anger, she lost the ability to walk and remained that way the rest of her life.[35]

Maral Baba's staff was also included in one the charges against Zhünïskhan, where it was charged that people would come to his house and spend the night by the staff, and that he used the offerings pilgrims brought as a source of income. Sïrlïbay Bürkïtbayŭlï rejected these charges as nonsense, emphasizing that Zhünïskhan or his family would never have kept such an important and incriminating relic in their own home.[36]

Zhünïskhan possessed another sacred relic. We have seen how, according to the hagiography, Zhünïskhan remained in prison to treat the sick "enemies of the people," even though he could have been released through his miraculous powers. Zhünïskhan had a fur cap (*börïk*) that he used to heal the sick. Specifically, when he placed it on the head of a patient named Zhüsïpbek, the patient recovered. Later, the authorities released Zhünïskhan, and he gave the cap to Zhüsïpbek. As for Zhüsïpbek, he was later released, returned to his people, and became the kolkhoz chairman. He would talk about Zhünïskhan-*ishan*'s goodness for the rest of his life. He also treated the sick (whether it was with that cap is not indicated), and preached religion to the people, until his death in 1976.[37] The holy fur cap as a relic appears to have had Sufi associations, specifically connected to Bahāʾ ad-Dīn Naqshband, since in a

---

[35] Nŭrtayŭlï, *Islam zhäne Maral Baba*, 64, 67–68.
[36] Sïrlïbay Bürkïtbayŭlï, *Maral ishannïng nŭr shapaghatï*, (Qostanay: n.p., 1998), 59.
[37] Nŭrtayŭlï, *Islam zhäne Maral Baba*, 67.

Kazakh poem devoted to the great Sufi, the author mentions his skill in crafting such a cap.[38]

A similar sacred relic, a holy dervish cap (*qasiyettĭ gülä-täzh*), was in the possession of a branch of Ayqozha-ishan's descendants. Specifically, it had belonged to Ayqozha's grandfather Naurïz, and he passed it to his son, Temĭr. Temĭr passed it to Ayqozha. All three, we are told, wore the *gülä* on their heads. "Whoever wore the *gülä* on his head, the people kneeled before him, went along with what he said, and considered him a *pir*. If someone if they became very ill, they would bring the *gülä*, spray water [*ŭshïqtap*] over them, and cast spells [*zhazïlïp ketken*]." The *gülä* then passed to Ayqozha's son, Ibadulla, and from him, to his son Baltaqozha. Baltaqozha passed it to his son, Äzzam-ishan. Äzzam-ishan traveled among the nomads (*el*), and was in the steppe (*Arqa*). He wore the *gülä* when it was necessary, and the rest of the time he kept it in a clean place. During the period of the most severe repression, from 1929 until 1931, the family, fearing the relic would be found by the activists, and be used as a charge to exile the entire lineage, they buried the *gülä*, place three yurt poles over it, set it on fire, and fled to Tajikistan.[39]

The accounts of the Gulag miracles, set during the worst period of Stalinist repression, commemorate the terrible losses suffered by the *ishan* lineages, as well as their survival. But the miracle stories serve another purpose, besides the memorialization of ancestors and their miracles, and the physical continuity of the lineages. They demonstrate, metaphorically and expressly, the social role of the *khoja* and *ishan* linages in Kazakh society, as the bearers of Islamic ethics, norms of behavior, and piety. The miracle narratives also demonstrate the unbroken chain connecting the ancestors (*äruaqs*), the saints, and future generations, that defines both the genealogical community (*shezhĭre*) and the chain of Sufic initiation (*silsila*). Despite the terrible human toll of the 1920s and 1930s, the hagiographies emphasize, through the accounts of Gulag miracles, that the saints who experienced Stalinist repression did not surrender their ethical convictions, forsake their ancestors and descendants, or accept the Soviet verdict on religion. Nevertheless, for the lineages to survive, for *ishans* to maintain their role in Kazakh society, and for the Soviet system to mobilize the *khojas* and *ishans* in the Second World War and beyond, *ishans* and the Soviet state needed to find an accommodation. The manner in which this adjustment is reflected in the hagiographies is the subject of our next chapter.

---

38 *Khwāja Bahā ʾ ad-Dīn khażratlarīning qiṣṣasī*, (Kazan: Karimov, 1903), 3–4.

39 Äshĭmŭlï, *Sïr boyïndaghï äuliyeler*, 110–111.

CHAPTER 5. ACCOMMODATION, SOVIETIZATION, AND ISLAMIZATION

There is a story that circulates among the Kazakhs of the Qïzïl Qŭm Desert, in Uzbekistan, about a *khoja* named Däuït-Qozha Berdïsügïrŭlï (1901–1976), who was a descendant of Müsïrälï-Qozha, and hence from the Kereyt *khoja* lineage. From the age of 15 he offered blessing to the people, performed *zikr* for them [*zïkïr salïp*], and treated the mentally ill, who were brought to him with their hands and feet bound. He was a shepherd, and then from 1943 until 1945 he served in the war, and was demobilized in 1946. After the war he worked as a shopkeeper, harvester, and kolkhoz foreman [*brigadir*]. As he kept the religious path, and would not abandon it, an activist [*belsendï*] interfered in his activities. At some point in 1943, when he was tending livestock, his count came up short 4 or 5 sheep. So, he was sentenced and thrown in the Kattakurgan prison. One day the prison supervisor who was visiting the jail noticed that the door of a cell was staying open, and he mentioned it to the warden. The warden kept an eye on it for two or three days, and to his surprise, nobody escaped. The incident reached the ears of the city leader, and finally he asked for advice from a respected community leader (*aqsaqal*) of the city's Kazakh residents, named Äzïm-maqsŭm, who happened to also be a descendant of Müsïrälï Pir.[1] Äzïm-maqsŭm visited the prison and recognized Däuït-qozha. After the *aqsaqal* explained the situation to the warden, Däuït-qozha was let out. The *raion* chief summoned Däuït-qozha, and told him, "We are unable to so honor the spirits [*äruaq*] of your ancestors. Let's send you to war, instead of to prison." Without having to think on it for very long, Däuït-qozha agreed, went off to war, and ended up on the Leningrad Front. During his three years of military service, he remained unscathed, and returned unharmed.[2]

This story, which combines a Gulag miracle with a narrative of a *khoja's* military experience during the Second World War, neatly symbolizes how, during and after the Second World War, *khojas* and the Soviet authorities were able to reach a sort of *modus vivendi*. The Soviet authorities, while unable to publicly acknowledge the *khojas'* religious power, could ill afford to exclude them from projects that required the willing participation of the Soviet citizenry. For their part, the *khojas* would make their contribution to the Soviet project, while continuing to serve their own religious communities, as Däuït-

---

1 The title *maqsŭm* suggests he was the son of an *ishan* himself.

2 Seyt-Omar Sattarŭlï *Qozhalar shezhïresï,* (Almaty: Atamŭra, 2015), 492–493.

Qozha did by serving on the front and then working as a shopkeeper, harvester, and kolkhoz foreman, but at the same time offering his ancestral spirits to the community to heal the mentally ill.

The hagiographies reflect this evolving relationship between *ishan* lineages and the Soviet state. On the one hand, in such a relationship lineages acquiesced to becoming part of Soviet society. This process of accommodation was strongly accelerated during the Second World War, thanks to the total mobilization of Soviet citizens; in this sense, the war experience involved the Sovietization of the lineages. This aspect of Sovietization is evident in the narrative, where Däuĭt-qozha willingly goes as a Soviet soldier to defend his homeland, the Soviet city of Leningrad,. However, the hagiographies also reveal that the *ishan* lineages, and especially the *khojas* – who saw their position in Kazakh society as Islamizers, and as the bearers of Islamic social and religious norms – explained their role in the new arrangement in a time-tested manner, as Islamizers of the Soviet system. An unmistakable example of that tendency is a Bashkir legend, in which in 1941 Gabrakhman Rasulev is summoned to the Kremlin, where Stalin asks him how he can defeat the Germans. Rasulev explains that reciting the *shahada* is the key to victory. Stalin acquiesces, and thus becomes a Muslim.[3] Just as Däuĭt-qozha's ancestor, Baba Tükles, has been described as not only an Islamizer of nomads but also as an Islamizer of the native religious traditions of the steppe nomads,[4] so did the *ishan* lineages seek to maintain their role in Islamizing various aspects of Soviet labor on the collective farm and in the professions that *khojas* and *ishans* entered. Historians have documented this sort of Islamization of Soviet rural institutions. Stéphane Dudoignon and Christian Noack have studied these processes extensively in the presentation of case studies of Islamic culture on collective farms in Central Asia, the North Caucasus and the Volga-Ural after the Second World War, and following the collapse of the Soviet Union.[5] In Dudoignon and Noack's volume, Ashirbek Muminov's study of two kolkhozes in southern Kazakhstan demonstrates especially clearly the activities of Sufis and other

[3] S. Ä. Kildin et al., *Bashqortostan - äüliälär ile*, (Ufa: Kitap, 2012), 225–226.

[4] Devin DeWeese, *Islamization and Native Religion in the Golden Horde: Baba Tükles and the Conversion to Islam in Historical and Epic Tradition*, (University Park, Pennsylvania: The Pennsylvania State University Press, 1994), 51–66.

[5] Stéphane Dudoignon and Christian Noack, "Introduction," *Allah's Kolkhozes: Migration, De-Stalinization, Privatisation, and the New Muslim Congregations in the Soviet Realm*, Stéphane Dudoignon and Christian Noack eds. (Berlin: Klaus Schwarz Verlag, 2011), 9–46.

holy figures in rural southern Kazakhstan, and their religious role in these communities.[6]

Sacred Lineages and the Second World War

Adolf Hitler's invasion of the Soviet Union on June 22nd, 1941, and the four years of total war that followed it, compelled the Soviet government to rely on former elements of society who had been the targets of purges and repression before the war, whether formerly purged Red Army officers, members of religious organizations, or *ishans*. Beginning in the autumn of 1941, at the time of supreme military crisis, Stalin began mobilizing religious leaders to lend their support to the war effort. This mobilization included, most prominently, the Russian Orthodox Church, but also Muslim, Jewish, and Buddhist religious leaders, and even smaller groups, such as the Baptists and other Protestant communities.[7]

Since the establishment in 1788 of the Orenburg Muslim Spiritual Assembly, whose jurisdiction encompassed the Volga-Ural region and those portions of the Kazakh steppe then under Russian control, officially registered imams were expected to encourage and report the loyalty of their congregants to the Russian state. In wartime, loyalty included support for the war effort. In this regard, Stalin's mobilization of Muslim religious leaders was not new. It appears evident from the actions of Muslim religious leaders during the Second World War that they simply followed the example of Muslim religious leaders in the Volga-Ural region and the Crimea during the First World War, in fundraising, and giving Islamic sanction to the war effort. Stalin's efforts in that direction followed closely the mobilization of Muslim religious leaders by Imperial Russia during the First World War.[8] Already in the autumn of

---

6 Ashirbek Muminov, "From Revived Tradition to Innovation: Kolkhoz Islam in the Southern Kazakhstan Region and Religious Leadership (through the Cases of Zhartï-Töbe and Oranghay since the 1950s)," *Allah's Kolkhozes: Migration, De-Stalinization, Privatisation, and the New Muslim Congregations in the Soviet Realm,* Stéphane Dudoignon and Christian Noack eds. (Berlin: Klaus Schwarz Verlag, 2011), 307–366.

7 For the publication of numerous archival documents addressing the role of Muslim, and non-Muslim, religious leaders and organizations in supporting the Soviet war effort, see. V. A. Akhmadullin, *Patrioticheskaia deiatel'nost' dukhovnykh upravlenii musul'man v Velikoi Otechestvennoi Voine*, (Moscow: Islamskaia Kniga, 2015); see also D. Iu. Arapov ed. *Islam i sovetskoe gosudarstvo (1944–1990). Sbornik dokumentov,* vyp. 3 (Moscow: Izdatel'skii dom Mardzhani, 2011), 28–39.

8 Liutsian Klimovich, *Islam v Rossii*, (Moscow: Gosudarstvennoe antireligioznoe izdatel'stvo, 1936), 268–372; it is perhaps symbolic of much historical writing from the

1941, Gabrakhman Rasulev was raising substantial funds among Muslims in the Volga-Ural region to support the Soviet war effort; it was in this period that he had his famous meeting with Stalin himself in the Kremlin. Stalin also met with Ishan Khan Töre Babakhan, a member of an Uzbek *khoja* lineage from Sayram, in Kazakhstan. These men were to become muftis in the newly constituted Soviet muftiates. Rasulev was to head the Muslim Religious Administration for European Russia and Siberia (DUMES), based in Ufa, and Babakhan was to head the Central Asian Muslim Religious Administration (SADUM), based in Tashkent, and having jurisdiction over Turkmenistan, Uzbekistan, Kyrgyzstan, and Tajikistan, as well as Kazakhstan, which was removed from the authority of DUMES.[9]

One of the characteristics of the Soviet state's relationship with Muslim religious leaders was the tendency to favor Salafi-oriented scholars, including *jadids*. This favoritism began in the 1920s, and became strongly evident in the Brezhnev era.[10] As we have seen, in the 1920's Sufism was openly attacked in the journals of Soviet muftiates, and in the 1930s *ishan* lineages had become a targeted community for repression. However, the exigencies of the war emergency led to a truce, even in the persecution of Sufis. As Jeff Eden has demonstrated in the declarations of jihad against Nazi Germany, issued and published in 1943 by Babakhan, who had been associated with strongly anti-Sufi circles in Uzbekistan before the war, we find believers encouraged to defend the shrines and other holy places of Central Asia against the Nazis.[11]

Stalin era that in Klimovich's study, one of the most comprehensive treatments of the "Muslim clergy's" role in the Russian war effort during the First Word War, the author denounces the very same activities that would endorsed by Stalin five years later, although, admittedly, in a quite different political context.

9 For an informed discussion of the wartime creation of SADUM, see Eren Tasar, *Soviet and Muslim: the Institutionalization of Islam in Central Asia*, (New York: Oxford University Press, 2017), 15–76; On the reestablishment of DUMES, see S. G. Rakhmankulova, *Mufti Gabrakhman Rasulev, starshii syn Ishan Khazreta Rasuleva,* (Cheliabinsk: n.p., 2000), 121–128; L. A. Iamaeva, "Gabrakhman Rasulev," *Islam na territorii byvshei Rossiiskoi* imperii 4, (Moscow: Izdatel'skaia firma 'Vostochnaia Literatura', 2003), 68–69; A. Iu. Khabutdinov, *Rossiiskie mufti ot ekaterinskikh orlov do iadernoi epokhi* (Nizhnii Novgorod: Makhinur, 2006), 54–57.

10 Shamsiddin Bobokhonov, *Mufti Ziiauddinkhan ibn Eshon Babakhan: zhizn' i deiatel'nost'*, (Tashkent: O'zbekiston milli entsiklopediyasi, 1999), 189–207; Bakhtiiar Babadzhanov, "O fetvakh SADUM protiv 'neislamskikh obychaev," *Islam na postsovetskom prostranstve: vzgliad iznutri*, Aleksei Malashenko and Martha Brill Olcott eds. (Moscow: Carnegie Center, 2001), 170–183.

11 Jeff Eden, "The Soviet Jihad against Hitler: Ishan Babakhan Calls Central Asian Muslims to War." *Journal of the Economic and Social History of the Orient* 59 (2016), 252–253.

These shrines, of course, are if anything manifestations of Sufi thought and practice, and were traditionally targets for denunciations by anti-Sufi theologians and jurists; later they became targets again of SADUM and DUMES fatwas.

The establishment of muftiates during the war was accompanied by the reopening of mosques, and their staffing with officially appointed and vetted imams. While the number of mosques that were reopened was a small fraction of the number that had existed in the 1920s, some members of formerly persecuted *ishan* lineages did became imams. For example, Shaykhan Qari Ata Kamalŭlï (1891–1977), a grandson of Shāh-i Aḥmad aṣ-Ṣābawī, was appointed imam of the mosque in Ayagöz in 1945. The way his appointment came about, we are told, is that his daughter translated a letter from Arabic into Russian her father had written to Stalin and Marshal Kliment Voroshilov, asking for the position of imam. The request was granted, and Shaykhan Qari held the position until his death 1977.[12] Maral Baba's grandson, Süleyman-ishan Eseyŭlï (1888–1969) served as imam of the Aytbay Mosque in Qïzïlorda from 1947 until 1965. He made his loyalty to the Soviet state public during his tenure, declaring "I am not in opposition to Soviet policy; it is the duty from God of every believer in his time to support the policy of the current state.[13] A descendant of Ayqozha-ishan, Zhapar-maghzïm Seydakhmetŭlï (1890–1973), managed to avoid persecution, and during the war the Soviet authorities appointed him imam in a *raion* center in South Kazakhstan oblast'. He is said to have raised 20,000 rubles for the war effort, and remained imam of that mosque until his death.[14]

The *ishan* lineages, as Soviet citizens, also supported the war effort by its men serving in the Soviet military. Compulsory military service had been a major catalyst of the 1916 rebellion in Central Asia, but the Soviet government successfully imposed conscription on Kazakhs around 1929. The proportion of members of *ishan* lineages who served and were killed during the war appears impossible to estimate. Sakhibzada Saparŭlï, a grandson of Shāh-i Aḥmad aṣ-Ṣābawī, related that seven members of the family were reported killed during the war, and a further ten were missing in action and never returned, while four came home wounded.[15] What proportion of the lineage

---

[12] Asqar Mangabay (Uäli)ŭlï, *Äziz äulet: Shakhiakhmed Khazret pen onïng ïnïsï Fatikh imamnïng häm olardïng ŭrpaqtarïnïng shezhïresï*, (Almaty: Öner, 2001), 90.

[13] Säden Nŭrtayŭlï, *Islam zhäne Maral Baba*, 69; Öteulï Änïs Zhaqïpŭlï, "Maral baba nemeresï, Eseyŭlï Süleyman ishan turalï bïr üzïk sïr," 92.

[14] Shaydarbek Äshïmŭlï, *Sïr boyïndaghï äuliyeler*, (Almaty: Atamŭra, 2000), 143.

[15] Mangabay (Uäli)ŭlï, *Äziz äulet*, 90.

this represents is not stated, but in one Bashkir village, for example, out of 259 men who left to serve, 145 were reported killed or missing, and only 114 returned home. [16] One healer (*täuĭp*), descended from the Qongïrat saint Qŭrban Ata, lost seven of his nine sons during the war. [17] At the same time, the hagiographies and genealogies identify numerous *ishans* who survived their service and returned home. Ikramsha Äubakĭrŭlï, a descendant of Maral Baba, had an illustrious career in the Red Army, evidently as a professional officer. He fought, we are told, against the Japanese in the Battle of Lake Khasan. Then he fought in the Winter War against Finland, and then in the entirety of the Great Patriotic War. After the war, he stayed in the army, and was promoted to Colonel. Then he was stationed in the Ukrainian Military District and obtained the rank of Major General, finally marrying a Jewish woman, to whom, the account relates, he revealed that he was a Muslim. Ikramsha's cousin, Aqlima Ïsqaqŭlï, left for the front in August 1941 and survived the war. Before he left, his father Ïsqaq Ishan predicted Aqlima would survive the war and return to his people, while experiencing "40,000 carnages." Ïsqaq also foretold his own death at the age of 85, and predicted that Aqlima would not die before his 85th birthday. According to the account, Aqlima returned home in October 1945, and his father's prophecy about his own death came to pass soon after his son's return. [18] The chairman of a village *soviet* named Palmakhan Bekzhanŭlï, of the Mangghïtay people (a branch of the Qongïrat tribe), and a descendant of a saint known as Aytzhan Äuliye, near Sozaq, related that the day the war started, his ancestor entered his dream, and his *äruaqs* protected Palmakhan from bullets, and enabled to return home safely. [19] Akhmetzhan Mŭkhammetghali, the grandson of Shāh-i Aḥmad's brother Fatikh, served in the war and brought back to the settlement of Oyïq a Ukrainian wife he had met in Germany who, we are told, assimilated well into Kazakh life. [20] Zhandarbek Ishan, a descendant of Isabek Ishan is also remembered as a war veteran, and this experience clearly contributed to his religious authority.

In the hagiographies, the military service of the members' lineages in the Second World War are mentioned alongside the other evidence of their service

---

[16] Khazgali Iapparov, *Nashe shezhere*, (Ufa: Kitap, 1999), 126.

[17] Shaydarbek Äshĭmulï, *Sïr boyïndaghï äwliyeler,* 111.

[18] Nŭrtayŭlï, *Islam zhäne Maral Baba*, 55–56, 59.

[19] Eskermes Zhaqsïmbetov, *Äzĭret qaratau, äuliyenĭng kenĭ edĭ*, (Shymkent: Zhĭbek zholï, 2000), 42; Qazïbek Täzhiyev, *Äz äuliyeler* V, *Qazïnalï ongtüstĭk* 22, (Almaty: Nŭrlï älem, 2011), 7.

[20] Mangabay (Uäli)ŭlï, *Äziz äulet*, 233.

to their communities, in keeping with the role of *ishans* in the Muslim community. If recounting the service of holy lineages through Soviet institutions is evidence of the lineages' Sovietization, the hagiographies are conscious of the other side of this equation, namely, the *ishans'* role as Islamizers. For example, we see the *äruaqs* protect their kin in the Red Army, thereby contributing to the larger Soviet effort. This Islamizing role is also evident in the story of the Ukrainian war bride who assimilates into Muslim Kazakh life.

ISHANS AND SOVIET CAREER PATHS

In conjunction with their sacred prestige in Kazakh society, *ishan* lineages often specialized in professions that demonstrated their service to their communities. Before the Soviet era, these professions were, most prominently, Islamic education and law, medicine, and irrigation. Islamic education and law had been effectively outlawed in the Soviet Union by 1926, restricting the profession of Islamic law to a handful of Muslim legal scholars after 1943, to include at least a few *ishans*. However, we find in the hagiographies and genealogical treatises frequent mention of members of *ishan* lineages who trained in Soviet medical and engineering institutes to become doctors and hydraulic engineers. On the one hand, Soviet credentials and training enabled them to function as part of the Soviet workforce, and brought new technologies and scientific disciplines into their communities, and, perhaps, better outcomes. On the other, the religious prestige of their lineages and the longstanding association of their ancestors with these professions aided in the assimilation of Soviet technology and training – and Sovietization – of their communities through the added prestige of acquiring Soviet academic and professional credentials. At the same time, from the perspective of Kazakh communities, we can also understand that the association of the *ishans'* religious prestige and holiness with Soviet professions and technology was evidence of – from the *ishans'* perspective – the Islamization of Soviet credentials, and of the Soviet system more broadly. Such a view would be wholly consistent with the historical Kazakh perception – and especially the *ishans'* self-perception – of *ishan* lineages as Islamizers of Kazakh society, to include Soviet Kazakh society. The frequent mention of Soviet doctors and engineers in the hagiographies and genealogical treatises, and their explicit connection with ancestral healers and irrigation engineers (*mŭrabs*) provides strong evidence for such an association.

As noted above, among Turkmens managing water resources and irrigation infrastructure was a task often entrusted to *khojas*, stemming from their traditional role as mediators in disputes between lineages. *Ishan* lineages appear to have had a similar role in the lower Syr Darya Valley, where Kazakhs became increasingly dependent on irrigated agriculture over the course of the 19th century. Maral Baba's son, Qalqay, is remembered for "teaching the people irrigated agriculture." He built canals and dams, and initially irrigated an 80-hectare parcel of land. Additionally, Qalqay is credited with sedentarizing the Kazakhs in the Qarmaqshï area. One of Maral Baba's great-grandsons, Seyilkhan the son of Saruar-ishan, obtained Soviet training and credentials as a hydraulic engineer, and was said to have been involved in the building of the Ferghana Canal. [21] Lineages descended from religious scholars, known as *akhuns*, were similarly involved in irrigation and agriculture along the Syr Darya before 1917. The most famous of these was Nŭrtaza-akhun, who is remembered as a hydraulic engineer and agronomist. The title of *mŭrab* was passed down to his descendants into the Soviet era. His son Egenberdĭ held the position, and his grandchildren Zäyla and Älkhazh were *mŭrabs* in the Qŭmzhïghanaq kolkhoz, where, we are told, they dug many canals and off-shoots. His great-grandson, Saqap Seyilkhanŭlï was trained in hydraulic engineering, and became the chief *mŭrab* at the Aydarlï kolkhoz.[22]

For *ishan* lineages, by far the largest area for overlap in specialization between the pre-Soviet and Soviet period was the medical field. Kazakh traditional medicine was closely bound with religious authority, and to a large degree remains so today.[23] Kazakh medical specialists included the *täuïp, emshĭ, baqsï*, and others, and ethnographers have focused particular attention on the magical aspects of Kazakh medicine. Medicine (*ʿilm-i ṭibb*), was also an Islamic science, and was taught in the *madrasa*, particularly in Bukhara. It was not uncommon for Kazakh *ishans* and other scholars who were studying in Central Asia include that discipline in their curriculum, and particularly

21 Nŭrtayŭlï, *Islam zhäne Maral Baba*, 34, 44, 69.

22 Zh. A. Zhontayeva and Sh. Sh. Äbdĭbayev, *Sïr elĭnĭng mädeni mŭralarï*, (Qïzïlorda: n.p., 2005), 86–87.

23 See, Bruce Privratsky, *Muslim Turkistan*, (Richmond, Surrey: Curzon, 2001), 193–235; Soviet scholars also have presented relatively nuanced evaluations of Kazakh folk medicine; see, T. Sh. Sharmanov and B. A. Atchabarov eds, *Ocherki po istorii narodnoi meditsiny Kazakhstana*, (Alma-Ata: n.p., 1978); for important parallels with Kazakh tradition, see V. Z. Gumarov, *Bashkirskaia narodnaia meditsina*, (Ufa: Bashkirskoe knizhnoe izdatel'stvo, 1985).

herbal medicine. The experience of formal training in medicine evidently facilitated the shift from studying the Islamic science of medicine to studying Soviet medicine. Many of the *ishan* lineages we have examined associated themselves with medicine from their earliest beginnings. Maral Baba's father Qŭrman was remembered as the healer (*emshĭ*) of Abïlay Khan, and Maral himself is identified in Russian documents from the 1820s as being a healer among the Kazakhs. Similarly, the 18th century saint Er Seytpenbet was remembered as a doctor specializing in herbal medicine.[24]

Already before the Revolution some *ishans* were obtaining access to Russian medical training. Shāh-i Aḥmad aṣ-Ṣābawī's son, Safar-maghzŭm (1861–1921) was the *pir* of the Sätek people in Sholaqqorghan, near Turkistan, and in 1885 the Säteks sent Safar to Tashkent to study. There, he entered a Russian *gimnaziia* and obtained medical training. Upon his return, he would treat the local community using Russian medicine and drugs.[25] Maral Baba's grandson, Ämit-ishan, went to Tashkent in 1919, and then continued his studies, where he obtained the *shatïrkhat* degree. Among the subjects he studied in Bukhara was medicine, and he specialized in treating patients with herbal compounds. He became a specialist in internal illnesses, and his home was described as being "like a doctor's house, filled with dishes and bottles of all sorts of different sizes." Ämit's three surviving sons, Qasïmkhan, Asqar, and Äbĭlda all became doctors. Qasïmkhan worked as a doctor among the stockbreeders of the Qara Qŭm Desert, and, we are told, received medals from the government for his efforts. Ämit-ishan's youngest son Äbĭlda worked as a surgeon, including at the hospital at the Baykonur Cosmodrome for several years. Another of Ämit's sons, Asqar, received formal training in Soviet medical institutions, and worked as the chief of the district (*raion*) medical office. He evidently continued his father's specialty of treating internal illnesses. However, Asqar's home also functioned as an unofficial headquarters for Maral Baba's lineage, as the central contact point (*qara shangïraq*) for the lineage's descendants throughout Kazakhstan, and "all issues were resolved from this house." Asqar and Äbĭlda's sons and daughters also followed the ancestral path, and studied at medical institutes.[26]

Ishan lineages were not the only Kazakh groups to make the shift from traditional medicine to Soviet medical institutes. The descendants of Sayrabay-täuĭp (1748–1824), a descendant of the Qongïrat saint Qŭrban Ata

[24] Zhontayeva, *Sïr elĭnĭng mädeni mŭralarï*, 90.
[25] Mangabay (Uäli)ŭlï, *Äziz äulet*, 197–198.
[26] Nŭrtayŭlï, *Islam zhäne Maral Baba*, 60–63.

was in his time a well-known healer.[27] One of his descendants became a kolkhoz chairman in Tajikistan, and his children and grandchildren all entered the medical field. One daughter was a dentist and doctor in Qïzïlorda, and became an instructor in the medical college. Another son was a therapist, and another daughter was studying in medical school in Almaty. Two other sons were medics. Äshïmŭlï tell us, "His ancestor's spirit [*äruaq*] entered the professor, academic, doctor of medicine, hero of the people, and physician Mŭkhtar Äliyev. Along with Mŭkhtar, his descendants produced four doctors."[28]

Ishan lineages continued their service to their communities as practitioners of traditional Kazakh medicine, including herbal medicine and various sorts of religion-based diagnostic and treatment methods. In this capacity, they are one of many varieties of traditional practitioners who were active in Kazakhstan during the Soviet period, and down the present day. In particular, in the hagiographies, we find many accounts of an *ishan's* treatment of the mentally ill, which combine their medical expertise with their ability to perform miracles. Accounts of *ishans* treating the mentally ill, including Russians, are ubiquitous in the hagiographies. In the typical account, patients are brought to *ishans* with their hands and feet bound and are miraculously cured, as a result of the *ishans'* use of a variety of healing techniques which they specialized in, such as reciting prayers and litanies, or using knives and whips in the healing ceremony.[29] Ospan-ishan Qalqayŭlï would use a whip to treat "those who were possessed by jinns and were brought to him bound hand and foot, [and] they would come back to their senses, and become lucid." Another descendant of Maral Baba, Qaus Ishan was one of the important healers in Zhosalï, who treated patients using medicines as well as a knife. However, he would treat the mentally ill with prayers. While he was in exile in Uzbekistan another descendant of Maral Baba, Ïsqaq Ishan Aldazharŭlï healed a mentally ill patient using breath (*dem salu*).[30] Another *ishan* who used breath to heal the mentally ill was Omartöre Ishan, a descendant of the saint Qïlïshtï-äuliye.[31] Mŭkhamatshaykh Kamalŭlï, a descendant of Shāh-i Aḥmad aṣ-Ṣābawī, who from 1945 until 1977 served as the officially recognized imam of the mosque in Ayagöz, healed mentally ill patients using

[27] On Qŭrban Ata, see Zhaqsïmbetov, *Äzïret qaratau*, 53–55.

[28] Äshïmŭlï, *Sïr boyïndaghï äuliyeler*, 110.

[29] For an overview of these healing techniques, and of the role of *khojas* in healing, see Privratsky, *Muslim Turkistan,* 195–197.

[30] Nŭrtayŭli, *Islam zhäne Maral Baba*, 47, 52–53, 61.

[31] Äshïmŭlï, *Sïr boyïndaghï äuliyeler*, 304.

prayers and performing *zikr* (*zĭkĭr salu*).[32] A similar account exists for Zhandarbek Qozhakhmetŭlï in the Pavlodar region.[33]

In the hagiographies, it was the degree to which a figure conformed to the ideal of an *ishan* during the Soviet era, rather than what positions he held, that was the measure of *ishan* status. A case in point is Baqït, the son of Süleyman Ishan who served as imam in Qïzïlorda. Baqït, we are told, headed the Qïzïlorda *oblast* teachers' college for many years. According to the hagiography, "his personality was as soft as silk. He was a humble person and used to smile and grin. When he was inspecting the schools, he would never frighten anyone. He never took bribes and never thought of oppressing anyone. He was a very cultured young man. He was a genuine *ishan* of the era of the former Soviet government."[34] Similarly, we read how Gharifolla Safarŭlï (1894–1972) had originally studied religious subjects in Kazan and Ufa, and after learning his brother had been arrested, switched over to the study of law, and became a Soviet judge. We are told that "he was not interested in property, and he did not take bribes." Not only did he display the decency expected of *ishans* in his professional life, but he fulfilled the lineage's role of Islamizer. We are told that in 1934, he married a German woman, who became a convert to Islam, took the name Ghaliya, and bore him six children.[35]

The holiness of a *khoja* named Eräli-qozha Äkimŭlï (1893–1970), a descendant of Khorasan Ata, is exemplified by his political achivements, These include becoming the chairman of his community's fishing kolkhoz, on the Aral Sea, through his authority among his people. He is remembered for having navigated his people through the famine of 1931–1932, the Purges of 1937, and the Great Patriotic War, when, we are told, the Aqshatau Kolkhoz of which he was the chairman, provided great benefit to the Soviet Union when it was most hard-pressed. Although the account cites no specific miracles, his success as a khoja and Soviet leader of his people is attributed to his his quality of maintaining a connection to his ancestral spirits (*äruaqtï*).[36]

---

32 Mangabay (Uäli)ŭlï, *Äziz äulet*, 90–91.

33 B. Zeynullin, "Aqköl-zhayïlma basqamïs auïlï," in: *Isabek Ishan,* E. M. Arïn ed., (Pavlodar: Sïtin, 2011), 204.

34 Nŭrtayŭli, *Islam zhäne Maral Baba*, 70.

35 Mangabay (Uäli)ŭlï, *Äziz äulet*, 205.

36 Tängïrbergen Därmenov, *Ishandar ötken ghŭlama, khaber bergen Alladan* II, (Qïzïlorda: Tŭmar, 2015), 39–44.

SAINTS ON THE COLLECTIVE FARM: TRACTOR AND RAIN MIRACLES

The integration of the *ishan* lineages into Soviet society, and their own Islamization of that society are evident in a series of other miracle narratives, this time appearing in the context of economic production on the collective farm, usually set in the postwar era. While these miracles are not as numerous as the Gulag miracles, they symbolize the integration of the *ishan* lineages into Soviet society. A good example of an *ishan* who made his accommodation with the Soviet authorities, while using his ability to perform miracles that benefitted the community he served was Baqïr-maghzïm Ïbïrayïmshaykhŭlï (1895–1977), a grandson of Ayqozha Ishan. His grandfather had sent his sons to each of the six branches [*ata*] of the Qongïrat tribe [*ru*], known as the *altï ata* ("six branches", but literally, "six ancestors"). The Qïrghïzalï clan [*ru*] of the Qongïrat's six branches [*altï ata*] who lived in a place called Ïntïmaq, on the slopes of the Qaratau, made Baqïr their imam and *pir* in 1907, and he lived in that community for 70 years. He was not persecuted during the Stalin years, supposedly because during the Sozaq uprising in 1930, fulfilling the traditional *khoja* role of mediators, he saved the life of an NKVD commander whom the rebels had captured and were intending to execute. It was said that the NKVD commander had Baqïr's name "recorded in a book," establishing him as "friend of the Soviet Union," which saved him from persecution. Despite his status as an *ishan*, Baqïr became a member of the kolkhoz, and worked raising horses. He is also remembered for performing miracles on the collective farm:

> In March and April 1957, it did not rain. A drought started and lasted into May. The sun kept baking. There wasn't a cloud in the sky. The people of Ïntïmaq assembled, slaughtered livestock at the tomb of Ŭzïn Ata and performed the rain (*tasattïq*) prayer. The Qur'an was recited for the saint. Baqïr-maghzïm went up in front of everyone, tears were flowing both his eyes, and he gave a blessing. Then at that moment a cloud shaped like a yurt appeared, and it began drizzling, and then raining. People who participated in that *tasattïq* ceremony and witnessed the miracle today live in Qosüyïngkĭ.[37]

Ulan Bigozhin recorded a miracle involving Zhandarbek Ishan, a descendant of Isabek Ishan Mŭratŭlï, that illustrates the religious role that *ishans* adopted in the communities in the postwar era. This miracle took place on a collective farm in Pavlodar *oblast*, in 1953. Following a bad winter storm, when the snow on the ground hardened into ice, making it impossible for horses to forage, the chiefs of a collective farm sent fodder to a remote horse farm in the midst of severe cold (*sarï ayaz*). The tractor, hauling a large sledge with

[37] Äshĭmŭlï, *Sïrgha tolï Sïr boyï*, 295–298.

fodder, broke down at nightfall in the middle of the steppe. When some of the travelers began to panic, Zhandarbek Ishan began praying, and, although public prayer was almost unheard of at that time, the others began praying, too. Zhandarbek was a good tractor mechanic, and after his prayer, thanked God for reminding him of something he had forgotten, got up, and began working on the tractor. He then said *bismillah*, pulled the tractor's ignition, and started it up. Bigozhin has emphasized that this particular miracle demonstrated how Muslim sainthood, personified by a sacred lineage, could and did coexist on the Soviet collective farm with the ethics of socialist labor. The miracle story also highlights Zhandarbek's prestige as a Soviet *khoja*, based on his deeds as a Soviet citizen, as a kolkhoz tractor mechanic, as a decorated "veteran of labor," and a veteran of the Second World War, as well as his *khoja* lineage.[38]

Ishans and Soviet Patriotism

Eren Tasar has discussed the Islamic dimensions of Soviet patriotism that emerged among Central Asians during and after the Second World War, emphasizing the participation and experience of Muslims in the war, as well as Stalin's recognition and sponsorship of a Soviet Muslim establishment as leading to a sort of "reconciliation" between the Soviet state and Muslim believers. [39] In the hagiographies of the Kazakh *ishans*, as we have seen, this Soviet patriotism is strongly evident in the pride the members of the *ishan* lineages showed in their own, or their ancestors', participation in defeating Nazi Germany. In a blessing (*aq bata)* recorded in 1984 on audiotape, the war veteran Zhandarbek Ishan called on God to help the believers stand firm against the "fascist Germans."[40] This sort of Soviet patriotism has transferred itself to the independent states of Central Asia. One of the purposes of publishing and circulating Kazakh hagiographies and shrine catalogs is to establish a place in independent Kazakhstan and Kazakh nationalism for the *ishan* lineages and their shrines and ancestors. Ergash Tomatov, known by the

---

[38] Ulan Bigozhin, *Shrine, State, and Sacred Lineage in Post-Soviet Kazakhstan*, Unpublished Ph.D. Dissertation, Indiana University, Bloomington, 2017, 91–92, 94; for the Kazakh version of the same account, see Zhŭmabek Qamzin, "Kögĭdĭr kümbezlĭ oylar," in: *Isabek Ishan,* E. M. Arĭn ed., (Pavlodar: Sĭtin, 2011), 154.

[39] Eren Tasar, *Soviet and Muslim: The Institutionalization of Islam in Central Asia, 1943–1991*, (New York: Oxford University Press, 2017), 16–17.

[40] Akhmetolla Qazhĭ, "Atamĭzdĭng ŭrpaqtarĭna arnaghan bata-tĭlegĭ," in: *Isabek Ishan,* E. M. Arĭn ed., (Pavlodar: Sĭtin, 2011), 215.

pen-name Elnazar, was an ethnic-Uzbek Second World War veteran from Kazakhstan. He published a series of Uzbek-language pamphlets in Turkistan in the 1990's that were sold in the vicinity of the tomb of Ahmad Yasavi. The writings in these pamphlets connect his own wartime experience with Sufism in general, and Ahmad Yasavi in particular. However, we also see his works invoking Uzbek nationalism, connecting Ahmad Yasavi and Amir Timur, and composing verse devoted to the former First Secretary of the Community Party of the Uzbek SSR Sharof Rashidov, to Soviet construction projects, to the Uzbek literary figure Abdullo Qodiriy, and of course, his own wartime experiences as a Red Army soldier.[41] This sort of Soviet patriotism, expressed in explicitly Islamic religious contexts and within Islamic compositional genres, is difficult to isolate from the official propaganda issued by the Soviet Islamic establishment of SADUM in Tashkent, and illustrates the relationship between the Sovietization of Central Asian Muslim society and the Islamization of Soviet Central Asia, and its impact in the independent Central Asian states.

[41] Elnazar, *Yassaviy va Arslonbob*, (Turkistan: Turkiston bosmakhonasi, 1991), 41–42; Elnazar, *Yassaviy va Temur Köragon*, (Turkistan: Turkiston bosmakhonasi, 1993), 26; Elnazar, *Muhammad payghambar va Ahmad Yassaviy,* (Turkistan: Turkiston bosmakhonasi, 1995), 38.

CONCLUSION

Historians examining Islam in the Soviet Union have typically emphasized a story of rupture – the rupture of local institutions, the rupture of educational tradition, and the rupture of trans-national networks and bonds. They have also tended to focus on Muslim legal scholars, their networks, and their institutions. "Islam," according to the content of much scholarship, is an intellectual phenomenon, characterized above all by scholarship, law, ritual, and the institutions associated with them. To be sure, these elements of Muslim culture were crippled by Stalinism, leaving only a remnant to be coopted or to function underground. The hagiographies and genealogical treatises of the Kazakh *ishan* lineages that contain these remarkable miracle stories set in the Gulag serve to remind us that "Islam in the Soviet Union" can be understood more broadly, to include institutions rooted in Sufism, and that rather than rupture, continuity – and especially meaningful continuity – was also present.

The stories of the *ishan* lineages are important sources for the social history of Kazakh society as a whole, showing the economic and political role of holy lineages within Kazakh society more broadly, and across different historical periods and geographic boundaries. Far from inhabiting some "frontier" or "borderland," as too many historians thoughtlessly describe the region, the stories of the lineages are geographically centered. They describe the rise and fall of borders, empires, and economic and political systems. It is the lineages that are permanent, and the empires, jurisdictions, frontiers, and ideological systems that are transitory. This point is obvious to the authors and their public, but lost on historians who fail to appreciate, or even acknowledge, the self-definitions of communities who showed, and show, little interest in essentialist foreign conceptions of "national identity." They also represent a specific type of Sufism, where hereditary lineage displaces (or rather, assimilates) the *tariqat*, but where Sufi ethics and imperatives remain anchored by the social role of the *ishans* as "Islamizers," that is, as bearers of Islamic ethics and norms to their communities, and as the living bonds to saints and ancestral spirits. The stories show that such a conception of the *ishans'* social role survived Stalinism, the Second World War, and the entire Soviet era, in part thanks to the lineages' ability to maintain their sacred role by surviving the trials, and by Islamizing elements of Kazakh Soviet culture. While these hagiographies were written in the post-Soviet era, it would be mistaken to dismiss them as merely folklore of the "re-Islamization" of the former Soviet Union. The authors of the hagiographies have written public documents, with verifiable chains of transmission to oral sources, and there is no reason to doubt the stories they relate derived from their families' experiences in the Soviet era.

The stories reveal a specifically Sufi reaction to totalitarian atrocity. These Muslims were capable of responding to intense, even genocidal, oppression without mandatory recourse to narrowly politicized responses, such as jihad or invocations of the Apocalypse (which were in fact more commonly encountered in the Russian Empire than the Soviet Union). In fact, it was the Soviet authorities, using their own Muslim scholars, who invoked jihad against the Third Reich, rather than Muslims invoking it against Stalin, at least in the Soviet Union. These *ishan* narratives show us that these Sufis' responses to Stalinism were neither passive, nor even particularly pietistic. Rather, the Gulag miracles contain an unalloyed critique of Stalinism, while also accommodating it, to enable *ishan* lineages to maintain their role as Islamizers of the society around them. That these Gulag narratives are political statements cannot be denied, although they are not the sort of political statements we find reference to in many studies of "Sufism in the Soviet Union," or of "Political Islam."

Ultimately, the accounts of these Sufi lineages deserve a hearing among religious responses to 20th century totalitarianism. Not only do they inform us about Kazakh social history, Islam in the Soviet Union, and Stalinism, but they are worthy of attention in their own right, as a deeply thoughtful – and above all, collective – responses to one of the great crimes of the 20th century.

APPENDIX: MIRACLES IN THE GULAG AND TSARIST PRISONS

1. Appaq Ishan

It was the 30s when they raised up the cry of the Soviet state, "Drive the *khojas*, and mullahs with whips, like sheep." This cry put pressure on the major religious figures and forced them into exile. They persecuted them, accusing them in the following manner: "Appaq Ishan, his son Bakhibulla, and [Appaq's] younger brother Sabïr, these three *ishans* went to the people and tried to foment discord, saying, 'Famine is coming. Think of the coming days. Keep your spare food. Don't give it up.' They came out against the Soviet government's excellent policy." Appaq Ishan, who held the Holy Qaz Ata as his *pir*, was aware through his power [*qŭdïret*] that bad oppression was coming to the people, and what he did to protect his son, his younger brother, and his people was correct. So, they threw Appaq Ishan in jail.

After his first night in jail, Appaq Ishan summoned the guard, and said, "My dear, you are a Muslim. The air is bad in the dark cell. Let some fresh air in. No one will run away. I give my word. Open the door." A young Kazakh with epaulettes said, "Old man, they call this place a prison. You didn't come here as a guest. There are no older brothers, younger brothers, in-laws, or distant relatives here. There are just criminals. The door won't be opened. It's kept firmly locked." Looking at him disapprovingly, Appaq Ishan said, "My son, you're young. Don't get high and mighty. The *äruaqs* will open it themselves. Don't worry!" That night, the door of Appaq Ishan's cell opened, and fresh air entered the cell. The guard saw that the door was open. He made a big fuss, and said, "Who opened it?" When he looked, the lock was in its place, the key was on his belt. The news sped from the prison commandant to the senior commander. The next day, all of the prison's guards and chiefs were there, and they watched the door of Appaq Ishan's cell. After midnight, at the time for getting air, the lock squeaked, and the iron door opened wide. Unseen, with magical power, the door was not broken, and opened with the lock intact. The prison commandant said to the young guard, "It turns out there's a great saint here. Put the saint in a separate cell with his companions."

The next day Appaq Ishan changed his cell. Without a long delay, the investigation was completed, and there would be a sentence. Before the sentence, the judge asked for his last words. Appaq Ishan replied, "Fine, I am the one who said, 'Famine is coming. Keep your extra food, don't pay your taxes, consider the future.' I said that as advice. I am someone with a direct connection with God. My saint Qaz Ata, who prays with my angels, said, 'A terrible disaster is coming to Kazakhstan. A terrible famine that will slaughter the Kazakhs is starting. Save yourself. Protect the people, and [your] many family members.' For that reason, I sent the *ishans*, *khojas*, and mullahs to go and preach among the people. I said I did everything I could. Now that terrible famine has just started. What will you say to the people who, without finding bread, have flowed from every corner of Kazakhstan for sustenance?" When the investigators asked, "Who opened the door?" he answered, "The spirit of my saint Qaz Ata." The judge laughed at the Ishan's answer and sentenced the Ishan to be exiled to Pavlodar *oblast*.

In prison. An order was given to send Appaq Ishan, Bakhibulla, and Sabïr to Almaty, and they put the three "culprits" in a special Red car that had come from Moscow. The ones in it were religious figures who had been tried in Russia. All of them were thin, exhausted, hungry, and dirty, and they looked at the ones who had just joined them shyly. The common people [*qara khalïq*] and his relatives had given Appaq Ishan two sacks of bread and rolls, and two sacks of meat, as food for the road. Appaq Ishan, who saw the miserable condition of those who had travelled a long distance, ordered to his son and younger brother who were with him: "Open the mouth of your sack to show mercy to those who have become so thin and worn out." Bakhibulla took off his jacket and spread it out on the wooden floor of the railcar. He opened the mouth of one of the bags, and with both hands, poured the rolls [*toqash*] onto the robe, and they struggled and fought over the rolls. Appaq Ishan said to his son, "No, that's not acceptable, my son. Pick up your jacket." Then he spread out the long, wide, white covering [*zhamïlghï*] he had on, and place it on the floor. He poured all of the rolls that were in the open bag onto the covering. Then he opened the second bag, and he emptied that out. Then when the *bauïrsaq* were poured out, it was finished. Then the horse sausage and intestine, and mutton from the remaining two bags were put in front of the people who were hungry. That way, he gave to the starving people the offerings that the *khojas* in Äuliye-Ata had sent and who had waited, saying "Appaq Ishan is coming." The train went for a long time, and after 36 hours, before it reached Almaty, the religious people who had been driven from Russia, placed Appaq Ishan on two mattresses, and would not let his feet touch the ground. They brought him and lifted him on the long road to prison.

Appaq Ishan worked tirelessly [imparting] to those in prison to be clean, pure, to have faith, to study the law of creation and the Holy Qur'an, to take direction from the Prophet Muhammad's hadiths, to hold eternally in the human heart the merciful light of the Islamic faith, and through that, to place in every heart the law of being human [*adami bolmïs*]. That being the case, when Appaq Ishan died, the prisoners grieved bitterly, and said to the guards placed by the door: "Believe us, none of those who were driven to prison will run away. Appaq Ishan is a saint in the true sense of the word. He taught us to live like human beings, to exist like human beings, and to know the difference between human and animal, between good and bad, between despoiling and protecting. He established order in the prison. Give us permission. He summoned us onto the path of humanity. Let us take Appaq Ishan, who fell on this path, on his final journey, with our own hands. We guarantee that not one of us who participates in taking the saint out will run away," and they raised their voices calmly in request.

Sainthood follows the path of Appaq Ishan, who memorized the hadiths of the Prophet Muhammad, the great inheritance left for mankind; he fed his soul, and and placed in his memory the Holy Qurʾān, which was like the shining light of the Islamic faith. The old men say he touched the blessing of his great master, the saint Qaz Ata, who was considered his *pir*, and who always supported him.[1]

2. *Äzzam-ishan Baltaqozhaŭlï*

Äzzam-ishan was suddenly arrested without cause and put in jail. When it was time for the daily prayers, the prison door opened on its own accord, Äzzam Ishan went out, did his ablutions, and performed the prayers. One day the chief of the prison saw Äzzam Ishan who had gone out and done the ablutions, and cursed at the guard, "Why is he going out?" The guard replied, "Comrade Chief, when he went out the locks opened on their own, and when he came back, it was like it had been before." As a result, he fired that guard and put in another one. That same thing happened again. The prison chief was waiting for [Äzzam-ishan], caught him, struck him once or twice with a whip, and said, "Who gave you permission to go out?" Äzzam made a little smile and went into the cell. At that moment two black snakes coiled around the jailer's neck. Then the jailer said, "Shoot the heads of these snakes, get [Äzzam-ishan] Baltayev!" The executioner's pistol wouldn't shoot. The jailer asked for Äzzam-ishan's forgiveness. Äzzam-ishan said, "I'll forgive you when you stand on the threshold with water and a pitcher. The jailer said, "Oh, I apologize!" Then, Äzzam Ishan went out, recited a Qur'anic verse, and made

---

[1] Qazïbek Täzhiyev, *Äz äuliyeler* V, *Qazïnalï ongtüstïk* 22, (Almaty: Nŭrlï älem, 2011), 107–108, 111.

the two snakes disappear. After that, Äzzam Ishan walked around the prison freely. Nŭrdĭlla Paluanŭlï, who was a secretary and translator at the prison, was a witness. He was a descendant of Bozhban Ata of Zhangaqorghan. Nŭrdĭlla had kept telling the head jailer to free him. He had not harmed anyone and was a scholar. He greatly helped in returning Äzzam-ishan to his people.

The chief jailer said, "Fine, I'll free him, if he answers one question." The executioners brought Äzzam-ishan to the jailer. Then the chief jailer greeted him and spread out a map of the world on the table. "If you make the world fit into one point for me, you are free." Nŭrekeng [Nŭrdĭlla] heard the question and feared how Äzzam-ishan might answer the question. Then Äzzam-ishan said, "When I think about it and ponder it, God Almighty puts an answer in my mind, and I will tell that." The jailer replied, "Say it." "The point that is referred to is the pupil of my eye." When Nŭrekeng interpreted the *ishan's* reply for the chief jailer, he got up from his seat, was satisfied, and let him out of prison. Äzzam-ishan went back to his homeland and joined his kin. He was buried at the shrine of Ayqozha Ishan, that is by the Besarïq Station, in Zhangaqorghan raion.[2]

3. *Inayat-maghzïm*

He was the great-grandson of Ayqozha Ishan, the son of Omar-maghzïm (the son of Remetulla). He was born in Qarasopï in Zhangaqorgan District. He followed the ancestral path and graduated from a madrasa in Bukhara. When the persecution started, he was forced to flee his people and he was exiled to Tajikistan. After that he went to a village called Shömĭsh in place called Kitap, in Uzbekistan. After that he went to Zhetĭsay. One day a person from Zhangaqorghan named Ïdïrïs came to Zhetisay to say hello to him. Ïdïrïs used to rustle cattle. When he was sitting in Inayat-maghzïm's house a KGB officer came. Ïdïrïs said, "They're coming for me, and he was very frightened. The KGB officers told Inayat, "We came for you. Let's go." Asking to perform the daily prayer before going, Inayat performed the prayer. They left the house. After passing some sand hills, he got permission to perform two supplementary *namazes*. After he performed those prayers, the pistols that the KGB officers were holding in their hand broke in two. Then they both sensed why this had happened, and begged forgiveness of Inayat. They said, "You haven't seen us, and we haven't seen you," and they went back to where they had come from. Another time KGB officers seized him, took him to the

[2] Shaydarbek Äshĭmŭlï, *Sïr boyïndaghï äuliyeler*, (Almaty: Atamŭra, 2000), 111–114.

riverbank, and intended to shoot him. He requested to be allowed to perform two supplementary prostrations. […] When he said, I will take the pistols of the KGB officers, they disappeared. Then they begged him, "We've done wrong! Give us our weapons back! We'll let you go safely." Inayat-maghzïm recited a prayer, returned the weapons, and they went back. […]

His miracles: in a place called Qolbasï, next to Samarqand, his son Sündetulla was pasturing a camel and he fell asleep, and the camel wandered into a cotton patch. The water officer who saw that seized the boy and beat him, and severely cursed his parents. Inayat-maghzïm was performing his prayers when he heard it and didn't stop them. After that, the water officer [*sushï*] went to his house and fell gravely ill. He immediately sent his children and told them to summon the *ishan*. But he died before Inayat Ishan agreed to go. That person in his will told his children to respect the *ishan* and his descendants. That family deeply respected Inayat-maghzïm, and the *ishan* lived among them for 10 years. During the time of repression Inayat-maghzïm's brother Omar-maghzïm lived in the Zhayïlma section of Zhangaqorghan. At that time one of the village activists, Tölegen, the son of Bayet came and informed him, "Omeke, if you don't leave tonight, they will arrest you." So then from his kinsman Ismat he took two camels, and in the night went away to Bukhara across the Qara Qŭm Desert. He encountered many difficulties along the way. Thanks to the miracles of Inayat, Omar and his son were able to make it safely to Bukhara. In 1999 Inayat's son Akhmetkhan, the oblast' imam in Aktau, gave a 20-year memorial feast for his father.[3]

4. Äbduayt Ishan

He is descended from Ïsqaqbab. He studied in a Bukharan madrasa. He also studied with his father Mammat Shükïr and served in the Turkistan Mosque. During the repressions, he was not left in peace among his people, and was forced to flee to Tajikistan. However, he had dream in which Khoja Aḥmad Yasavī told him to come back to his homeland. He was arrested 17 times. Twice he didn't stay locked up for more than 17–21 days. The other times he was jailed for 3–4 days, and he was released. At night the locked doors were opened, and at night he would go out, perform the ablutions, and perform the prayers. After a while he went to Uzbekistan, to Bekobod, by Khawas. After

---

[3] Shaydarbek-qazhï Äshïmŭlï, *Sïrgha tolï Sïr boyï: tarikhi-tanïmdïq zhazbalar* (Almaty: Foliant, 2009), 292; Äshïmŭlï, *Sïr boyïndaghï äuliyeler* 117–118.

that he was able to go to Afghanistan. Then he saw Ahmad Yasavi in a dream, who told him to return home three times. Äbduayt said, "If I go back, they will persecute me." Then Ahmad Yasavi lifted his head and said, "Look at me. The head of your ancestor Ahmad Yasavi is above the clouds and his feet are on the ground." Äbduayt Ishan grew frightened and looked down. Ahmad Yasavi said, "No one will persecute [you]. Go back to your home." In November of 1964 Khrushchev was removed and Brezhnev came. Gradually conditions changed, and in 1965 he moved to Turkistan, and settled in a place called Qŭshata.[4]

5. *Mŭkhamedzhan Ishan*

He was the grandson of Ayqozha and was known as Mhän Ishan. He was educated in the old way and served as imam in the mosque in Zhuantöbe. He was arrested around Bäygeqŭm in 1937. What happened was this. When he was sitting by the Qalghandarya River he caught a catfish. The catfish was pulling away from the riverbank. In a moment he cried out and called the nearby villagers for help, and they brought in and killed the catfish (after that he got the name Mhän). After that the village activists especially arrested the *ishans*. When he was in jail, his ancestors gave him a revelation, and he said, "Go out" three times. Then the door opened on its own, and he put on women's clothes and escaped. In the morning the guard did not notice (miraculously). As a result, he returned safely to his people, and he died in 1939.[5]

6. *Nïghmet Makhmut Ishan*

He was born in 1894 in Zhangaqorghan's 9th *auïl*. He was one of the mullahs among the people who were educated in Arabic. He opened a mosque on the bank of Ütïrlï Lake and trained a few students. He was arrested and put in prison on charges that he was a leader of a branch of the Aral counter-revolutionary organization that was based abroad, and that he organized moving residents of Zhangaqorghan *raion*. When he was in prison he would perform the prayers five times a day. When it was time to perform the prayers, the doors would open on their own, and the chief of the prison became frightened. People who were in the company of him were amazed at the saint's ability to perform miracles. He was unjustly charged and served eight years,

---

4 Äshïmŭlï, *Sïr boyïndaghï äuliyeler*, 121

5 Äshïmŭlï, *Sïrgha tolï Sïr boyï*, 277.

and in 1951 he was released, and he returned to his people. He died in 1982. He is buried at the Qarasopï Mazar in a place called Zhanga-arïq, on the Zadar'ia Sovkhoz.[6]

7. Babkhozha Ishan (1890–1976)

He was the father of Ibadulla Bayghozhin. He was also a descendant of [the *khoja*] Babazhan. During the famine years people fled to China, Mongolia, and Uzbekistan, but he did not separate himself from [his ancestor] Khorasan Ata and his native land, and he helped the local people as best he could. He would bury people, so they would not be eaten by scavengers, and he would wash the bodies. As a result, they held Babqozha as a *pir*, and honored him. His father Äbdĭmälĭk was an *ishan* of Khorasan Ata's lineage, and the local people would call his son Babkhozha. He was educated and had studied in a *madrasa*, and he healed people by reciting the Qur᾽ān and casting spells. His holiness was such that the chairman of the kolkhoz spoke with the village headman [*auïlnay*] and they brought witnesses and said that Babkhozha had accepted a dowry [*qalïng*] when he had accepted the *auïlnay's* sister-in-law. He was accused of being an enemy of the people and he was sentenced in 1936 and imprisoned for a time in Byelorussia. Within a year the judge's wife lost nine of her children. The judge's kin and learned elders gathered, and told him to absolve Babqozha, and the leader brought a document absolving him, and they released him.[7]

8. Shabar Ishan Esenŭlï

At the beginning of the 1920's the Soviet government began watching the religious figures among the people, and they began crowding the well-known religious figures into prison. That reached the remote Mangghïstau region in 1929, and in 1931 it culminated in a great punitive campaign called the crushing of the Aday rebels. One of the Sufis [*pĭradar*] who was snared in the lasso of unjust punishment was Shabar Esenŭlï. He was descended from Tünqatar, the son of Zhangay Qozhanazar. According to oral information, it is said he was an age-mate to the poet Öskĭnbay Qalmambetŭlï.

Repression reached the Aday people in 1928. In the summer of that year many communities [*el*] fled to Turkmenistan. There was a second migration

[6] Äshĭmŭlï, *Sïrgha tolï Sïr boyï*, 277.

[7] Äshĭmŭlï, *Sïr boyïndaghï äuliyeler*, 341.

in the spring of 1930. The *ishan*, who was waiting for a good outcome stayed behind both times. The people who looked to his wishes waited to see what God would bring. Finally, the limits of his patience ran out, and the Red activists came after him. He tried to flee to Khorezm but was caught when he was approaching Senek Plain. He was arrested along with his kinsman Balseyĭt, bound, and sent to Fort Shevchenko, and from there to Gur'ev (Üyshĭk), and Shabekeng [Shabar] was put in prison there.

When he was imprisoned the *ishan* did not forego a single daily prayer. When he was touching his forehead in prostration to the floor in his cell, a foolish young guard insulted him. The illuminated Sufi who had never said a bad thing in his life, probably cursed him. When that stupid young man got home he could not urinate. That situation continued until morning, and it was like the Torment of the Grave. His father, an old man, repeatedly queried him. His son told him that at work he had resused to allow a mullah, who had a foot in the grave and was bent over, to perform the prayers, and that this this mullah had cursed him. His son admitted his mistake. The old man then went to the chief of the prison, explained the situation, and met with the *ishan*. With tears in his eyes, he said, "He is my only son. He went to that job probably because it was the talk of this era. Rather, he goes around without free will. Dear one, please forgive my son's heedlessness, his thoughtlessness." The *ishan* strongly pleaded with him and said, "My word, what you have just said. I again yielded to human weakness and was guilty in my speech." Although he was not in the hallway, he came and treated the boy who was moaning and close to death as a result of the urine in his body, and he let flow the urine that had been unable to go through his body. The old man all the same found a solution, and he brought the *ishan's* family to his house, and hosted them well. "In any case, it is a brave risk. Break out of the prison. I have kinsmen in Narïn. I will entrust you to them. From that side there will be no problem, and they won't find you."

The Ishan flatly refused and did not agree with the old man's proposal, saying, "I hated your only son. I will stay for his sin. And after the blessing and experiencing the house of a Muslim, this will be my last breath." What he said then came to pass. The news of the *ishan* being shot was given to his relatives. That old man marked [his grave] to the best of his ability, and honored it until he died, and would tell trustworthy people that story.[8]

---

[8] Äbĭlqadïr Span, *Aday qasïretĭ* (Almaty: Nŭrlï Älem, 2011), 107–110.

9. Däuĭt-Qozha Berdĭsügĭrŭlï (1901–1976)

He was a descendant of Qosïm-qozha, the son of Müsĭrälĭ. He lived in Uzbekistan, in Navai oblast, Tamdï raion, in the village of Kerĭz. His genealogy was as follows: Müsĭrälĭ → Qosïm → Zhandïghŭl → Ŭlan → Zholdan → Berdĭsügĭr → Däuĭt. His mother Zhangïl Botabayqïzï was from the Sïrïm lineage [*ru*]. He was well known among the Qïzïl Qŭm Kazakhs; his seniors called him Däke and Qozheke, and his juniors called him Qozha-atam. From the age of 15 he offered blessing to the people, performing *zikr* for them [*zĭkĭr salïp*], and treated the mentally ill. From the ages of 55 to 75 he would treat the mentally ill, who came from him from everywhere with their hands and feet bound.

Since Däuĭt-qozha unswervingly and exclusively maintained only the religious path, an activist [*belsendĭ*] interfered in his work. He looked after livestock as a shepherd, then from 1943 until 1946, he was in the war, and after that he worked as a shopkeeper, harvester, and kolkhoz foreman [*brigadir*]. During the war, while he was tending livestock, he came up short 4 or 5 sheep, and he was sentenced to imprisonment, and was put in the Kattakurghan prison. One day the prison supervisor noticed that the door of a cell was staying open, and he told it to the prison chief. When the warden kept an eye on it for two or three days, he was surprised that no one was escaping. The incident reached the ears of the city chief, and finally he asked for advice from a respected elder from among the Kazakh residents of the city named Äzĭm Maqsum (his lineage was from one of the six sons form from Müsĭrälĭ's senior wife). Going to the prison, Äzĭm Maqsŭm recognized Däuĭt-qozha, and after he had explained the situation, he was let out. The *raion* chief summoned him [Däuĭt-qozha], and said, we are unable to so honor the spirits [*äruaq*] of your ancestors. Let's send him to the war instead of to imprisonment." Without pondering on it, our ancestor agreed, set off for the war, and wound up on the field of Leningrad. In three years of being in the war, no enemy bullet reached his body, and he returned unharmed.[9]

10. Batïrkhan Tobaghabïlŭlï

Tobaghabïl sons were named Batïrkhan and Khazikhan. Batïrkhan studied and became an *aqïn*. During the Soviet era activists were sent to do the work of collectivization. Suddenly, he and his age-mate Ämire were tossed in the jail in Qarmaqshï. Qalqay-ishan appeared to Batïrkhan in a dream. "There is a nail

---

[9] Seyt-Omar Sattarŭlï *Qozhalar shezhĭresĭ,* (Almaty: Atamŭra, 2015), 492–493.

on the side of the stove. With that take a brick from the side of the window and get out that way." The two of them did that and escaped from the jail. But it was not over, and in 1937 he was accused of being from an *ishan's* family and arrested on the charge of being an enemy of the people, and he was exonerated in 1954.[10]

11. Äbdĭrakhman Qalqayŭlï (Ämit Ishan)

The echo of the Soviet Government's extreme Red policy that resulted in the banishment of those on the religious path touched him as well. He was persecuted because he was from Maral Baba's lineage. As a result, he left his people and went to a foreign land. He went to the city of Kurgantepe in Tajikistan and settled there. He changed his first and last names and carried on. Finally, in 1946 he returned to his people under the name Bayghazï Täzhibayev. The reason he went to Qostanay was to avoid prison. But wherever he went, he would miss his relatives and kinsmen. Ämit-ishan spent a few months hiding in a yurt that had been pitched in a place hidden from the eyes of the people. He had nobody with him except an old student [*qalpe*] who would be with him. When the people were asleep, the sound of very many cavalrymen was heard on the outskirts of the tent. There was no end to the crowd of rattling soldiers passing by. Ämit-ishan went outside and after it was time to milk the mare, he returned. Even when the dawn was starting to break, the clopping of horses' hooves was audible. In a flash the cavalry was going by the yurt. Based on the sound of the clopping, it was probably thousands. Ämit got out of bed, got dressed, and went out. After a while he returned completely unconcerned, as if he were sleeping. Not revealing the secret, [his companion] had awakened and covered himself with the blanket and was shaking, out of his mind with fear. Involuntarily, he was compelled to ask, "What, is this a miracle?" Ämit-ishan said casually, to calm his student, "This is the host of the 40,000. Don't be afraid. It's to protect us from the enemy. In that way, Ämit-ishan had Maral Baba's host of 40,000 *äruaqs*.

When he fled there some kinsmen told him that their younger brother was the raion chief, and he went there and noted his circumstances. They talked openly, and finally he told him about his difficult circumstances. It was that young man who let Ämit-ishan set up a yurt outside of the city and offered him protection from a distance. He had a younger brother who was sick. When he explained that, he brought out the possessed young man. The chief said,

---

[10] Säden Nŭrtayŭlï, *Islam zhäne Maral Baba*, 46.

"Cure him for me. Let that be the help that you do for us." Ämit agreed and he drove off the spirit possessing him by reciting prayers and using breath. He cured him, and [the boy] regained his former good health.[11]

12.Zhünĭskhan Ündemesŭlĭ (1902–1976)

He was born in 1902 in the winter encampment of Qapïrïq, in Kamyshnin District in Qostanay. He spent most of his life in Aralköl. He someone who was just, helped widows, orphans, and the poor, and did not hold back his help. When he was a young man, his ancestor Maral Baba appeared to him in a dream and said, "Give the people religious service." This period was a difficult time. It was when the government did not like religious people. But the *äruaqs* kept appearing in his dream and would not give him peace. There were whole days when he could not get sleep. One day his mother Mïnggoy said that the spirit of his father Ündemes-ishan was coming and going and he was saying to give the green staff he inherited from Maral Baba to Zhünĭskhan, and that in any case he needed to bond with them. She took the staff from the chest and gave it to him. In the end, he kept to his father's path.

One day an official from the district came to the Zhanga Tŭrmïs kolkhoz that had been organized in Qayïndï and summoned him into the office. He confronted Zhünĭskhan with being from an *ishan* lineage and cursed at him. This was the period in the 1930s when if you said, "Cut the hair," they would remove the head. As a result of that, the official became tormented. That official whose abdomen swelled up and who groaned in pain pleaded with Zhünĭskhan for forgiveness. He treated that petty tyrant and cured him.

In 1937 Zhünĭskhan was accused of being an enemy of the people and was locked in jail. But he got out of the jail whose outside was locked and went and stayed at his relatives' house. When he was locked up again, he got out again. Later, when the head jailer got tired of this, he stopped doing it, and put himself in line. A fellow villager named Zhüsĭpbek who was locked up with him had bad headaches and his calves ached unbearably. This happened frequently, and he began to decline. Who would protect the "enemies of the people" in prison? Zhünĭskhan put his fur cap on Zhüsĭpbek. He recovered. That holy cap healed him. Zhünĭskhan got out of prison after three and a half years. One day he gave that cap to Zhüsĭpbek. Later, after Zhüsĭpbek returned to his people he became the kolkhoz chairman. He talked about the *ishan's* goodness for the rest of his life. Before the war Zhünĭskhan was released for

---

[11] Nŭrtayŭlï, *Ishan zhäne Maral Baba*, 60–61.

good, and he returned to his *auïl* and went to work. He treated the sick. He preached religion to the people. Zhünĭskhan died in Aralköl in 1976.[12]

13.Shämshĭ Ishan Remetŭlï (1868–1938)

He was one of those falsely accused by the Soviet government of supporting foreign counter-revolutionary movements. He was born in 1868 in Sortöbe, in the Özgent region, and his father was Remet Ishan. The source for this information was Zŭlpïqar Mŭsakhanov, a longstanding leader in the *raion*. Mŭsakhanov came to Zhangaqorghan in 1929 or 1930 with his father, and he worked as a timekeeper in Äshĭm Kenzheŭlï's brigade in the kolkhoz. [Mŭsakhanov related], "In the afternoon, after finishing work, we were planning to return to the *auïl*. My father held my horse for me, entered through a door on the west side of the train station, and hesitated. After he came, I asked about it, he said, "Zhamhŭr Ishan and Shamshĭ Ishan are locked up here. They are charged with being religious leaders [*dĭnbasïlar*]. I performed the noon [*besĭn*] prayer with them and left." When Mŭsakhanov asked how they joined his father, if they were in jail, he replied, "Their door was unlocked. Whenever they wanted, they went out, did the ablutions, and performed the prayers. When their door was locked, they opened it. So they couldn't keep them from leaving."[13]

14.Aqlima Aldazharŭlï

"There was a time when I was working in the fire department in Qïzïlorda. This was in 1947. We were working under a paramilitary system. Suddenly a young man named Shämshidin Nŭrtazayev, the driver of a fire truck, had me locked up without cause in the underground jail for two days. He was a son-in-law of Akhmet-ishan. His wife Khadiysha was born from the ishan's junior wife. I was very upset. Qalqay-ishan appeared in my dream. 'The guilt [*ayïp*] has fallen. Two days will pass, you will see on the third say.' Like [Qalqay-ishan] had said, the punishment [*ayïp*] fell on his wife, without Shämshidin experiencing the guilt of his treachery. On the third day, exactly at noon an *albastï* attacked and killed his pregnant wife Khadiysha. His daughter was a

---

[12] Nŭrtayŭlï, *Islam zhäne Maral Baba*, 67–68.

[13] Äshĭmŭlï, *Sïrgha tolï Sïr boyï,* 300–301.

six-month old child, and her death fell on her," recalled the old man Aqlima-qart, with regret.[14]

15. Kamal Ishan, the son of Shāh-i Aḥmad's wife Khadisha.

Kamal's last wife who had been given to him was Balïsh Bĭbi, of the Baraq Tama people [*ru*]. For various reasons, Kamal was exiled to Astrakhan soon after he had married Balïsh-bĭbi. Unable to bear such torment, Kamal soon passed away in Astrakhan. [...] Although they only lived together a short time, Balïsh Bĭbi mentioned the miracles the people saw him perform while he was in prison in Astrakhan. The greatest of these miracles was when some fisherman had gone out onto the sea to fish. A storm came up and people were drowning. The chief of the prison said, "Your Holiness, reveal your sainthood. If you intervene for these unfortunates' lives, and bring them to safety, I promise to release you from prison." Kamal beseeched God, prayed with all his strength, and asked for God's mercy. The ship reached the shore safely. After at, everyone in the prison called Kamal "His Holiness" [*khazĭret*]. However, after a short while, the saint fell ill, and he died on an island near Astrakhan. One misfortune is that no one knows where the saints body is resting. Searching for Kamal-maghsŭm's grave is one of the duties of all the descendants of Shāh-i Aḥmad.[15]

---

[14] Nŭrtayŭlï, *Islam zhäne Maral Baba*, 56.

[15] Asqar Mangabay (Uäli)ŭlï, *Äziz äulet: Shakhiakhmed Khazret pen onïng ĭnĭsĭ Fatikh imamnïng häm olardïng ŭrpaqtarïnïng shezhĭresĭ*, (Almaty: Öner, 2001), 80–81.

BIBLIOGRAPHY

Abashin, Sergei. "Ishan," *Islam na territorii byvshei Rossiiskoi imperiia: entsiklopedicheskii slovar* I, (Moscow: Vostochnaia Literatura, 2006), 164–166.

——. "Tura," *Islam na territorii byvshei Rossiiskoi imperiia: entsiklopedicheskii slovar* I, (Moscow: Vostochnaia Literatura, 2006), 387–388.

——. *Sovetskii kishlak*, (Moscow: Novoe literaturnoe obozrenie, 2015).

Abdulakhatov, Nodirbek et al., *Farghona azizlari taqdiri*, (Tashkent: Abu Matbuot-Kansalt, 2012).

ʿAbdullāh al-Muʿāẓī *al-Qaṭrat min biḥār al-ḥaqāʾiq fī tarjuma aḥwāl mashāʾikh aṭ-ṭarāʾiq*, (Orenburg: Dīn wa maʿīshat maṭbuʿasī, n.d.).

Abdulsattar. *K Voprosu o mususl'manskikh ishanakh*, (Kazan: Lito-tipografiia Imperatorskago Universiteta, 1895).

Abil', A. "Maral-Ishan: kharakter i ideinye osnovy natsional'no-osvboditel'nogo dvizheniia," in: *Soltüstĭk Qazaqstan öngĭrĭndegĭ täwelsĭzdĭk üshĭn küres tarikhï – Istoriia bor'by za nezavisimosti v Severnom Kazakhstane*, (Almaty: Atamŭra, 2011), 215–221.

Absattar Qŭttïqozhaŭlï, *Ükasha Ata tarikhi*, (n.p., n.d.).

Aḥmad b. Ḥāfiẓ al-Dīn al-Barāngawī, *Tārīkh al-Barāngawī*, Manuscript Institute of Tatarstan, 39/34.

Ahmad, Abu Talib. "Japanese Policy towards Islam in Malaya during the Occupation: A Reassessment, *Journal of Southeast Asian Studies* 33/1 (2002), 107–122.

Akhmadullin, V. A. *Patrioticheskaia deiatel'nost' dukhovnykh upravlenii musul'man v Velikoi Otechestvennoi Voine*, (Moscow: Islamskaia Kniga, 2015).

Akhmetolla Qazhï, "Atamïzdïng ŭrpaqtarïna arnaghan bata-tĭlegĭ," in: *Isabek Ishan,* E. M. Arïn ed., (Pavlodar: Sïtin, 2011), 214–215.

Akhmetqaliŭlï, Nïghi. "Isabek Ishan kĭm?" in: *Isabek Ishan* (Pavlodar: Sïtin baspakhanasï, 2011), 68–71.

Aldazhumanov, K. S. et. al. eds. *Nasil'stvennaia kollektivizatsiia i golod v Kazakhstane 1931–1933 gg.: Sbornik materialov i dokumentov*, (Almaty: Fond XXI vek, 1998).

Algar, Hamid. "Bābā Sankū," *Encyclopedia Iranica* III Fasc. 3, 295.

Alieva, Svetlana. *Tak eto bylo: national'nye repressii v SSSR 1917–1952* I-III, (Moscow: Insan, 1993).

Amangel'diev, B. R. *Vosstanie 1916 goda v Turgaiskom uezde i Amangel'dy Imanov*, (Almaty: Alatau, 2015).

Aminev Z. G., and L. A. Iamaeva, *Regional'nye osobennosti islama u bashkir*, (Ufa: Dizain PoligrafServis, 2009).

ʿAqid b. ʿUlūmchī Qarmāṣāqōf, *Manāqib-i pīrān-i ʿazīzān* (Kazan: Tipografiia Imperatorskago Universiteta, 1909).

Arapov, D. Iu. ed. *Islam i sovetskoe gosudarstvo (1944–1990). Sbornik dokumentov,* vyp. 3 (Moscow: Izdatel'skii dom Mardzhani, 2011).

Arïn, Erlan, ed. *Isabek Ishan*, (Pavlodar: Sïtin, 2011).

Auezova, Zifa-Alua. "Conceiving a People's History: the 1920–1936 Discourse on the Kazakh Past," in: *The Heritage of Soviet Oriental Studies*, Michael Kemper and Stephan Conemann eds., (New York: Routledge, 2011), 241–261.

Ayaghan B. et. al. *1932–1933 zhïldardaghï asharshïlïq aqiqatï – Pravda o golode 1932–1933 godov*, (Almaty: Ligera-M, 2012).

Aytbayev, Erbol. "Qalmaq äyelīnīng säueleyīlīgī," in: *Isabek Ishan* (Pavlodar: Sïtin baspakhanasï, 2011), 22–24.

Babadzhanov B. M., ed. *Sobranie fetv po obosnovaniiu zikra dzhakhr i sama'*, (Almaty: Daik Press, 2008).

——. *Kokandskoe khanstvo: vlast', politika, religiia*, (Tashkent: Yangi Nashr, 2010).

——. "O fetvakh SADUM protiv 'neislamskikh obychaev," *Islam na postsovetskom prostranstve: vzgliad iznutri*, Aleksei Malashenko and Martha Brill Olcott eds. (Moscow: Carnegie Center, 2001), 170–183.

——. *Zhurnal "Ḥaqīqat" kak zerkalo religioznogo aspekta v ideologii dzhadidov,* TIAS Central Eurasian Research Series No. 1 (Tokyo: University of Tokyo, 2007).

Babadzhanov, Bakhtiyar ed., *Manaqib-i Dukchi Ishan*, (Almaty: Daik Press, 2004).

Bashir, Shahzad. *Sufi Bodies: Religion and Society in Medieval Islam*, (New York: Columbia University Press, 2011.

Basilov, V. N. "Honour Groups in Traditional Turkmenian Society," in: *Islam in Tribal Societies: From the Atlas to the Indus*, edited by Akbar S. Ahmed and David M. Hart, London: Routledge & Kegan Paul, 1984), 220–243.

Basilov, V. N. and Dzh. Kh. Karmysheva, *Islam u kazakhov*, (Moscow: Institut Etnologii i antropologii im. N. N. Miklukho-Maklai, 1997).

Bayqŭlov, T. *Äuliye-Ata öngīrīndegī asharshïlïq* (Almaty: Üsh qiyan, 2017).

Benda, Harry J. *The Crescent and Rising Sun: Indonesian Islam under Japanese Occupation, 1942–1945*, (The Hague and Bantung: Van Hoeve, 1958).

Bennigsen, Alexandre and S. Enders Wimbush. *Mystics and Commissars: Sufism in the Soviet Union*, (London: C. Hurst, 1985).

Bigozhin, Ulan. *Shrine, State, and Sacred Lineage in Post-Soviet Kazakhstan*, Unpublished Ph.D. Dissertation, Indiana University, Bloomington, 2017.

Bobokhonov, Shamsiddin. *Mufti Ziiauddinkhan ibn Eshon Babakhan: zhizn' i deiatel'nost'*, (Tashkent: Özbekiston milliy entsiklopediyasi, 1999).

Bobrovnikov, Vladimir, and Michael Kemper, "Miuridizm," *Islam na territorii byvshei Rossiiskoi imperii* 5, (Moscow: Vostochnaia Literatura," 2013), 98–99.

Boltina, V. D. and L. V. Shevelëva eds. *Iz istorii islama v Pavlodarskom Priirtysh'e, 1919–1990*, (Pavlodar: Department arkhivov Pavlodarskoi oblasti, 2001).

Boranbayev, Zharïlqasïn, *Shïghïs shayïrlarïnïng songï – Shädī Aqïn,* (Almaty: Bīlīm, 2014).

Bregel, Yuri. *Bibliography of Islamic Central Asia* I-III, (Bloomington, Indiana: Research Institute for Inner Asian Studies, 1995).

——. *Khorezmskie turkmeny v XIX veke*," (Moscow: Izdatel'stvo Vostochnoi literatury, 1961).

Bürkītbayŭlï, Sïrlïbay. *Maral ishanning nŭr shapaghatï* (Qostanay: n.p., 1998)

Bustanov, Al'frid, "Rukopis' v kontekste Sibirskogo islama," in: A. G. Seleznev et al., *Kul't sviatykh v Sibirskom islame: spetsifika universal'nogo*, (Moscow: Izdatel'skii dom Mardzhani, 2009), 156–192.

——. *Knizhnaia kul'tura Sibirskikh musul'man,* (Moscow: Izdatel'skii dom Mardzhani, 2013).

——. "The Narrative of Ishaq Bab and the Lore of Holy Families in Western Siberia: a Preliminary Discussion," in, *Islamizatsiia i sakral'nye rodoslovnye v Tsentral'noi Azii* I, eds. Devin DeWeese and Ashirbek Muminov, (Almaty: Daik Press, 2013), 496–533.

Conquest, Robert. *The Nation Killers*, (London: MacMillan, 1970).

——. *The Soviet Deportation of Nationalities*, (New York: MacMillan, 1960).

Därmenov, Tängïrbergen. *Ishandar ötken ghŭlama, khaber bergen Alladan* II, (Qïzïlorda: Tŭmar, 2015).

Dayrabay Tïnïshbek et al. eds., *Bekshentayŭlï Seyïtzhan, Dabïlŭlï Moldakhmet, Bäykenov Älibek: shïgharmalar*, (Astana: Foliant, 2009).

Dayrabay, Tïnïshbek and Moldabek Akhmetov eds. *Biler sözĭ – kiyelĭ (Sïr elĭnĭng bilerĭ khaqïnda)* (Almaty: n.p., 2012).

Demidov, Sergei. *Turkmenskie ovliady*, (Ashkhabad: Izdatel'stvo Ylym, 1976).

Denny, Frederick. "Prophet and *Walī*: Sainthood in Islam," *Sainthood and its Manifestations in World Religions,* Richard Kieckhefer and George D. Bond eds., (Berkeley: University of Californa Press, 1988), 69–97.

DeWeese, Devin, and Ashirbek Muminov eds. *Izlamizatsiia i sakral'nye rodoslovnye v Tsentral'noi Azii* I-II, (Almaty: Daik Press, 2008–2013).

DeWeese, Devin. "Baba Kamal Jandi and the Kubravi Tradition among the Turks of Central Asia," *Der Islam*, 71/1 (1994).

——. "Disordering' Sufism in Early Modern Central Asia: Suggestions for Rethinking the Sources and Social Structures of Sufi History in the 18th and 19th Centuries," *History and Culture of Central Asia*, Bakhtiyar Babadzhanov and Yayoi Kawahara eds. (Tokyo: TIAS: Department of Islamic Area Studies, 2012), 259–279.

——. "Islam and the Legacy of Sovietology: a Review Essay on Yaacov Roi'i's *Islam in the Soviet Union*," *Journal of Islamic Studies* 13/3 (2002), 298–330.

——. "A Khwarazmian Saint in the Golden Horde: Közlük Ata (Gözli Ata) and the Social Vectors of Islamization," *Revue des Études des mondes Musulmans et Méditerrané* 143, 107-132.

——."Re-Envisioning the History of Sufi Communities in Central Asia: Continuity and Adaptation in Sources and Social Frameworks," *Sufism in Central Asia: New Perspectives on Sufi Traditions, 15th-21st* Centuries, Devin DeWeese and Jo-Ann Gross, eds. (Leiden: Brill, 2018), 21–74.

——. "Shamanization in Central Asia," *Journal oft he Economic and Social History oft he Orient* 57 (2014), 326–363.

——. "Sacred History for a Central Asian Town: Saints, Shrines, and Legends of Origin in Histories of Sayrām, 18th-19th Centuries," *Revue des mondes musulmans et de la Méditerranée* 89–90 (2000), 245–295.

——. "Yasavian Legends on the Islamization of Turkistan," *Aspects of Altaic Civilization III: Proceeding of the Thirtieth Meeting of the Permanent International Altaistic Conference*, (Bloomington, Indiana, 1990), 1–19.

——. *Islamization and Native Religion in the Golden Horde: Baba Tükles and the Conversion to Islam in Historical and Epic Tradition*, (University Park, Pennsylvania: Pennsylvania State University Press, 1994).

Di Cosmo, Nicola et al. eds. *The Cambridge History of Inner Asia: the Chingisid Era,* (Cambridge: Cambridge University Press, 2009).

Dudoignon, Stéphane A. "Local Lore, the Transmission of Learning, and Communal Identity in Late 20th Century Tajikistan, The *Khujand-Nāma* of 'Ārifjān Yakhyāzād Khujandī," *Devout Societies vs. Impious States? Transmitting Islamic Learning in Russia, Central Asia, and China through the Twentieth Century*, (Berlin: Klaus Schwarz Verlag, 2004), 213–241.

Dudoignon, Stephane and Christian Noack, "Introduction," *Allah's Kolkhozes: Migration, De-Stalinization, Privatisation, and the New Muslim Congregations in the Soviet Realm,* Stephane Dudoignon and Christian Noack eds. (Berlin: Klaus Schwarz Verlag, 2011), 9–46.

Dudov, Makhmud et al. *Pravozashchitniki repressirovannykh narodov*, (Moscow: n.p., 1996).

Dulat Tŭrantegĭ and Zharïlqasïn Boranbap, *Baba Tüktĭ Shashlï Äzĭz*, (Shymkent: Zhĭbek zholï, 1996).

Dütpayev, Tĭlegen qazhï Moldabayŭlï. *Sarïköl qazhïlarï men taqualarï* (Qostanay: Qostanay baspa üyĭ, 2012).

Düysenbayev, Daniyarbek. *Domalaq Ana*, (Almaty: Mŭrattas, 1991).

Eden, Jeff. "The Soviet Jihad against Hitler: Ishan Babakhan Calls Central Asian Muslims to War." *Journal of the Economic and Social History of the Orient* 59 (2016), 237–264.

——. *The Life of Muḥammad Sharīf: A Central Asian Sufi Hagiography in Chaghatay,* (Vienna: Verlag der Österreichischen Akademie der Wissenschaften, 2015).

——. *Warrior Saints of the Silk Road: Legends of the Qarakhanids*, (Leiden: Brill, 2018).

Eliach, Yaffa. *Hasidic Tales of the Holocaust*, (New York: Vintage Books, 1988).

Engsebayev, T. A. *Qanzhïghalï shezhĭresĭ*, (Pavlodar: EKO, 2004).

Ergöbekov, Qŭralbek. *Bäydĭbek Baba men Domalaq Ana,* (Shymkent: Zhĭbek zholï, 1999).

Eshmŭkhambetov, Sŭltanbek, *Suan shezhĭresĭ*, (Almaty: Zhalïn, 1993).

Fisher, Alan. *The Crimean Tatars*, (Palo Alto: the Hoover Institution, 1978).

Frank, Allen J. "Islamic Shrine Catalogues and Communal Geography in the Volga-Ural Region: 1788–1917" *Journal of Islamic Studies*, VII/2 (July, 1996), 265–286.

——. "Muslim Sacred History and the 1905 Revolution in a Sufi History of Astrakhan," *Studies on Central Asian History in Honor of Yuri Bregel*, Devin DeWeese ed., (Bloomington, Indiana: Research Institute for Inner Asian Studies, 2001), 297–317.

——. "Sufis, Scholars and Divanas of the Qazaq Middle Horde in the Works of Mäshhür-Zhüsip Köpeyulï," *Islam, Society and States across the Qazaq Steppe,* Niccolo Pianciola and Paolo Sartori, eds. (Vienna: Austrian Academy of Sciences, 2013), 213–232.

——. *Bukhara and the Muslims of Russia: Sufism, Education, and the Paradox of Islamic Prestige*, (Leiden: Brill, 2012).

——. *Islamic Historiography and 'Bulghar' Identity among the Tatars and Bashkirs of Russia*, (Leiden: Brill, 1998).

Frank, Allen J. and Mirkasyim Usmanov, eds. *Materials for the Islamic History of Semipalatinsk: Two Manuscripts by Aḥmad-Walī al-Qazānī and Qurbān-ʿAlī Khālidī* (Berlin: Das Arabische Buch, 2001).

Galiautdinov, I. G. *'Tarikh Nama-i Bulgar' Tadzhetina Ialsygulova*, (Ufa: Kitap, 1998).

Gavrilov, M. *Risolia sartovskikh remeslennikov: izsledovanie predanii musul'manskikh tsekhov*, (Tashkent: Tipografiia pri kantselarii General-Gubernatora, 1912).

Ghïlmani, Saduaqas. *Biographies of the Islamic Scholars of Our Times* I-II, Ashirbek Muminov et al. eds. (Istanbul: IRCICA, 2018).

Goloshchekin, F. I. *O kollektivizatsii v kazakskom aule*, (Alma-Ata: Partizdat, 1932).

Gross, Jo-Ann Gross. "Multiple Roles and Perceptions of a Sufi Shaikh: Symbolic Statements of Political and Religious Authority," in *Naqshbandîs: cheminements et situation actuelle d'un ordre mystique musulman* (Actes de la Table Ronde de Sèvres, 2–4 mai 1985), ed. Marc Gaborieau, Alexandre Popovic, and Thierry Zarcone (Istanbul/Paris: Éditions Isis, 1990; Varia Turcica, v. 18), pp. 109–121.

Gumarov, V. Z. *Bashkirskaia narodnaia meditsina*, (Ufa: Bashkirskoe knizhnoe izdatel'stvo, 1985).

Guseva, N. F. *Ishanizm kak sufiiskaia traditsiia Srednei Volgi v XX veke: formy, smysly, znachenie*, (Moscow: Medina, 2013).

Ḥājjī Muṣliḥ ad-Dīn, "Qïrïmda shaykhlïq wa ahl-i taṣawwuf," *'Aṣrī musulmān* 1924 (1), 5–6.

Heck, Paul L. "Introduction," in: *Sufism and Politics*, Paul L. Heck ed. (Princeton: Markus Weiner Publishers, 2007), 1–22.

Hermansen Marcia K. "Interdisciplinary Approaches to Islamic Biographical Materials," *Religion*, 18 (1988), pp. 163–182.

Hoare, Marko Attila. *The Bosnian Muslims in the Second World War: a History*, (Oxford: Oxford University Press, 2014).

Iamaeva, L. A. "Gabrakhman Rasulev," *Islam na territorii byvshei Rossiiskoi* imperii 4, (Moscow: Izdatel'skaia firma 'Vostochnaia Literatura', 2003), 68–69.

Iapparov, Khazgali. *Nashe shezhere*, (Ufa: Kitap, 1999).

Ihrig, Stephan. *Atatürk in the Nazi Imagination*, (Belknap Press: Cambridge Massachusetts, 2014).

Iliyasova, Rïszhan. *Dalam tŭnghan shezhïre*, (Almaty: Zerde, 2007).

Īshān Muḥammad-Ḥarrāṣ Āydārōf al-Qārghālī, *Īshānlargha khiṭāb!* (Sterlitamak: Nur, 1911).

Ishmukhametov, Z. A. *Sotsial'naia rol' i evoliutsiia islama v Tatarii*, (Kazan: Tatarskoe knizhnoe izdatel'stvo, 1979).

Iskhaki, Gaiaz. *Idel-Ural*, (Kazan: Tatarskoe knizhnoe izdatel'stvo, 1991).

Istoriia Kazakhstana v persidskikh istochnikakh I, Ashirbek Muminov, ed. (Almaty: Daik Press, 2005).

Ivanov, P. P. *Khoziaistvo dzhuibarskikh sheikhov (K Istorii feodal'nogo zemlevladeniia v Srednei Azii)*, (Moscow-Leningrad: Izdatel'stvo Akademii Nauk SSSR, 1954).

Kamalov, S. K. *Karakalpaki v XVIII-XIX vekakh*, (Tashkent: Fan, 1968).

Karmysheva, B. Kh. *Ocherki etnicheskoi istorii iuzhnykh raionov Tadzhikistana i Uzbekistana*, (Moscow: Glavnaia Redaktsiia Vostochnoi Literatury, 1976).

Kashshāf Tarjumānī, "Dīnī tashkīlātlarïmïznïng älikkī wa ḥazirgī aḥwālī," *Islām majlisī*, February 1925 (5–6), 194–204.

Katanov, N. F. "Predaniia Tobol'skikh tatar o pribytii v 1572 g. mukhammedanskikh propovednikov v g. Isker," *Ezhegodnik Tobol'skago Gubernskago Muzeia*, VII (1897), 51–61.

——. "Musul'manskiia skazaniia o zhezle Moiseia," *Izvestiia obshchestva arkheologii, istorii i etnografii pri Kazanskom Universitete*, XVI/1 (1900), 87–93.

Katz, Steven T. et al. eds. *Wrestling with God: Jewish Theological Responses during and after the* Holocaust, (New York: Oxford University press, 2007).

Kazakhsko-Russkie otnosheniia II, (Alma-Ata: Akademiia Nauk Kazakhskoi SSR, 1964).

Keller, Shoshana. *To Moscow, not Mecca: the Soviet Campaign against Islam in Central Asia, 1917–1941*, (Westport, Connecticut: Praeger, 2001).

Khabutdinov, A. Iu. *Rossiiskie mufti ot ekaterinskikh orlov do iadernoi epokhi* (Nizhnii Novgorod: Makhinur, 2006).

Khakimov Rafael. *Repressiyalängän tatar ädipläre,*" (Kazan: Tatar kitap näshriyäte, 2009).

Khalid, Adeeb. *Islam after Communism: Religion and Politics in Central Asia* (Berkeley and Los Angeles, University of California Press, 2007).

Khwāja Bahā' ad-Dīn khażratlarïning qiṣṣasī, (Kazan: Karimov, 1903).

Kildin S. et al. eds., *Bashqortostan – äüliälär ile,* (Ufa: Kitap, 2012).

Kindler, Robert. *Stalins Nomaden: Herrschaft un Hunger in Kasachstan* (Hamburg: Hamburger Edition, 2014).

Klimovich, Liutsian. *Islam v Rossii*, (Moscow: Gosudarstvennoe antireligioznoe izdatel'stvo, 1936).

Koigeldiev, M. K. *Stalinizm i repressii v Kazakhstane 1920–1940-kh godov*, (Almaty: Zerde, 2009).

Kraft, N. N. "Vdokhovennyi kirgiz Maral Kurmanov," *Iz kirgizskoi stariny*, (Orenburg: Lito-tipografiia Sachkova, 1900), 83–90.

"Kratkii obzor sovremennago sostoianiia i deiatel'nosti musul'manskago dukhovenstva," *Sbornik materialov po musul'manstvu* I, V. I. Iarovyi-Ravskii ed., (St. Peterburg: Topgrafiia Rozenoer, 1899) 3–47.

Kudriashov, G. E. *Perezhitki religioznykh verovanii chuvash i ikh preodolenie,* (Cheboksary: Chuvashskoe Gosudarstvennoe Izdatel'stvo, 1961).

Kuzeev, R. G. *Bashkirskie shezhere*, (Ufa: Bashkirskoe knizhnoe izdatel'stvo, 1960).

Kuznetsov, S. K. "Otryvki iz dorozhnykh zametok co vremia etnograficheskoi ekskursii po viatskoi gubernii v 1880 godu," *Uchenye Zapiski Kazanskago Universiteta* 1882 (2–3), 312–328.

Liubimova, Galina. "Sibirskaia traditsiia pochitaniia sviatykh mest v kontekste narodnoi istoricheskoi pamiati," *Studia Mythologica Slavica* XVI (2013), 27–45.

Lykoshin, N. S. *Pol zhizni v Turkestane*, (Petrograd: Berezovskii, 1916).

Madanov, Khamit. *Kĭshĭ zhüzdĭng shezhĭresĭ,* (Atamŭra-Qazaqstan, 1994).

Mangabay (Uäli)ŭlï, Asqar. Äziz äulet: *Shakhiakhmed Khazret pen onĭng ĭnĭsĭ Fatikh imamnĭng häm olardĭng ŭrpaqtarĭnĭng shezhĭresĭ*, (Almaty: Öner, 2001).

Manmoury, Jean Louis, ed. *Sublimes paroles et idioties de Nasr Eddin Hodja*, (Paris: Phébus, 2002).

Mashhür-Zhüsĭp Köpeyŭlï, *Shïgharmalarï* I-XIII, (Pavlodar: Pavlodar University, 2003–2008).

Materialy po istorii Kazakhskoi SSR IV (Moscow:-Leningrad: Izdatel'stvo Akademii Nauk SSSR, 1940).

McChesney, R. D. "Reliquary Sufism: Sacred Fiber in Afghanistan," *Sufism in Central Asia: New Perspectives on Sufi Traditions, 15th-21st Centuries*, Devin DeWeese and Jo-Ann Gross eds. (Leiden: Brill, 2018), 191–237.

Mikhailov, Valeriy. *The Great Disaster: Genocide of the Kazakhs* (London: Stacey, 2014).

Milani, Milad. *Sufi Political Thought*, (Routledge: New York, 2018).

Minnullin, Il'nur. *Musul'manskoe dukhovenstvo i vlast' v Tatarstane (1920–1930-e gg.* (Kazan: Akademiia Nauk Respubliki Tatarstan, 2006).

Mirahmad Mirkholdor öghli, *Sayram tarikhi,* (Shymkent: Chimkent shahar bosmakhonasi, 1991).

Mïrzabay, B. B. "Kiyelĭ 'kök asalar' turalï," *Aralo-Kaspiiskii region v istorii kul'tury Evrazii*, (Almaty-Aqtöbe: Arïs, 2011), 211–214.

Morokhin, N. V. *Nizhegorodskie mariitsy*, (Ioshkar-Ola: Ministerstvo kul'tury Respubliki Mari El, 1994).

Motadel, David. *Islam and Nazi Germany's War*, (Belknap Press: Cambridge Massachusetts, 2014).

Mozaffari, Zarif. *Ishannar-Därvishlär*, (Kazan: Janalif, 1931).

Mukanov, M. S. *Iz istoricheskogo proshlogo (rodoslovnaia plemen kerei i uak)*, (Almaty: Qazaqstan, 1998).
Mukerjee, Madhusree. *Churchill's Secret War: the British Empire and the Ravaging of India during World War II* (New York: Basic Books, 2010).
Mŭkhammed-Sadïq Qashghari, *Tazkira-yi 'azizan*, Aytzghan Nurmanova ed., Qazaqstan tarikhï turalï derektemelerĭ IV, (Almaty: Daik Press, 2006).
Muminov, Ashirbek. "Die Qožas – Arabische Genealogien in Kasachstan," *Muslim Culture in Russia and Central Asia Vol. 2: Inter-Regional and Inter-Ethnic Relations*, Anke von Kügelgen et al. eds., (Berlin: Klaus Schwarz Verlag, 1998), 193–209.
Mustafina, R. M. *Predstavleniia, kul'ty, obriady u kazakhov*, (Almaty: Qazaq universitetĭ, 1992).
Mŭsayev Alpïsbay, *Äyteke bi aymaghïnïng etnomädeni mŭrasï*, (Aqtöbe: n.p., 2006).
Näsenov, Bolatbek. *Khalïq zhaularï: keng dalanïng küyreuĭ* (Almaty-Novosibirsk: n.p., 2006).
Nekrich, Aleksandr. *The Punished Peoples*, (New York: Norton, 1981).
Nicosia, Francis. *Nazi Germany and the Arab World*, (Cambridge: Cambridge University Press, 2014).
Nŭrtayŭlï, Säden. *Islam zhäne Maral Baba* (n.p., n.p., n.d.).
——. *Keng dalanïng ŭlïlïghï*, (Almaty: n.p., 2018).
"O musul'manskom dukhovenstve, sufiiakh, i ishanakh," *Tserkovnye vedomosti,* 22 October 1898, 1454–1455.
Ohayon, Isabelle. *La sédentarisation des Kazakhs dans l'URSS de Staline*, (Paris: Maisonneuve et Larose, (2006).
Oleshchuk, F. *O reaktsionnoi roli musul'manskogo dukhovenstva*, (Alma-Ata: Partizdat TsK KP(b)K, 1937).
Ōrāntāy ibn Qūrïmtāy Qïpchāqī, *Naṣīḥat al-qazāqīya*, (Kazan: Karimov, 1900).
Orazov, R. E. *Qarqara qŭzhatï*, (Almaty: An Arïs, 2016).
Öteulĭ Änis Zhaqïpŭlï, "Maral baba nemeresĭ, Eseyŭlï Süleyman ishan turalï bĭr üzĭk sïr," *Qasiyettĭ Maral Ishan,* Öteulĭ Änĭs Zhaqïpŭlï ed., (Qïzïlorda: Tŭmar, 2005), 91–94.
——. "Maral ishan ŭrpaqtarïna qŭrïlghan sot ükĭmĭnen song," *Qasiyettĭ Maral Ishan*, Öteulĭ Änis Zhaqïpŭlï ed. (Qïzïlorda: Tŭmar, 2005), 89–91.
——. *Qasiyettĭ Maral Ishan,* (Qïzïlorda: Tŭmar, 2005).
Paul, Jürgen. "Hagiographic Literature," *Encyclopedia Iranica* XI, fasc. 5, 536–539.
——. "Hagiographische Texte als historische Quelle," *Saeculum,* 41/1 (1990), 17–43.
Peshchereva, E. M. "Organization of Craftsmen in Central Asia in the Late XIXth and Early XXth Centuries, *XXV Mezhdunarodnyi kongress vostokovedov,* III, (Moscow, 1963), 519–522.
Pianciola, Niccolò. "Interpreting an Insurgency in Soviet Kazakhstan: The OGPU, Islam and Qazaq 'Clans' in Suzak, 1930," *Islam, Society and States across the Qazaq Steppe,* Niccolò Pianciola and Paolo Sartori, eds. (Vienna: Austrian Academy of Sciences, 2013), 297–336.
——. *Stalinismo di frontiera: Collonizzazione agricola, sterminio dei nomadi e costruzione statale in Asia centrale (1905–1936)* (Vicenza: Viella, 2009).
Privratsky, Bruce. *Muslim Turkistan,* (Richmond, Surrey: Curzon, 2001).
Qamzin, Zhŭmabek. "Kögĭdĭr kümbezlĭ oylar," in: *Isabek Ishan,* E. M. Arïn ed., (Pavlodar: Sïtin, 2011), 151–164.
Qazaq ŭlt-azattïq qozghalïsï v. 19, Adaiskoe vosstanie 1929–1931 gg., (Astana: Astana Poligrafiia AQ, 2001).

Qïrghïzbayev, Ötesh. *Sozaq köterīlīsī,* (Almaty: Arqas, 2003).

Qurbān-ʿAlī Khālidī, *An Islamic Biographical Dictionary of the Eastern Kazakh Steppe, 1770–1912*, Allen J. Frank and Mirkasyim Usmanov eds., (Leiden: Brill, 2005).

——, *Tawārīkh-i khamsa-yi sharqī*, (Kazan, Kazakov, 1910).

Rakhmankulova, S. G. *Mufti Gabrakhman Rasulev, starshii syn Ishan Khazreta Rasuleva*, (Cheliabinsk: n.p., 2000).

Renard, John. *Friends of God: Islamic Images of Piety, Commitment, and Servanthood,* (Berkeley: University of California Press, 2008).

Rey-Goldzeighuer, Annie. *Aux origins de la guerre d'Algérie: de Mers-el-Kébir aux massacres Nord-Constantinois*, (Paris: La Decouverte, 2002).

Riadnin, M. *Päränzhige qarsï küres ashïp ädet, ghurïpqa töngkeris kirgizilsin*, (Qïzïl-Orda: Qazaghïstan baspasï, 1930).

Romodin V. A. ed. *Materialy po istorii kirgizov i Kirgizii*, (Moscow: Nauka, Glavnaia Redaktsiia Vostochnoi Literatury, 1973).

Rosliakov, A. A. "K voprosu o miuridizme v Turkmenii," Izvestiia Akademii Nauk Turkmenskoi SSR, No. 5, 1962, 21–25.

Rouhier-Willoughby, Jeanmarie. "The Gulag Reclaimed as Sacred Space: Negotiation of Memory at the Holy Spring of Iskitim," *Laboratorium* 1 (2015), 51–70.

Saidakhmedov, I. A., M. Iu. Iunuskhodzhaeva and G. Iu. Astanova, "Agiograficheskie sochineniia kak istochnik dlia izucheniia dukhovnoi i politicheskoi zhizni Vostochnogo Turkestana," *Iz Istorii Srednei Azii i Vostochnogo Turkestana XV-XIX vv,* (Tashkent: Fan, 1987), 149–162.

Saparbekülï, Sadïqbek. *Kanpeske qorïtïndïsï*, (Qïzïl Orda: Qazaghïstan baspasï, 1929).

Sarkin, N. *Chudodeistvennyi zhezl Moiseia po musul'manskim skazaniiam i posokh kirgizskikh dervishei*, (Kazan: Tipo-litografiia Imperatorskago Universiteta, 1904).

Sartori, Paolo. "The Tashkent *ʿUlamāʾ* and the Soviet State (1920–1938): A Preliminary Research Note Based on NKVD Documents," *Patterns of Transformation in and around Uzbekistan*, Paolo Sartori and Tommaso Trevisani eds. (Reggio Emilia: Diabasis, 2007), 161–184.

Sartori, Paolo. "Of Saints, Shrines, and Tractors: Untangling the Meaning of Islam in Soviet Central Asia," *Journal of Islamic Studies* (2019), 1–40.

Schwarz, Henry G. "The Khwājas of Eastern Turkestan," *Central Asiatic Journal* 20 (1976), 266–296.

Sela, Ron. *Ritual and Authority in Central Asia: the Khan's Inauguration Ceremony,* Papers on Inner Asia, No. 37, (Bloomington Indiana: Research Institute for Inner Asian Studies, 2003).

Seleznev A. G. et al. *Kul't sviatykh v sibirskom islame: spetsifika universal'nogo,* (Kazan: Izdatel'skii Dom Mardzhani, 2009).

Sēmey Bōlāṭ ōblāstī ōskāmen uyāzīna qārāghān qazāqlārnïng āshlïqdan zārlïqlārī, (Orenburg: Waqït, 1912).

Seyt-Omar Sattarülï, *Qozhalar shezhīresī,* (Almaty: Atamüra, 2015).

Sharmanov, T. Sh. and B. A. Atchabarov eds. *Ocherki po istorii narodnoi meditsiny Kazakhstana*, (Alma-Ata: n.p., 1978).

Shayakhmetov, Mukhamet. *The Silent Steppe: the Memoir of a Kazakh Nomad under Stalin*, (New York: The Rookery Press, 2006).

Shaydarbek Äshīmülï, *Sïr boyïndaghï äuliyeler*, (Almaty: Atamüra, 2000).

——. *Sïrgha tolï Sïr boyï: tarikhi-tanïmdïq zhazbalar* (Almaty: Foliant, 2009).
Smirnov, N. A. *Musul'manskoe sektanstvo*, (Moscow: Bezbozhnik, 1930).
Snesarev, G. P. *Khorezmskie legendy kak istochnik po istorii religioznykh kul'tov Srednei Azii*, (Moscow: Nauka, 1983).
Sovetskaia derevnia glazami OGPU-NKVD III/1 1930–1931, A. Berelovich et al. eds., (Moscow: ROSSPEN, 2003).
Span, Äbïlqadïr. *Aday qasïretï* (Almaty: Nŭrlï Älem, 2011).
Spisok lits, lishennykh izbiratel'nykh prav po gorodu Alma-Ata i prigorodnomu raionu, noiabr' 1934 (Alma-Ata: Poligrafkniga, 1934).
Starostin, Andrei, Ol'ga Seniutkina, and Rustam Bikbov, "Antisovetskaia organizatsiia ishanizma v Molotovskoi oblasti," *Islam na Urale: Entsiklopedcheskii slovar'*, (Moscow-Nizhnii Novgorod: Medina, 2009), 37–39.
Stasevich, I. V. "Sovremennye formy kul'ta sviatykh u kazakhov Orenburgskoi oblasti (RF) i Aktiubinskoi oblasti (RK)," *Aralo-Kaspiiskii region v istorii kul'tury Evrazii*, (Almaty-Aqtöbe: Arïs, 2011), 224–227.
Sugawara, Jun, and Yayoi Kawahara (eds.), *Mazar Documents from Xinjiang and Ferghana* 1, (Tokyo, Research Institute for Languages and Cultures of Asia and Africa, 2006).
Sügïrbayev, Tangat. *Qïzïlzhar öngïrïnïng ziyalï qauïmï*, (Petropavl: n.p, 2010).
Suleimenov, B. ed., *Materialy po istorii kazakhskikh khanstv XV-XVIII vekov*, (Alma-Ata: Nauka, 1969).
Suleimenov, R. B. and V. A. Moiseev, *Iz istorii Kazakhstana XVIII veka*, (Alma-Ata: Izdatel'stvo Nauka Kazakhskoi SSR, 1988).
Süleymenov, Zh. "Maral-Ishan: Ŭlt-azattïq küresïnïng rukhani köshbasshïsï," in: *Soltüstïk Qazaqstan öngïrïndegï täwelsïzdïk üshïn küres tarikhï – Istoriia bor'by za nezavisimosti v Severnom Kazakhstane*, (Almaty: Atamŭra, 2011), 309–315.
Tajeddin Yalchïgol, *Risaläi gazizä* I-II, (Kazan: Iman, 2001).
Tänekeyev, S. *1916. Qarqara-Alban köterïlïsï*, (Almaty: An Arïs, 2016).
Tasar, Eren. *Soviet and Muslim: the Institutionalization of Islam in Central Asia*, (New York: Oxford University Press, 2017).
Tazagül Qazbek-ishanqïzï, "Äkem Qazbek turalï," *Qasiyettï Maral Ishan*, Öteulï Änïs Zhaqïpŭlï ed., (Qïzïlorda: Tŭmar, 2005), 106–108.
Täzhiyev Qazïbek and and S. Ömïrzaqov eds. *Äz äuliyeler* I-VI, *Qazïnalï ongtüstïk* vol. 22. (Almaty: Nŭrlï älem, 2011).
Thum, Rian. *Sacred Routes of Uyghur History*, (Cambridge, Massachusetts: Harvard University Press, 2014).
Tïleuqabïlŭlï, Tölepbergen. *Kïshï zhüz Älïm atalïghïnïng shezhïresï*, 2-nshï basïlïm, (Almaty: Shapaghat-Nŭr, 2006).
Tillett, Lowell. *The Great Friendship*, (Chapel Hill: University of North Carolina Press, 1969).
Tokumbaev, Kemel. "Tatarskii plast v musul'manskoi kul'ture Vostochnogo Kazakhstana," in: *Tatary na vostoke Kazakhstana*, (Ust'-Kamenogorsk: Tatarskii kul'turnyi tsentr VKO, 2008), 28–38.
Tügelbayev, Ädïlqaq. "Aqköldï äuliyelï atandïrghan," in: *Isabek Ishan* (Pavlodar: Sïtin baspakhanasï, 2011), 13–21.
Uehling, G. *Beyond Memory: the Crimean Tatars' Deportation and Return*, (New York: Palgrave, 2004).
Üsenbayev, Tengïzbay. *Alshïn shezhïresï*, (Qïzïlorda: Tŭmar, 2003).

von Kügelgen, Anke. "Die Entfaltung de Naqšbandīya muğaddidīya im mitteleren Transoxanien vom 18. Bis zum Beginn des 19. Jahrhunderts," *Muslim Culture in Russia and Central Asia from the 18th to the Early 20th Centuries Vol. 2,* Berlin: Klaus Schwarz Verlag, 1998), 101–151.

Zarcone, Thierry. "L'Hagiographie dans le monde turc," *Saints orienteaux,* Denis Aigle ed., (Paris: De Boccard, 1995), 55–67.

——. "Political Sufism and the Emirate of Kashgaria (End of the 19th Century): The Role of the Ambassador Ya'qūb Xān Tūra," in: *Muslim Culture in Russia and Central Asia from the 18th to the Early 20th Centuries Vol. 2,* Berlin: Klaus Schwarz Verlag, 1998), 153–165.

Zeynullin, B. "Aqköl-zhayïlma basqamïs auïlï," in: *Isabek Ishan,* E. M. Arïn ed., (Pavlodar: Sïtin, 2011), 195–197.

Zhaqsïmbetov, Eskermes. *Äzīretī Qaratau, äuliyenīng kenī edī,* (Shymkent: Zhībek zholï, 2000).

Zhontayeva, Zh. A. and Sh. Sh. Äbdībayev, *Sïr elīnīng mädeni mŭralarï,* (Qïzïlorda: n.p., 2005).

Zhŭmabayev, Sotsial. *Eseney estelīgī,* (Petropavl: n.p., 2010).

—. *Ŭlïlar tughan ölke* (Petropavl: n.p., 2006).

Zhŭmabayev, Sotsial, and Kärīm Zhalmaqanov, *Bīrzhannïng belgīsīz ghŭmïrï – Nŭralï shezhīresī* (Petropavl: n.p. 2009).

Zhünīsbayev, K. "Qazaqstannïng XVII-XVIII ghasïrlardaghï tarikhïna baylanïstï qazaq tīlīndegī keybīr tarikhi derekter turalï," *Voprosy istorii Kazakhstana i Vostochnogo Turkestana,* Trudy Instituta Istorii, Arkheologii i Etnografii imeni Ch. Ch. Valikhanova, tom 15, (Alma-Ata: Izdatel'stvo Akademii Nauk Kazakhskoi SSR, 1962, 154–170.

Zhünīsbekov, Bolat ed. *Alash-Alzhir* II (Almaty: Sarïarqa, 2011).

MAPS

Moscow
Ulugh Saba (Bogatye Saby)
Kazan
RUSSIA
Ufa
Petropavlovsk
Omsk
Troitsk
Tobol
Qostanay
Ishim
Irtysh
Äuliyeköl
Aqköl (Isabek Ishan)
Pavlodar
Orenburg
Ekibastuz
Aralköl
Astana
Aqtöbe
Qayindi
Don
Volga
Ural
KAZAKHSTAN
Zhezqazghan
Ayagöz
Üyshik (Atyrau)
L. Balkhash
Astrakhan
Aral Sea
Qazalï
Maral Baba
Qarmaqshï (Zhosalï)
Qïzïlorda (Aqmeshit)
Mangghystau
Bäygequm
Fort Shevchenko
Zhuantobe
Sozaq
Oyiq
Qulja
Aqtau
Senek
Ayqozha Ishan
Qushata
Almaty
Shayan
Turkistan
Auliye-Ata (Taraz)
Black Sea
UZBEKISTAN
Qaratau
Shymkent
Caspian Sea
GEORGIA
Keriz
Sayram
KYRGYZSTAN
Khorezm
Sir Darya
Tashkent
Khoqand
ARMENIA
AZERBAIJAN
Amu Darya
Bekabad
Bukhara
Samarkand
CHINA
TURKMENISTAN
Kitap (Kitob)
Shahr-i Sabz
TAJIKISTAN
Kurgantepe
IRAN
Sources: Esri, USGS, NOAA

KAZAKHSTAN
Zhezqazghan
Ural
Üyshik (Atyrau)
Qazalī
Maral Baba
Qarmaqshī (Zhosalī)
Aral Sea
Sir Darya
Qīzīlorda (Aqmeshit)
Fort Shevchenko
Mangghystau
Zhuantobe
Bāygequm
Sozaq
Aqtau
Beket Ata
Senek
Zhangaqorghan
Sholaqqorghan
Oyiq
Qushata
Ayqozha Ishan
Turkistan
Auliye-Ata (Taraz)
Shayan
Qaratau
Amu Darya
UZBEKISTAN
Shymkent
Sayram
Keriz
Caspian Sea
Khorezm
Tashkent
Aydar Kul
Khoqand
Bekabad
Kattakurgan
Samarkand
Bukhara
TURKMENISTAN
Kitap (Kitob)
Shahr-i Sabz
TAJIKISTAN
Kurgantepe
Sources: Esri, USGS, NOAA

INDEX

VERÖFFENTLICHUNGEN ZUR IRANISTIK

HERAUSGEGEBEN VON BERT G. FRAGNER UND FLORIAN SCHWARZ

(Nr. 1–21: Veröffentlichungen der Iranischen Kommission,
Nr. 22–29: Veröffentlichungen der Kommission für Iranistik,
Nr. 30–31: Herausgegeben von Bert G. Fragner
Nr. 32–68: Herausgegeben von Bert G. Fragner und Velizar Sadovski)

Nr. 1: Manfred Mayrhofer, Onomastica Persepolitana. Das altiranische Namengut der Persepolis-Täfelchen. Unter Mitarbeit von János Harmatta, Walter Hinz, Rüdiger Schmitt und Jutta Seiffert. 1973 (SBph, 286. Band)

Nr. 2: Karl Jahn, Die Geschichte der Kinder Israels des Rašīd ad-Dīn. 1973 (Dph, 114. Band)

Nr. 3: Manfred Mayrhofer, Zum Namengut des Avesta. 1977 (SBph, 308. Band, 5. Abhandlung)

Nr. 4: Karl Jahn, Die Frankengeschichte des Rašīd ad-Dīn. Einleitung, Übersetzung und Kommentar. 1977 (Dph, 129. Band)

Nr. 5: Ronald Zwanziger, Zum Namen der Mutter Zarathustras. (Sonderdruck aus Anzeiger, 114/1977)

Nr. 6: Rüdiger Schmitt, Die Iranier-Namen bei Aischylos. (Iranica Graeca Vetustiora. I). 1978 (SBph, 337. Band)

Nr. 7: Manfred Mayrhofer, Supplement zur Sammlung der altpersischen Inschriften. 1978 (SBph, 338. Band)

Nr. 8: Karl Jahn, Die Indiengeschichte des Rašīd ad-Dīn. Einleitung, vollständige Übersetzung, Kommentar und 80 Texttafeln. 1980 (Dph, 144. Band)

Nr. 9: Oswald Szemerényi, Four Old Iranian Ethnic Names: Scythian – Skudra – Sogdian – Saka. 1980 (SBph, 371. Band)

Nr. 10: Rüdiger Schmitt, Altpersische Siegelinschriften. 1981 (SBph, 381. Band)

Nr. 11: Kaikhusroo M. JamaspAsa, Aogəmadaēcā. A Zoroastrian Liturgy. 1982 (SBph, 397. Band)

Nr. 12: R. E. Emmerick and P. O. Skjærvø, Studies in the Vocabulary of Khotanese I. 1982 (SBph, 401. Band)

Nr. 13: Manfred Mayrhofer, Lassen sich Vorstufen des Uriranischen nachweisen? (Sonderdruck aus Anzeiger, 120/1983)

Nr. 14: Reinhard Pohanka, Zu einigen Architekturstücken von Tell-e Zohak bei Fasa, Südiran. (Sonderdruck aus Anzeiger, 120/1983)

Nr. 15: Wilhelm Eilers, Iranische Ortsnamenstudien. 1987 (SBph, 465. Band)

Nr. 16: Reinhard Pohanka, Die Masdjed-e Djoume in Darab, Südiran. (Sonderdruck aus Anzeiger, 121/1984)

Nr. 17: R. E. Emmerick and P. O. Skjærvø, Studies in the Vocabulary of Khotanese II. 1987 (SBph, 458. Band)

Nr. 18: Wolfgang Felix, Antike literarische Quellen zur Außenpolitik des Sāsāniden-staates. Erster Band (224–309). 1985 (SBph, 456. Band)

Nr. 19: Reinhard Pohanka, Burgen und Heiligtümer in Laristan, Südiran. Ein Surveybericht. 1986 (SBph, 466. Band)

Nr. 20: N. Rastegar und W. Slaje, Uto von Melzer (1881–1961). Werk und Nachlaß eines österreichischen Iranisten. 1987 (SBph, 477. Band)

Nr. 21: Ladislav Zgusta, The Old Ossetic Inscription from the River Zelenčuk. 1987 (SBph, 486. Band)

Nr. 22: Wolfram Kleiss, Die Entwicklung von Palästen und palastartigen Wohnbauten in Iran. 1989 (SBph, 524. Band)

Nr. 23: Nosratollah Rastegar, Zur Problematik einiger handschriftlicher Quellen des neupersischen Namenbuches. 1989 (SBph, 525. Band)

Nr. 24: Dorit Schön, Laristan – eine südpersische Küstenprovinz. Ein Beitrag zu seiner Geschichte. 1990 (SBph, 553. Band)

Nr. 25: Rüdiger Schmitt, Epigraphisch-exegetische Noten zu Dareios' Bīsutūn-Inschriften. 1990 (SBph, 561. Band)

Nr. 26: Jost Gippert, Iranica Armeno-Iberica. Studien zu den iranischen Lehnwörtern im Armenischen und Georgischen. Band I–II. 1993 (SBph, 606. Band)

Nr. 27: R. E. Emmerick and P. O. Skjærvø, Studies in the Vocabulary of Khotanese III. 1997 (SBph, 651. Band)

Nr. 28: Xavier Tremblay, Pour une histoire de la Sérinde. Le manichéisme parmi les peuples et religions d'Asie Centrale d'après les sources primaires. 2001 (SBph, 690. Band)

Nr. 29: Rüdiger Schmitt, Die iranischen und Iranier-Namen in den Schriften Xenophons. (Iranica Graeca Vetustiora. II). 2002 (SBph, 692. Band)

Nr. 30: Rüdiger Schmitt, Meno-logium Bagistano-Persepolitanum. Studien zu den altpersischen Monatsnamen und ihren elamischen Wiedergaben. Unter redaktioneller Mitwirkung von Velizar Sadovski. 2003 (SBph, 705. Band)

Nr. 31: Antonio Panaino, Rite, parole et pensée dans l'Avesta ancien et récent. Quatre leçons au Collège de France (Paris, 7, 14, 21, 28 mai 2001). Edité par Velizar Sadovski, avec la collaboration rédactionnelle de Sara Circassia. 2004 (SBph, 716. Band)

Nr. 32: Roman Siebertz, Die Briefmarken Irans als Mittel der politischen Bildpropaganda. 2005 (SBph, 722. Band)

Nr. 33: Rüdiger Schmitt, Iranische Anthroponyme in den erhaltenen Resten von Ktesias' Werk. (Iranica Graeca Vetustiora. III). 2006 (SBph, 736. Band)

Nr. 34: Heiner Eichner, Bert G. Fragner, Velizar Sadovski und Rüdiger Schmitt (Hrsg.), Iranistik in Europa – gestern, heute, morgen. Unter redaktioneller Mitarbeit von Hannes Hofmann und Vera Giesen. 2006 (SBph, 739. Band)

Nr. 35: Uto v. Melzer, Farhangnevīs. Materialien zu einem Persisch-deutschen Wörter-buch. Hrsg. von Nosratollah Rastegar. Band I–IV. 2006 (Dph, 339. Band)

Nr. 36: Manfred Mayrhofer, Einiges zu den Skythen, ihrer Sprache, ihrem Nachleben. 2006 (SBph, 742. Band)

Nr. 37: Siegfried Weber, Die persische Verwaltung Kaschmirs (1842–1892). Band 1–2. 2007 (SBph, 754. Band)

Nr. 38: Farhangnevīs. Datenbank zu Uto von Melzers lexikographischen Materialien: Persisch-Deutsch/Deutsch-Persisch. Hrsg. von Nosratollah Rastegar. 2007 (CD-ROM)

Nr. 39: Rüdiger Schmitt, Pseudo-altpersische Inschriften. Inschriftenfälschungen und moderne Nachbildungen in altpersischer Keilschrift. 2007 (SBph, 762. Band)

Nr. 40: Thamar E. Gindin, The Early Judaeo-Persian Tafsīrs of Ezekiel: Text, Translation, Commentary. Vol. I: Text. 2007 (SBph, 763. Band)

Nr. 41: Antonio Panaino und Velizar Sadovski, Disputationes Iranologicae Vindobonenses, I.: Antonio Panaino, Chronologia Avestica. Velizar Sadovski, Epitheta und Götternamen im älteren Indo-Iranischen. 2007 (SBph, 764. Band)

Nr. 42: Helmut Slaby, Bindenschild und Sonnenlöwe. Die Geschichte der österreichisch-iranischen Beziehungen bis zur Gegenwart. Nachdruck. 2010 (SBph, 770. Band)

Nr. 43: Tommaso Gnoli, The Interplay of Roman and Iranian Titles in the Roman East (1st–3rd Century A.D.). 2007 (SBph, 765. Band)

Nr. 44: Thamar E. Gindin, The Early Judaeo-Persian Tafsīrs of Ezekiel: Text, Translation, Commentary. Vol. II: Translation. 2007 (SBph, 766. Band)

Nr. 45: Thamar E. Gindin, The Early Judaeo-Persian Tafsīrs of Ezekiel: Text, Translation, Commentary. Vol. III: Commentary (*in Vorbereitung*)

Nr. 46: Bert G. Fragner, Ralph Kauz, Roderick Ptak und Angela Schottenhammer (Hrsg.), Pferde in Asien: Geschichte, Handel und Kultur / Horses in Asia: History, Trade and Culture. 2009 (Dph, 378. Band)

Nr. 47: Giorgio Rota, La Vita e i Tempi di Rostam Khan. Edizione e traduzione italiana del Ms. British Library Add 7,655. 2009 (SBph, 790. Band)

Nr. 48: Fridrik Thordarson, Ossetic Grammatical Studies. 2009 (SBph, 788. Band)

Nr. 49: Rüdiger Schmitt und Gerhard Brugmann (Hrsg.), Aus Karl Brugmanns Jugenderinnerungen. Eingeleitet und mit Anmerkungen versehen von Rüdiger Schmitt. 2009 (SBph, 786. Band)

Nr. 50: Velizar Sadovski, Untersuchungen zu Sprache und Stil des ältesten Indo-Iranischen (Veda und Avesta). (Stilistica Indo-Iranica, II.) (*in Vorbereitung*)

Nr. 51: Velizar Sadovski und David Stifter (Hrsg.), Iranistische und indogermanistische Beiträge in memoriam Jochem Schindler (1944–1994). 2012 (SBph, 851. Band)

Nr. 52: Ralph Kauz, Giorgio Rota und Jan Paul Niederkorn (Hrsg.), Diplomatisches Zeremoniell in Europa und im Mittleren Osten in der frühen Neuzeit. 2009 (SBph, 796. Band)

Nr. 53: Giorgio Rota, Under Two Lions. On the Knowledge of Persia in the Republic of Venice (ca. 1450–1797). 2009 (SBph, 793. Band)

Nr. 54: Manfred Mayrhofer, Indogermanistik: Über Darstellungen und Einführungen von den Anfängen bis in die Gegenwart. 2009 (SBph, 787. Band)

Nr. 55: Ela Filippone, The Fingers and their Names in the Iranian Languages. (Onomasiological Studies of Body-Part Terms, I). 2010 (SBph, 811. Band)

Nr. 56: Olav Hackstein, Apposition and Nominal Classification in Indo-European and Beyond. 2010 (SBph, 798. Band)

Nr. 57: Geschichte Wassaf's. Persisch herausgegeben und deutsch übersetzt von Hammer-Purgstall. Neu herausgegeben von Sibylle Wentker nach Vorarbeiten von Klaus Wundsam. Band 1. 2010 (SBph, 802. Band)

Nr. 58: Gisela Fock, Die iranische Moderne in der Bildenden Kunst: Der Bildhauer und Maler Parviz Tanavoli. 2011 (SBph, 815. Band)

Nr. 59: Geschichte Wassaf's. Deutsch übersetzt von Hammer-Purgstall. Herausgegeben von Sibylle Wentker nach Vorarbeiten von Elisabeth und Klaus Wundsam. Band 2. 2010 (SBph, 803. Band)

Nr. 60: Toshifumi Gotō: The Old Indo-Aryan Morphology and its Indo-Iranian Background. 2013 (SBph, 849. Band)

Nr. 61: Yuri Stoyanov, Defenders and Enemies of the True Cross. The Sasanian Conquest of Jerusalem in 614 and Byzantine Ideology of Anti-Persian Warfare. 2011 (SBph, 819. Band)

Nr. 62: Barbara Karl, Treasury – Kunstkammer – Museum: Objects from the Islamic World in the Museum Collections of Vienna. 2011 (SBph, 822. Band)

Nr. 63: Şevket Küçükhüseyin, Selbst- und Fremdwahrnehmung im Prozess kultureller Transformation. Anatolische Quellen über Muslime, Christen und Türken (13.–15. Jahrhundert). 2011 (SBph, 825. Band)
Nr. 64: Geschichte Wassaf's. Deutsch übersetzt von Hammer-Purgstall. Herausgegeben von Sibylle Wentker nach Vorarbeiten von Elisabeth und Klaus Wundsam. Band 3. 2012 (SBph, 827. Band)
Nr. 65: Antonio Panaino und Velizar Sadovski, Disputationes Iranologicae Vindobonenses, II. 2013 (SBph, 845. Band)
Nr. 66: Geschichte Wassaf's. Deutsch übersetzt von Hammer-Purgstall. Herausgegeben von Sibylle Wentker nach Vorarbeiten von Elisabeth und Klaus Wundsam. Band 4. 2016 (SBph, 878. Band)
Nr. 67: Luke Treadwell, Craftsmen and coins: signed dies in the Iranian world (third to the fifth centuries AH). 2011 (Dph, 423. Band, gleichzeitig: Veröffentlichungen der Numismatischen Kommission, Band 54)
Nr. 69: Amr Taher Ahmed, La « Révolution littéraire ». Étude de l'influence de la poésie française sur la modernisation des formes poétiques persanes au début du XXe siècle. 2012 (SBph, 829. Band)
Nr. 70: Roman Siebertz, Preise, Löhne und Lebensstandard im safavidischen Iran. Eine Untersuchung zu den Rechnungsbüchern Wollebrand Geleynssen de Jonghs (1641–1643). 2013 (SBph, 835. Band)
Nr. 71: Walter Posch, Osmanisch-safavidische Beziehungen 1545–1550: Der Fall Alḳâs Mîrzâ. Teil 1 und Teil 2. 2013 (SBph, 841. Band)
Nr. 72: Niccolò Pianciola und Paolo Sartori (Hrsg.), Islam, Society and States across the Qazaq Steppe (18th – Early 20th Centuries). 2013 (SBph, 844. Band)
Nr. 73: Desmond Durkin-Meisterernst, Grammatik des Westmitteliranischen (Parthisch und Mittelpersisch). 2014 (SBph, 850. Band/Grammatica Iranica 1, hrsg. von Velizar Sadovski)
Nr. 74: Christine Noelle-Karimi, The Pearl in its Midst. Herat and the Mapping of Khurasan (15th–19th Centuries). 2014 (Dph, 463. Band)
Nr. 75: Bert G. Fragner, Ralph Kauz und Florian Schwarz (Hrsg.): Wine Culture in Iran and Beyond. 2014 (SBph, 852. Band)
Nr. 76: Alexander Lubotsky, Alanic Marginal Notes in a Greek Liturgical Manuscript. 2015 (SBph, 859. Band/Grammatica Iranica 2, hrsg. von Velizar Sadovski)
Nr. 77: Tilmann Trausch, Formen höfischer Historiographie im 16. Jahrhundert. Geschichtsschreibung unter den frühen Safaviden: 1501–1578. 2015 (SBph, 861. Band)
Nr. 78: Jeff Eden (transl. and annot.), The Life of Muḥammad Sharīf. A Central Asian Sufi Hagiography in Chaghatay. With an appendix by Rian Thum and David Brophy. 2015 (SBph, 864. Band)
Nr. 79: Rüdiger Schmitt, Stilistik der altpersischen Inschriften. Versuch einer Annäherung. 2016 (SBph, 875. Band/Grammatica Iranica 3, hrsg. von Velizar Sadovski)
Nr. 80: Andreas Wilde, What is Beyond the River? Power, Authority, and Social Order in Transoxania, 18th–19th Centuries. 2016 (SBph, 877. Band)
Nr. 81: Chiara Barbati, The Christian Sogdian Gospel Lectionary E5 in Context. 2016 (SBph, 874. Band)
Nr. 82: Nuryoghdi Toshov (Hrsg.), Īsh Murād b. Ādīna Muḥammad ʿAlavī: Jamshīdī ṭavāyifī fatḥī (The Subjugation of the Jamshīdīs). 2018 (SBph, 888. Band/Studies and Texts on Central Asia 1, hrsg. von Paolo Sartori)

Nr. 83: Nicholas Sims-Williams und François de Blois, Studies in the Chronology of the Bactrian Documents from Northern Afghanistan. With contributions by Harry Falk and Dieter Weber. 2018 (Dph, 505. Band)

IRANISCHE ONOMASTIK

HERAUSGEGEBEN VON BERT G. FRAGNER UND FLORIAN SCHWARZ

(Nr. 1–10: Herausgegeben von Bert G. Fragner und Velizar Sadovski)

Nr. 1: Rüdiger Schmitt, Das Iranische Personennamenbuch: Rückschau, Vorschau, Rundschau (mit einer Bibliographie zur Iranischen Personennamenkunde). 2006 (SBph, 744. Band)

Nr. 2: Sonja Fritz, Die ossetischen Personennamen. (= Iranisches Personennamenbuch, Band III, Faszikel 3). 2006 (SBph, 746. Band)

Nr. 3: Ulla Remmer, Frauennamen im Rigveda und im Avesta. 2006 (SBph, 745. Band)

Nr. 4: Ran Zadok, Iranische Personennamen in der neu- und spätbabylonischen Nebenüberlieferung. (= Iranisches Personennamenbuch, Band VII, Faszikel 1B). 2009 (SBph, 777. Band)

Nr. 5: Philippe Gignoux, Christelle Jullien, Florence Jullien, Noms propres syriaques d'origine iranienne. (= Iranisches Personennamenbuch, Band VII, Faszikel 5). 2009 (SBph, 789. Band)

Nr. 6: Rüdiger Schmitt, Iranische Personennamen in der neuassyrischen Nebenüberlieferung. (= Iranisches Personennamenbuch, Band VII, Faszikel 1A). 2009 (SBph, 792. Band)

Nr. 7: Nicholas Sims-Williams, Bactrian Personal Names. (= Iranisches Personennamenbuch, Band II, Faszikel 7). 2010 (SBph, 806. Band)

Nr. 8: Pavel B. Lurje, Personal Names in Sogdian Texts. (= Iranisches Personennamenbuch, Band II, Faszikel 8). 2010 (SBph, 808. Band)

Nr. 9: Rüdiger Schmitt, Iranische Personennamen in der griechischen Literatur vor Alexander d. Gr. (= Iranisches Personennamenbuch, Band V, Faszikel 5A). 2011 (SBph, 823. Band)

Nr. 10: Rüdiger Schmitt, Manfred Mayrhofer: Leben und Werk. Mit vollständigem Schriftenverzeichnis. 2012 (SBph, 828. Band)

Nr. 11: Matteo De Chiara, Mauro Maggi and Giuliana Martini (Hrsg.), Buddhism Among the Iranian Peoples of Central Asia (= Multilingualism and History of Knowledge, Volume I. Hrsg. von Jens E. Braarvig, Markham J. Geller, Gebhard Selz und Velizar Sadovski). 2013 (SBph, 848. Band)

Nr. 12: Olav Hackstein and Ronald I. Kim (Hrsg.), Linguistic Developments along the Silkroad: Archaism and Innovation in Tocharian (= Multilingualism and History of Knowledge, Volume II. Hrsg. von Jens E. Braarvig, Markham J. Geller, Gebhard Selz und Velizar Sadovski). 2012 (SBph, 834. Band)

Nr. 13: Rüdiger Schmitt und Günter Vittmann, Iranische Namen in ägyptischer Nebenüberlieferung. (= Iranisches Personennamenbuch, Band VIII). 2013 (SBph, 842. Band)

Nr. 14: Manfred Hutter, Iranische Personennamen in der hebräischen Bibel. (= Iranisches Personennamenbuch, Band VII, Faszikel 2). 2015 (SBph, 860. Band)

Nr. 15: Rüdiger Schmitt, Personennamen in parthischen epigraphischen Quellen (= Iranisches Personennamenbuch, Band II, Faszikel 5). 2016 (SBph, 881. Band)
Nr. 16: Iris Colditz, Iranische Personennamen in manichäischer Überlieferung (= Iranisches Personennamenbuch, Band II, Faszikel 1). 2018 (SBph, 889. Band)

IRANISCHES PERSONENNAMENBUCH

BEGRÜNDET VON MANFRED MAYRHOFER
HERAUSGEGEBEN VON RÜDIGER SCHMITT, HEINER EICHNER, BERT G. FRAGNER UND VELIZAR SADOVSKI

Band I: Die altiranischen Namen
Von Manfred Mayrhofer. 1979 (Sonderpublikation).

Faszikel 1, 2 und 3 in einem Band:
Faszikel 1: Die avestischen Namen.
Faszikel 2: Die altpersischen Namen.
Faszikel 3: Indices zum Gesamtband.

Band II: Mitteliranische Personennamen

Faszikel 1: Iranische Personennamen in manichäischer Überlieferung. Von Iris Colditz. 2018 (SBph, 889. Band/Iranische Onomastik, Nr. 16)

Faszikel 2: Noms propres sassanides en moyen-perse épigraphique. Von Philippe Gignoux. 1986 (Sonderpublikation)

Faszikel 3: Noms propres sassanides en moyen-perse épigraphique. Supplément (1986–2001). Von Philippe Gignoux. 2003 (Sonderpublikation)

Faszikel 5: Personennamen in parthischen epigraphischen Quellen. Von Rüdiger Schmitt, 2016 (SBph, 881. Band/Iranische Onomastik, Nr. 15)

Faszikel 7: Bactrian Personal Names. Von Nicholas Sims-Williams. 2010 (SBph, 806. Band/Iranische Onomastik, Nr. 7)

Faszikel 8: Personal Names in Sogdian Texts. Von Pavel B. Lurje. 2011 (SBph, 808. Band/Iranische Onomastik, Nr. 8)

Band III: Neuiranische Personennamen

Faszikel 3: Die ossetischen Personennamen. Von Sonja Fritz. 2006 (SBph, 746. Band/Iranische Onomastik, Nr. 2)

Band IV: Materialgrundlagen zu den iranischen Personennamen auf antiken Münzen: Nomina propria Iranica in nummis

Von Michael Alram. 1986 (Sonderpublikation)

Band V: Iranische Namen in Nebenüberlieferungen indogermanischer Sprachen

Faszikel 4: Iranische Namen in den indogermanischen Sprachen Kleinasiens: Lykisch, Lydisch, Phrygisch. Von Rüdiger Schmitt. 1982 (Sonderpublikation)

Faszikel 5A: Iranische Personennamen in der griechischen Literatur vor Alexander d. Gr. Von Rüdiger Schmitt. 2011 (SBph, 823. Band/Iranische Onomastik, Nr. 9)

Faszikel 6a: Iranische Namen in den griechischen Dokumenten Ägyptens. Von Philip Huyse. 1991 (Sonderpublikation)

Band VII: Iranische Namen in semitischen Nebenüberlieferungen

Faszikel 1A: Iranische Personennamen in der neuassyrischen Nebenüberlieferung. Von Rüdiger Schmitt. 2009 (SBph, 792. Band/Iranische Onomastik, Nr. 6)

Faszikel 1B: Iranische Personennamen in der neu- und spätbabylonischen Neben-überlieferung. Von Ran Zadok. 2009 (SBph, 777. Band/Iranische Onomastik, Nr. 4)

Faszikel 2: Iranische Personennamen in der hebräischen Bibel. Von Manfred Hutter. 2015 (SBph, 860. Band/Iranische Onomastik, Nr. 14)

Faszikel 5: Noms propres syriaques d'origine iranienne. Von Philippe Gignoux, Christelle Jullien, Florence Jullien. 2009 (SBph, 789. Band/Iranische Onomastik, Nr. 5)

Band VIII: Iranische Namen in ägyptischer Nebenüberlieferung

Von Rüdiger Schmitt und Günter Vittmann. 2013 (SBph, 842. Band/Iranische Onomastik, Nr. 13)